ARISTEAS OF
PROCONNESUS

νανσὶ δ’ οὔτε πεζὸς ἰών κεν εὕροις
ἐς Ὑπερβορέων ἀγῶνα θαυματὰν ὁδόν.

ARISTEAS OF PROCONNESUS

BY

J. D. P. BOLTON

FELLOW OF THE QUEEN'S COLLEGE
OXFORD

OXFORD
AT THE CLARENDON PRESS

OXFORD
UNIVERSITY PRESS

Great Clarendon Street, Oxford OX2 6DP

Oxford University Press is a department of the University of Oxford.
It furthers the University's objective of excellence in research, scholarship,
and education by publishing worldwide in

Oxford New York

Athens Auckland Bangkok Bogotá Buenos Aires Calcutta
Cape Town Chennai Dar es Salaam Delhi Florence Hong Kong Istanbul
Karachi Kuala Lumpur Madrid Melbourne Mexico City Mumbai
Nairobi Paris São Paulo Singapore Taipei Tokyo Toronto Warsaw

with associated companies in Berlin Ibadan

Oxford is a registered trade mark of Oxford University Press
in the UK and in certain other countries

Published in the United States
by Oxford University Press Inc., New York

© Oxford University Press 1962

The moral rights of the author have been asserted
Database right Oxford University Press (maker)

Special edition for Sandpiper Books Ltd., 1999

British Library Cataloguing in Publication Data

Data available

ISBN 0-19-814332-X

1 3 5 7 9 10 8 6 4 2

Printed in Great Britain
on acid free paper by
Bookcraft (Bath) Ltd.,
Midsomer Norton

TO
MY PARENTS

PREFACE

In the following pages I have tried, as far as possible, to present the reader with a developing argument; to advance only from established positions. However, it has occasionally been necessary to anticipate a conclusion, and anyway there are passages where reference, either forward or back, may prove helpful. Such cross-references within this book are indicated by numerals in square brackets: to a chapter, by roman numerals; to a page, by arabic. Arabic numerals preceded by the letter T refer to the Greek and Latin texts given on pages 207–14. References to other modern works are enclosed in round brackets, after the name either of the work or of its author; an arabic numeral indicating the page, a roman the volume (or, if off-set above the line, a work, as shown in the Bibliography on pages 215–17, where further details will be found).

The surviving fragments of Aristeas' *Arimaspea* will be found numbered as such in the first five of the above-mentioned texts, on pages 207–8. I have classified as fragments not only professed quotations from the poem but also summary matter which is specifically and solely ascribed by later authors to Aristeas or to the *Arimaspea*. My ordering of the fragments, which may perhaps at first appear haphazard, is in fact not so: the first gives the broad outline of the poem's contents, the second the poet's admission concerning the farthest people he reached and his dependence on their account for the regions beyond, the third a description of that people, the remainder their reports on their neighbours.

It remains to say that, where I refer to quotations by ancient authors of others whose work is otherwise lost to us, the reader may find, under the quoted author's name in the Index Locorum on pages 219–47, a reference to his collected fragments, if such a collection exists and is readily accessible. For example, on page 51 there is a reference to a statement of Ephorus preserved by 'Scymnus': if the reader looks in the index under '*Scymnus*' he will find a reference to the relevant lines of that author's poem, but if he looks under *Ephorus* he will find opposite *51* the appropriate fragment number of Ephorus in Jacoby's *Fragmente der griechischen Historiker*.

Narrow as the subject of this work is, it quickly revealed to me the breadth of my ignorance. I am conscious that the book must contain many imperfections; but it would contain more, had it not been for the friendly help and suggestions of colleagues, to all of whom I feel deeply grateful, and in particular to Mr. Geoffrey Bownas, Mr. J. G. Griffith, Dr. J. L. Harley, Professor David Hawkes, Professor Hugh Lloyd-Jones, Mr. Edgar Lobel, Mr. L. D. Reynolds, and Mr. J. P. Sullivan. I owe thanks too to the learned readers and staff of the Clarendon Press, and to its Delegates for permission to reproduce Plates I and III(*b*); similarly to the Trustees of the British Museum and to Messrs. Thames and Hudson for permission to reproduce Plates II and III(*a*) respectively. Finally, I must acknowledge a special debt to two scholars, with whose views on Aristeas I sometimes disagree: to Sir Maurice Bowra and Professor E. R. Dodds; for had it not been for some remarks they made to me long ago this book might never have been written.

J. D. P. B.

Oxford, October 1961

CONTENTS

LIST OF PLATES

(at end)

MAPS

(at end)

I

FOUNDATIONS

Ever since my childhood acquaintance with *Alice in Wonderland* I have had a fondness for griffins. Yet even at that age I felt that Carroll's amiable, ill-educated creature represented but shabbily the dignity proper to a conflation of the King of Birds and the King of Beasts, whose attributes should be grimness and fearful power. Far more satisfying was it years later, skulking through the solitudes of Galloway with the hunted Hannay of *The Thirty-Nine Steps*, to hear the poetic innkeeper quote with ironic but unconscious aptitude

> As when a Gryfon through the Wilderness
> With winged course ore Hill or moarie Dale,
> Pursues the *Arimaspian*, who by stelth
> Had from his wakeful custody purloind
> The guarded Gold.

I read Milton after I read Buchan; and when I did come upon the source of these lines, in the second book of *Paradise Lost*, my curiosity was properly aroused to know whence their author had drawn the inspiration for his magnificent picture. The answer was to provide another puzzle, to which this book suggests a solution.

In that part of his work where he passes from a discussion of the origin of the Scyths to a geographical description of their south Russian home and the more northerly parts of Europe and Asia, Herodotus states the following[1] [T. 1; 12; 2]:

Aristeas also, the son of Caystrobius, a native of Proconnesus [an island in the Sea of Marmara; Map II], says in the course of his poem that, possessed by Apollo, he reached the Issedonians. Above them dwelt the Arimaspi, men with one eye; still further, the gold-guarding griffins; and beyond these, the Hyperboreans, whose country extended to the sea. Except the Hyperboreans, all these nations, beginning with the Arimaspi, continually encroached on their neighbours. Hence it came to pass that the Arimaspi gradually drove the Issedonians from their country, while the Issedonians dispossessed the Scyths; and the Scyths, pressing upon the Cimmerians, who dwelt on the shores of the southern sea, forced them to leave their land.

The birthplace of Aristeas, the poet who sang of these things, I have already mentioned. I will now relate a tale which I heard concerning him at Proconnesus and Cyzicus [on the Asiatic mainland nearby]. Aristeas, they said, who belonged to one of the noblest families in the island, had entered one day a fuller's shop, when he suddenly dropped down dead. Hereupon the fuller shut up his shop, and went to tell Aristeas' kindred what had happened. The report of the death had just spread through the town, when a certain Cyzicenian, lately arrived from Artace [a seaport about five miles from Cyzicus], contradicted the rumour, affirming that he had met Aristeas on the road to Cyzicus, and had spoken with him. This man, therefore, strenuously denied the rumour; the relations however proceeded to the fuller's shop with all things necessary for the funeral, intending to carry the body away. But on the shop being opened, no Aristeas was found, either dead or alive. Six years afterwards he reappeared, they told me, in Proconnesus, and composed the poem which the Greeks now know as the *Arimaspea*, after which he disappeared a second time. This is the tale current in the two cities above mentioned.

What follows I know to have happened to the Metapontines in Italy two hundred and forty years after the second disappearance of Aristeas, as I discovered by calculations I made at Proconnesus and Metapontum. Aristeas then, as the Metapontines affirm, appeared to them in their own country in person, and ordered them to set up an altar in honour of Apollo, and to place near it a statue to be called that of Aristeas the Proconnesian. Apollo, he told them, had honoured them alone of the Italiotes with his presence; and he himself accompanied the god at the time, not however in his present form, but in the shape of a raven. Having said so much he vanished. Then the Metapontines sent to Delphi, and inquired of the god what they were to make of this apparition. The priestess in reply bade them attend to what the spectre said, 'for so it would go best with them'. Thus advised, they did as they had been directed; and there is now a statue bearing the name of Aristeas, close by the image of Apollo in the market-place of Metapontum, with bay trees standing round it. But enough has been said concerning Aristeas.

With regard to the regions which lie above the country whereof this portion of my history treats, there is no one who possesses any exact knowledge. Not a single person can I find who professes to be acquainted with them by actual observation. Even Aristeas, whom I have just mentioned—even he did not claim in his poem to have got further than the Issedonians, but on his own confession what he related of the regions beyond was hearsay, being the account which the Issedonians gave him of these countries.

At first sight, even though we discount the miraculous element in it, Herodotus' story is startling enough: at least two and a half centuries before his time, that is, not later than *c*. 675 B.C., a Greek penetrated far into the hinterland beyond the Black Sea and brought back with him an essentially true account of the pressure of the nomadic peoples of those regions upon their westerly neighbours. The fact that it contained this truth indicates that the author of the *Arimaspea* either had himself made the journey which he professed to have made, or was using information gained from someone who had. There is too a notable ring of honesty about the poet's confession that the limit of his journey was the country of the Issedonians, and that his knowledge of the parts beyond depended upon hearsay.

If the poem is really to be dated in the seventh century we are hardly entitled to assume that its contents were derivative— for from whom, at that time when the Greeks were only just beginning to establish a foothold on the northern coast of the Black Sea, would they be derived? On the other hand it is hard to believe that the first Greek penetration into Scythia was also to be the deepest, and it is therefore natural to wish to bring the date of the poem down to a time when the information it contained could be ascribed to the settled intercourse between native and Greek traders in the coastal marts, or when the appearance of a Greek among the tribes of the interior would not be so strange. This prompts the question, is there any indication that the *Arimaspea* was in fact composed in the seventh century?

We must dismiss for the time being the prima facie evidence for the early date, the 'two hundred and forty years' of Herodotus. This is relevant to the dating of Aristeas himself, but it would only be relevant to the dating of the *Arimaspea* if we were sure that Aristeas was its author; an assumption which we cannot yet make, when not only has his authorship but his very existence been denied by some scholars. I therefore confine myself here to evidence related to the poem, and postpone consideration of its authorship to a later chapter [VI]. If in the meantime I call its poet Aristeas, it is without prejudice and merely as a convenience to by-pass the phrase 'the author of the *Arimaspea*'.

The poem provides itself with an upper terminus by its mention of the ousting of the Cimmerians from their homeland about the Sea of Azov. Already towards the end of the eighth century these had moved southwards past the Caucasus, and clashed with the Assyrian empire. After a defeat in *c.* 679 by Esarhaddon they turned west into Asia Minor, killed the Phrygian king Midas in battle, and in the middle of the century sacked Sardis and Magnesia; their power was then broken, under Scythian and Assyrian attack, but Cimmerian settlements persisted for a longer or shorter time at Sinope, Antandrus, and in Cappadocia (Minns 42; Rostovtzeff [1] 36).

Whether these Cimmerians were in fact one people, who invaded Asia Minor at one time from one direction, is doubtful; but what matters for my purpose is certain enough—that northern invaders whom the Greeks called Cimmerians were active in Asia Minor from *c.* 680 till *c.* 630 B.C. This nearby activity would have closely concerned the audience of a Proconnesian Greek poet, and have justified an explanation by him of why the foreigners had left their own land.

If we could be sure that the reference to the Cimmerian migration in the poem was topical and not historical, we could date the *Arimaspea* fairly confidently between *c.* 670 and *c.* 620. Aristeas may have spoken as if the Cimmerian emigration from Scythia was completed, but the movement of peoples which caused it was still continuing. The movement ceased after the seventh century—the evidence of sixth-century graves shows that by then the Scythian kingdom was well established and settled in south Russia (Rostovtzeff [1] 41)—and was not renewed till nearly 400 years later, by the Sarmatians (Vernadsky 74).

Rawlinson understood Herodotus' present infinitives (ἐπιτίθεσθαι and ἐξωθέεσθαι) of the Arimaspi, Issedonians, and Scyths (contrasted with the aorist ἐκλιπεῖν of the Cimmerians) to stand for present indicatives in *oratio recta* [T. 1]; but they may stand for imperfects, and I have emended Rawlinson's translation to meet this possibility.

There can be little doubt that the *Arimaspea* was known to Alcman, who mentioned the Issedonians in the form Ἐσσηδόνες.[2] Nevertheless this variant is for Schmid–Stählin (i. 303) and for Meuli (154), who favours a sixth-century date for the poem, sufficient proof not only that Alcman did not hear of his 'Essedonians' from the *Arimaspea*, but that he did not know of the existence of such a work at all. This is hardly reasonable. It is true that in the one place where they are mentioned in the fragments of the *Arimaspea* they are called Ἰσσηδοί; but this cannot be treated as evidence that the poem was unknown to anyone who did not use the same form: that would disqualify Herodotus! Aristeas could have used both Ἰσσηδοί and Ἰσσηδόνες, *metri gratia* —we should indeed expect to find such variants in an early poem. It is not difficult to account for the slight change to Ἐσσηδόνες as a mishearing of an outlandish name;[3] Alcman would more probably have heard the poem recited than have read it. Again, if he did not get his knowledge of this remote tribe from the *Arimaspea*, whence did he get it? From some proto-Aristeas, or *Ur-Arimaspea*? Finally, this, though it is the weightiest, is not the only indication that Alcman drew on the poem [40 ; 43].

About Alcman's own dates we cannot, unfortunately, be certain. D. L. Page, in his circumspect discussion of the question in his edition of the *Partheneion* (164), concludes that we are not entitled to accept more than that he lived some time in the seventh century. He may have survived into the sixth; but it would not, I think, be held that his *floruit* could be later than *c.* 600. That the lower terminus for the *Arimaspea* must be about this time is confirmed by archaeological evidence. In 1904 there was discovered in a barrow at Kelermes, near the river Kuban beneath the north-western spurs of the Caucasus, a silver mirror. The back of its disk is divided radially into eight segments, in each of which some picture is engraved: the 'Winged Artemis'; sphinxes; lions, boars, and other creatures; and in one segment two shaggy savages fighting with a griffin. It was made about the beginning of the second quarter of the sixth century B.C., and is the work of a Greek [89 ff.].

Here is our earliest example in Greek art of the 'grypomachy', the battle between griffins and men, which was later to become quite a popular theme. It seems to indicate that already by *c.* 570 monsters who were opposed by human adversaries were located in the Scythian region by report. For the artist of the mirror these monsters were griffins; we may guess that the two savages are meant to be Arimaspi, though they do not appear to be one-eyed (they never are in fact so represented in art).

There is of course the possibility that the artist was filling in his panel with a subject which had no connexion with the destination of the finished article—a conventional subject, perhaps, like the sphinxes, or even one out of his own head: a fantasy which itself was later to give rise to the rumours of northern barbarians doing battle with griffins. I think this is improbable. If the subject were a conventional one in Greek art we might expect to have some earlier example of it; yet we have none. Nor was it a fantasy of the artist's own, for he had precedents for his scheme in Phoenician art, where we find fights depicted between men and griffins, the attitudes of the antagonists being strongly reminiscent of those on the Kelermes mirror [87]. Why should he have resuscitated this scheme? It is curious that the first Greek example of the grypomachy which we have should virtually coincide with the opening of the Scythian market. The obvious explanation is that the artist had heard from some source of men fighting griffins in the country for which his mirror was destined.

Whether this source was Scythian or Greek, the identification of the men's monstrous enemy with the *griffin* could only have been Greek; for we have no reason to suppose that the early Scythians were acquainted with this beast, whereas we know that the early Greeks were [88]. Was it the artist himself who, hearing a Scythian story, equated the monsters therein with griffins? Or did he receive it from another Greek, with the equation ready-made (if indeed the whole story was not a Greek fabrication)?

If we knew that the artist dwelt in Asia Minor, I should have no hesitation in concluding that his intermediary must have been a Greek, and was likely to have been the *Arimaspea*; but he was probably an inhabitant of one of the recently established entrepots on the north coast of the Black Sea: if so, the possibility of his having got the story from his Scythian neighbours would have to be considered. This possibility might seem to gain in attractiveness from the statement of Herodotus that the Scythians heard of the one-eyed men and the gold-guarding griffins from the Issedonians, and passed the account on to the Greeks (iv. 27: παρὰ δὲ Σκυθέων ἡμεῖς οἱ ἄλλοι νενομίκαμεν, καὶ ὀνομάζομεν αὐτοὺς σκυθιστὶ Ἀριμασπούς). But even if Herodotus can be trusted when he says this (implying either that the *Arimaspea* was not the source of the Greeks' belief in the Arimaspi, or that the Scythians rather than the Issedonians were the informants of its author), his visit to the Scythian coast took place more than a century after the making of the Kelermes mirror, when relations between Scythians and settlers were long-standing and close, and the trade-route to the far interior well established—not a very good parallel for conditions at the beginning of the sixth century.

I am inclined, therefore, to conclude that the grypomachy motif was suggested to the artist from an outside source, and that a Greek one—the *Arimaspea*—and to regard it as buttressing the evidence of Alcman for a lower terminus for the poem. This, combined perhaps with the testimony of Aristeas himself that migratory movement was still continuing in the Eurasian hinterland in his day, will date it with fair certainty between *c.* 670 and the end of the seventh century, at latest.

I have deferred consideration of the surviving fragments of the *Arimaspea* so far because, in an investigation so beset by problems and dubiety, the one firm rock is the notice in Herodotus. On this foundation we must build upwards and (I fear) outwards, and it seemed best to see what could be inferred about the date of the poem from Herodotus and earlier evidence, and then to

inquire how far the professed remnants of it square with the result
so obtained; for these remnants are preserved in late authors, and
their genuineness cannot be taken for granted.

Twelve lines are quoted in all, six by the Byzantine Tzetzes
(frr. 3–5), and six by the author, known as 'Longinus', of the
work *On the Sublime*, written probably in the first century of our
era (fr. 7) [T. 3; 5]:

fr. 3   Ἰσσηδοὶ χαίτῃσιν ἀγαλλόμενοι ταναῇσι

The Issedi glorying in their long hair

fr. 4   καί φασ᾽ ἀνθρώπους εἶναι καθύπερθεν ὁμούρους
πρὸς βορέω, πολλούς τε καὶ ἐσθλοὺς κάρτα μαχητάς,
ἀφνειοὺς ἵπποισι, πολύρρηνας πολυβούτας.

And they say that there are men neighbouring them above towards
Boreas, numerous and very doughty warriors, rich in horses and possessing many flocks and many herds of cattle.

fr. 5   ὀφθαλμὸν δ᾽ ἕν᾽ ἕκαστος ἔχει χαρίεντι μετώπῳ,
χαίτῃσι⟨ν⟩ λάσιοι, πάντων στιβαρώτατοι ἀνδρῶν.

Each has one eye in his comely forehead. They are shaggy with hairs,
toughest of all men.

fr. 7   θαῦμ᾽ ἡμῖν καὶ τοῦτο μέγα φρεσὶν ἡμετέρῃσιν.
ἄνδρες ὕδωρ ναίουσιν ἀπὸ χθονὸς ἐν πελάγεσσι·
δύστηνοί τινές εἰσιν, ἔχουσι γὰρ ἔργα πονηρά,
ὄμματ᾽ ἐν ἄστροισι, ψυχὴν δ᾽ ἐνὶ πόντῳ ἔχουσιν.
ἦ που πολλὰ θεοῖσι φίλας ἀνὰ χεῖρας ἔχοντες
εὔχονται σπλάγχνοισι κακῶς ἀναβαλλομένοισι.

This too we remark with great wonder: men dwell in the water,
far from the land in the midst of the sea. Unlucky wights they are, for
they suffer grievously, with their eyes on the stars but their life
amidst the waves. Assuredly, lifting up their hands to the gods, many
are the prayers which they must make, with entrails sorely tossed.

Fragments 3–5, which are quoted by Tzetzes in uninterrupted
succession, though not a syntactic whole hang together in sense,
especially if we accept Hubmann's emendation of φασ᾽ for the
nonsensical σφᾶς of the manuscripts in 4. 1: the subject of φασί
may then be the Issedonians of fr. 3 (Ἰσσηδοί: another form of
Ἰσσηδόνες, according to Stephanus Byzantius under the latter

name; also used by Zenothemis [67 f.]), and fr. 4 may refer to the
Arimaspi as fr. 5 clearly does.

The subject-matter of fr. 7 presents more difficulty. Who are
these unlucky people whom it mentions? In the context in which
he quotes it 'Longinus' is discussing the treatment of the storm-
theme by poets, and compares the ways in which Homer and
Aratus do it: any tempest-tossed sailors, then, would seem to be
meant, but these would cause no surprise to a Greek, to whom
the hardships of a nautical life would be almost proverbial (cf.
vit. Hom. Herodotea 262: ναῦται ποντοπόροι στυγερῇ ἐναλίγκιοι
ἄτῃ, πτωκάσιν αἰθυίῃσι βίον δύσζηλον ἔχοντες). Is Aristeas then not
speaking here in his own person, but ascribing these words to some
landsman to whom ships would be strange? This is the view of
Rhys Roberts in his edition of the treatise of 'Longinus' (218),
and of Tournier (29), who thinks that men totally unversed in seafaring are expressing their astonishment at hearing of the boldness
of Greek sailors. The former would identify the speaker as an
Arimaspian, the latter as one of the untoiling Hyperboreans, and
see Aristeas as satirizing, through their mouths, his countrymen's way of life. However, we know that the author of the
Arimaspea did not reach the Arimaspians, much less the Hyperboreans; so Bowra (4), while accepting this general interpretation
of the fragment, suggests that it may express the view of the
Issedonians.

There are two slight indications that here it is not the poet
himself who professes to be speaking. First, Homer never uses the
particle ἦ except in the mouth of one of his characters (l. 5; J. D.
Denniston, *The Greek Particles* 279); but it would be dangerous to
assume that Homer's practice must also have been that of a poet
in a different genre, who, relating or professing to relate his
own personal experiences, would be entitled to express personal
opinions (cf. Hes., *Op.* 333). Secondly, the use of the plural
ἡμῖν and ἡμετέρῃσιν in l. 1: if this is really the work of a seventh-
century author these words are unlikely to refer to himself,
or to himself and his Greek audience, or to the Greeks generally
(Bowra 4 f.).[4] This argument has more weight, but it takes the
genuineness of the fragment for granted.

Regarding this thesis it must be remarked that the Issedonians, a distant inland people, would know nothing about Greek, or any other, seafaring in the seventh century B.C. In other words, Aristeas must be making it up, and he must be making it up to get a dig at his fellow-Greeks through the mouth of a barbarian. If so, I find it hard to believe that these lines can be from the seventh-century *Arimaspea*, they being appropriate neither to the age nor to the faithful reporting for which the poem, as we shall see, was remarkable.

There is another possibility: that sailors, or at any rate sailors in the ordinary sense, are not meant, in spite of the context, which is not in itself conclusive ('Longinus' merely says that the author of this passage thought it would inspire terror) [26]. Thus Meuli (155) thinks the sufferers are a sort of lake-dwellers, inhabitants of houses raised on piles in the midst of the water (so too Schmid–Stählin i. 303). The author of *Airs Waters Places* (c. 15) says that the dwellers in the marshland of the Phasis had houses just like this—οἰκήματα ξύλινα καὶ καλάμινα ἐν τοῖς ὕδασι μεμηχανημένα —but these or similar are hardly appropriate here: it would be gross exaggeration to describe such as 'far from the land in the midst of the sea', and their inmates as seasick; and why, or how (through the roof?), would they keep their eyes fixed on the stars the while?

For Bethe (877) they are legendary sea-dwellers; similarly Bowra (3 f.) has ingeniously suggested that they might be Steganopods, web-footed men bobbing up and down in the waves. This idea is commended by the fact that Alcman mentioned Steganopods[5] (Strabo 43), and, as has been seen, he appears to have known the *Arimaspea*. Aristeas may have heard (from the Issedonians again?) of the men-fish of old Chinese tale [194], or a story like that told by a Russian traveller much later of the Samoyeds on the coast near the mouth of the river Ob: that, in the words of Hakluyt (i. 467), 'one moneth in the yeere they live in the sea, and doe not come or dwell on the dry land for that moneth'. Bowra is disinclined to press his suggestion, on the ground that such creatures would hardly be called 'men'; but as Simias can call the Half-Dogs 'men' [68] perhaps it is not

impossible. A stronger objection to this, as to Meuli's interpretation, is the statement that they keep their eyes fixed on the stars—
comprehensible of sailors, but why should mermen do so?

Before examining the language of these fragments to see if we
can extract clues to their date a question arises: are they by the
same hand? More than half a millennium separates the preserver
of one group of verses, 'Longinus', from their putative author,
more than a millennium and a half the preserver of the other,
Tzetzes. In the case of the latter, a double act of faith is needed:
we must assume that he took the verses all from the same source,
and that he is quoting them correctly. His habit was to rely on his
memory, vast but not always accurate (*Chil.* i. 275 ff; cf. e.g. T. 13,
χαλκεῖον for γναφεῖον).

A first impression, from the style of the two groups, is that they
are the product of one brain. This is somewhat confirmed by
metrical analysis. The two groups are clearly too small to justify
any firm pronouncements on this score, yet they are large enough
to yield some results. In such a case the argument from metre is
more trustworthy when it tends to establish unity of authorship
than the opposite. An author may have his idiosyncrasies (e.g.
Apollonius' liking for four-word lines), but is unlikely to display
them in almost every verse; thus if such an idiosyncrasy appeared
in one group but not in the other it could not be taken as evidence
of different authorship (and obviously we must know a great deal
of a poet's work before we can say that he always *eschews* certain
metrical phenomena, as for instance Callimachus is said to eschew
the bucolic diaeresis after a spondee).

By way of a check I have compared with these two groups a
number of six-line passages, syntactically complete, taken at
random from other authors: three from the *Iliad*, including one
from the (supposedly intrusive) *Dolonea*; three from the *Odyssey*,
including one from the (supposedly intrusive) second *Nekyia*;
three from Hesiod, including one from the (Hesiodic) *Shield*; two
Delphic oracles from Herodotus; and two passages each from
Callimachus, Apollonius, and Simias.[6]

The most conspicuous differences between the Tzetzes and
'Longinus' groups are (*a*) in the number of spondees in the first

four feet (thirteen examples to nine); (*b*) in the number of trochaic caesurae in the first four feet (four to nine); (*c*) in the use of diaeresis (four to seven). But judged on these three counts alone the *Dolonea* was much closer to *Iliad* i than the latter to *Iliad* xxii; and on counts (*a*) and (*b*) the discrepancy was as great or greater between the two passages of the *Works and Days* ((*a*) five to nine, (*b*) seven to three), as also between those from Apollonius ((*a*) eight to three, (*b*) six to three).

If attention is confined to trochaic caesurae in the first two feet only, a difference is revealed between the two groups (none to three) which is not paralleled elsewhere. But this is the only substantial discrepancy. In the case of (*a*) above the difference is more apparent than real, for *both* the *Arimaspea* groups are above the over-all average (seven) in the freedom with which they admit spondees in the first four feet. Likewise in their use of diaeresis ((*c*) above) they are *both* well below the average (eleven). In fact, in all the phenomena examined with the exception of the trochaic caesurae, both groups are found on the same side of the average with each other. It is indeed remarkable that the Tzetzes group again and again occupies the extreme wing: it shows the largest number of spondees in the first four feet; of successive spondees (two examples in the first two feet, and one example of three in succession in the first three; equal as runners-up are the 'Longinus' group and the *Hecale*, each with three examples of two successive spondees); the least use of the trochaic caesura in the first, second, and fourth feet (no examples at all); the least use of diaeresis; and the lowest average number of words to the line. But, though the 'Longinus' group is nearer to the average, in none of these cases, with the exception of the trochaic caesura already mentioned, is it far away from its companion. I conclude, therefore, that there are no adequate grounds on the score of metre for believing that the two groups are by different hands, and some grounds for believing that they are by the same hand.

There is one oddity of prosody: the lengthening *in arsi* of the last syllable of χαίτῃσι in χαίτῃσι λάσιοι. Homer frequently so lengthens before certain words beginning with λ, but λάσιος is not one of them (*Il.* i. 189 στήθεσσιν λασίοισι). It is found later where one would not expect it (e.g. Theocr. xxii. 121 ἀπὸ λαγόνος; xxv. 246 ὑπὸ λαγόνος), but here Tzetzes himself may simply have omitted the νῦ ἐφελκυστικόν, as elsewhere.

Accepting that the two groups are by the same author, let us now see if the language of either helps to give him a date.

Fr. 5. 2 χαίτησι⟨ν⟩ λάσιοι, πάντων στιβαρώτατοι ἀνδρῶν. Στιβαρός, applied by Homer and Hesiod to human limbs and parts of the body, is not found until much later applied to men themselves (Ar. Thesm. 639). A somewhat similar extension is to be re-marked in the use of λάσιος here: it refers not to a part of the body but to the whole man, as if he were a shaggy-coated animal like a ram (Il. xxiv. 125 ὀῒς λάσιος) (Bowra 8). So at least we may take it, rather than as meaning 'with long, unkempt hair', when we should have to go to Xenophon, I think, for the earliest parallel use of the dative (e.g. Anab. ii. 6. 9 τῇ φωνῇ τρηχύς; Cyrop. ii. 3. 6 οὔτε ποσὶν ταχὺς οὔτε χερσὶν ἰσχυρός. Hellen-istic Greek preferred this construction to the 'accusative of res-pect'—Schwyzer–Debrunner, Griechische Grammatik ii. 168).

Fr. 7. 2 ἐν πελάγεσσι. This epic dative plural is found in the Odyssey (v. 335), Archilochus (fr. 12. 1), and the Homeric Hymns (iii. 73; xxxiii. 15), but always in the phrase ἁλὸς ἐν πελάγεσσι (hence Empedocles' αἵματος ἐν πελάγεσσι, fr. 105. 1). It occurs unqualified in the Alexandrians (e.g. Call. H. iv. 36; Ap. Rhod. iv. 240), a usage foreshadowed in Euripides (Or. 990 πελάγεσι διεδίφρευσε).

Fr. 7. 3 ἔχουσι γὰρ ἔργα πονηρά. The word πονηρός, not found in the Homeric epics or hymns, has in early Greek the sense of 'having or incurring troubles': Heracles was πονηρότατος καὶ ἄριστος (Hes. frr. 138, 139 R.; cf. Solon, fr. 15. 1f. οὐδὲ μάκαρ οὐδεὶς πέλεται βροτός, ἀλλὰ πονηροὶ πάντες). Secondary seems to be the sense of 'causing troubles', which develops into the common Attic meaning of 'bad', pravus, with a strong moral tone when applied to people. Ἔργα πονηρὰ stands at the beginning of this secondary development, as it were a bridge between the two senses: when the adjective is first applied to things it must have the connotation of 'having' (not of course 'incurring') 'troubles'; but things can only be said to have troubles in the sense of causing them to sentient beings (cf. Theognis 274). So in the so-called 'Homeric epigram' 14. 20 (*vit. Hom. Herodotea* 458) the poet prays that the potters' workshop and its contents may be smashed by the Centaurs and the potters themselves may groan when they see the trouble they are being caused—αὐτοὶ δ' οἰμώζοντες ὁρῷατο ἔργα πονηρά. In this fragment of Aristeas it seems to be no more than a periphrasis for πόνους, as Homer's τιτὰ ἔργα for τίσις and Empedocles' ἔργα ῥευστά for ῥεύματα (*Il.* xxiv. 213; fr. 121. 3). It is a short step to regarding nuisances as bad, and, when the nuisances are people, as morally bad. The non-moral sense of πονηρός seems to have become so unusual by the fourth century that Aristotle can misapprehend the line οὐδεὶς ἑκὼν πονηρὸς οὐδ' ἄκων μάκαρ (Victorius: μακάριος—cf. [Plat.] περὶ δικαίου 374a)—of origin unknown—to mean 'no one is willingly *wicked*' (*E.N.* iii. 5. 4); though the sense of 'causing troubles' recurs in the following century in Callimachus (*H.* vi. 65 Ἐρυσίχθονι τεῦχε πονηρά).[7]

Fr. 7. 5 φίλας ἀνὰ χεῖρας ἔχοντες. This 'reflexive' use of φίλος with parts of one's body, common in early epic, is found hardly, if at all, in the Alexandrians (at Call. *H.* iii. 25, ⟨μήτηρ με⟩ ἀμογητὶ φίλων ἀπεθήκατο γυίων, it may not be reflexive, but mean 'dear to me'; and at Ap. Rhod. i. 281 and ii. 710 it may mean 'loving'). But the early usage still occurs in the fifth century, in Empedocles (fr. 115. 3 εὖτέ τις ἀμπλακίῃσι φόνῳ φίλα γυῖα μιήνῃ).

Fr. 7. 6 σπλάγχνοισι κακῶς ἀναβαλλομένοισι. An extraordinary phrase: what sort of a dative is it? Hardly a locative, as one does not pray in one's σπλάγχνα, which are usually the seat of the passions or dispositions; though Empedocles seems exceptionally to connect them with ratiocination once (fr. 4. 3 γνῶθι διατμηθέντος (διασσηθέντος Diels) ἐνὶ σπλάγχνοισι λόγοιο). Anyway a predicative participle with such a locative would be unusual. Bowra (7 f.) suggests that this is a bold use of the instrumental dative: 'while prayer is normally made with words, in this case it is made with cast-up bowels; ⟨Aristeas'⟩ sea-folk are too miserable to utter any words': their prayers actually consist of 'physical reactions of a painful and undignified character'. The expression would then be very striking, and that our author is audacious in his use of language seems to me to appear in ὄμματ' ἐν ἄστροισι ... ἔχουσι, though here the meaning is unmistakable. Nevertheless I think myself that this is a 'dative of the accompanying circumstances', conjoined with a participle sometimes in Homer (e.g. *Il.* xi. 555 ἀπονόσφιν ἔβη τετιηότι θυμῷ), though the construction occurs more frequently later, in Xenophon, both with the perfect and the present participles: ἱππεύς τις προσήλαυνε καὶ μάλα ἰσχυρῶς ἱδρῶντι τῷ ἵππῳ (*Hell.* iv. 5. 7); ηὐλίζεσθε ἐγκεχαλινωμένοις τοῖς ἵπποις (*Anab.* vii. 7. 6); τάφρον ὤρυττε κύκλῳ περὶ τὴν πόλιν, τοῖς μὲν ἡμίσεσι τῶν στρατιωτῶν προκαθημένοις σὺν τοῖς ὅπλοις τῶν ταφρευόντων, τοῖς δ' ἡμίσεσιν ἐργαζομένοις (*Hell.* v. 2. 4—a startling example).

This examination of linguistic usage has produced little positive result. There are two indications of lateness, in the extended use of στιβαρός and the unqualified πελάγεσσι; perhaps a third in the 'dative of the accompanying circumstances' (if such it is) qualified by a present participle in fr. 7. 6. Against these are the earlier, non-moral sense of πονηρός and the reflexive φίλος; but the former reappears in Callimachus, the latter in Empedocles, and it is obviously easier to account for an early usage in a late author than for a late usage in an early one. However, as we appear to be dealing with a poet who uses conventional epic language in a somewhat unconventional way, perhaps little weight can be attached to these considerations. It remains to see if a study of the literary relationships and style of the fragments adds any help.

It is notoriously difficult to date a work solely by its literary relationships (that is, by similarities of phraseology with other works), because it is rarely possible to be certain which is the creditor and which the debtor. So here there is a similarity between fr. 7. 4 ψυχὴν δ' ἐνὶ πόντῳ ἔχουσιν and Archilochus, fr. 21 ψυχὰς ἔχοντες κυμάτων ἐν ἀγκάλαις. This is so striking as to be hardly ascribable to coincidence; yet it takes us nowhere. So with other such similarities, mostly adduced by Tournier (22 ff.); these therefore need not concern us, but there are two places where it seemed that some result might be obtainable.

Literary borrowing is of two types: conscious and unconscious. The former, when it is not simple plagiarism, tends to be *cento*—

the conflation of words and phrases from another work. The latter
tends to be a process of fragmentation and digestion, in which
the borrowed matter is broken up and the words are dispersed over
a number of lines. Here, some word or idea that the author has
used causes him to recall subconsciously a passage from some
predecessor where the same word or idea appeared, and so
others from that same passage are drawn in the train of that re-
collection, suggested to him as he gropes for expression, and
reproduced anew. If we posit this as a rule of thumb—and it
could never be more—, we might say that conscious borrowing
implies repetition or compression of phrases, unconscious borrowing implies dispersion.

Has this any application to fr. 4? At *Il.* ix. 154/296 we find

ἐν δ᾽ ἄνδρες ναίουσι πολύρρηνες πολυβοῦται.

This is obviously related to Aristeas'

ἀφνειοὺς ἵπποισι, πολύρρηνας πολυβούτας,

and both to fr. 134 R. of the Hesiodic *Catalogus*:

ἔστι τις Ἑλλοπίη πολυλήιος ἠδ᾽ εὐλείμων,
ἀφνειὴ μήλοισι καὶ εἰλιπόδεσσι βόεσσιν·
ἐν δ᾽ ἄνδρες ναίουσι πολύρρηνες πολυβοῦται
πολλοὶ ἀπειρέσιοι, φῦλα θνητῶν ἀνθρώπων.

Here it would be tidy to see Aristeas as consciously borrowing
from the *Iliad*, and the Hesiodic poet as unconsciously 'digesting'
or dispersing Aristeas' line, so that the latter's ἀφνειοὺς ἵπποισι
produces ἀφνειὴ μήλοισι in the line *before* πολύρρηνες πολυβοῦται.
Going farther, one might derive the πολλοί and ἀνθρώπων of the
last line of the fragment of the *Catalogus* from the πολλοὺς and
ἀνθρώπους of the first two lines of this fragment of Aristeas.[8] However, inasmuch as the Hesiodic poet actually repeats *verbatim*
the line from the *Iliad*, whereas Aristeas does not, it seems just
as likely that the former was consciously borrowing from Homer,
and Aristeas laying the lines from the *Catalogus* under contribution. The case might be argued either way.

Perhaps less ambivalent is fr. 3

Ἰσσηδοὶ χαίτῃσιν ἀγαλλόμενοι ταναῇσι.

This is clearly related, by exact metrical correspondence, to *Il.*
XX. 222

θήλειαι, πώλοισιν ἀγαλλόμεναι ἀταλῆσι.⁹

A line of Xenophanes (fr. 3. 5),

αὐχαλέοι, χαίτῃσιν ἀγάλμενοι (Wilamowitz: ἀγαλλόμεν') εὐπρεπέεσσιν,

which repeats χαίτῃσιν ἀγαλλόμενοι of Aristeas but breaks the
metrical correspondence with Homer, seems therefore to be the
last of the series. If so, the line of Aristeas could not be later than
c. 465 B.C.

More remarkable, however, is the use in fr. 4 of the language
of the Ionian geographers. In the first two lines,

καί φασ' ἀνθρώπους εἶναι καθύπερθεν ὁμούρους
πρὸς βορέω, πολλούς τε καὶ ἐσθλοὺς κάρτα μαχητάς,

there are no less than four technicalities, if I may so call them:
ἀνθρώπους, καθύπερθεν, ὁμούρους, πρὸς βορέω. These are illustrated from Hecataeus of Miletus and Herodotus: ἐν δὲ πόλις
'Υώπη· οἱ δὲ ἄνθρωποι ἐσθῆτα φορέουσιν οἵην περ Παφλαγόνες
(Hec., fr. 287); ἄνθρωποι 'Ωπίαι (fr. 299); 'Υπερβορέων δὲ πέρι
ἀνθρώπων (Hdt. iv. 32; still in Dionysius Periegetes (656;
846)); τὰ κατύπερθε ἔλεγε ἀκοῇ (Hdt. iv. 16 *et saep. al.*); Σεσα-
ρηθίων πρὸς Βορέω οἰκέουσι Χελιδόνιοι (Hec., fr. 100); Ἀψινθίοισι
πρὸς μεσημβρίαν ὁμουρέουσι ⟨Χερρονήσιοι⟩ (fr. 163; cf. frr. 108,
203, 204, 207).

It was the practice of Hecataeus sometimes, after naming a
people, to add a note on their manners (e.g. frr. 154, 284, 323,
335). Comparable is Aristagoras' exposition of the map of the
world to Cleomenes (Hdt. v. 49. 5–7)—and ll. 2–3 of this fragment of the *Arimaspea*, which indeed reads like a rendering into
pedestrian verse of an extract of Hecataeus. As we have seen, the
ultimate source of the words πολύρρηνας πολυβούτας was Homer
(if it was not from a common stock of epic formulae), but
the phrase might have been used as a ready-to-hand version
of, say, πολυπρόβατοι in Hecataeus. If this were so, it would
account for the presence of κάρτα, a word unknown to epic, and

rarely used at all in dactylic verse (I note Callimachus, fr. 608, and uncertain readings in Empedocles (fr. 4. 1) and another fragment of Callimachus (75. 6)), but common in Ionic prose. However, all these 'technicalities' can be paralleled piecemeal from Homer, with the exception of ὅμουρος (πόλις μερόπων ἀνθρώπων Il. xx. 217; καθύπερθε Χίοιο Od. iii. 170; πρὸς Βορέαο ... πρὸς Νότου Od. xiii. 110). In a poem more concerned with topography one might expect them to be more concentrated, and this very fact might have helped to cause their frequency in the Ionian geographers, who would have drawn on the *Arimaspea*.

The style of these fragments is discussed with sympathetic discernment by Fränkel and by Bowra. But however strikingly he uses them, the author's choice of words seems to me tame: though borrowing the language of epic, he avoids the grander and rarer words[10] and compound adjectives (except for the Homeric πολύρρηνας πολυβούτας); repetitive: he uses ἔχειν three times in as many lines in fr. 7;[11] and tasteless: the choice of the epithet χαρίεντι is inept in a description of fierce and ugly savages (the line is perhaps the somewhat unhappy child of a marriage of Il. xvi. 798 ἀλλ' ἀνδρὸς θείοιο κάρη χαρίεν τε μέτωπον with Hes. Theog. 143 μοῦνος δ' ὀφθαλμὸς μέσσῳ ἐνέκειτο μετώπῳ).[12] A similar tastelessness, of thought in this case, is shown in the description of sea-sickness. In a high proportion of the lines the thought is completed in the first half, the remainder of the verse being filled with repetitious padding: fr. 7. 1 θαῦμ' ἡμῖν καὶ τοῦτο (μέγα φρεσὶν ἡμετέρῃσιν) 2 ἄνδρες ὕδωρ ναίουσιν (ἀπὸ χθονὸς ἐν πελάγεσσι) 3 δύστηνοί τινές εἰσιν (ἔχουσι γὰρ ἔργα πονηρά) 5 ἦ που πολλὰ θεοῖσι (φίλας ἀνὰ χεῖρας ἔχοντες) εὔχονται . . . fr. 4. 3 ἀφνειοὺς ἵπποισι (πολύρρηνας πολυβούτας). Though only in the last case is the second half of the line filled with a phrase which could be called formulaic, yet this phenomenon might be an indication of oral composition; but it might argue no more than lack of artistry. If these lines are in fact spurious, they must, in my opinion, at least precede the Alexandrian era, for there is no trace here of Alexandrian sophistication and polish.

To sum up the results of this examination: what appears to be a reminiscence in Xenophanes is the strongest evidence that these fragments were composed at the latest about 465 B.C. On the other hand there are indications of a later date in the extended use of στιβαρός, the unqualified πελάγεσσι, and perhaps the geographical terms (together with κάρτα) in fr. 4. But Aristeas may have been using the language of epic in a fresh and unconventional (perhaps colloquial?) way (cf. Bowra 8), and it is not by any means impossible that his poem helped to form the usages of the Ionian geographers later. Much more compelling evidence of spuriousness is fr. 7, if it purports to give the description by an Issedonian of the wretched life of Greek mariners. To use a barbarian as a mouthpiece for a sort of burlesque of an important Greek calling is out of keeping with what we know of the Greece of the seventh century B.C., and with what we shall otherwise discover about the nature of the *Arimaspea*.

I should not care to pronounce a final verdict, though I think the balance of the evidence here considered is rather against genuineness. But of this much I feel fairly certain: even if these fragments are not the very words of Aristeas, frr. 3–5 are based on him, through the mediation of Hecataeus or some Ionian geographer (apart from the 'technicalities', the unusual but warranted form Ἰσσηδοί, which a forger would be unlikely to invent, vindicates this). Their matter, then, at least will still deserve attention.

KNOWLEDGE OF THE *ARIMASPEA* IN
ANTIQUITY

IF the fragments discussed in the previous chapter are genuine
they are to be dated in the seventh century B.C.; if spurious, in
the fourth or very early third, before poets had come to form
their taste according to those canons which are called Alexandrian. It is most improbable that a forged *Arimaspea* would be
produced while the genuine work was still extant, and it was
still extant in the time of Herodotus.

The fourth century was not a period when literary forgery
was rife. Heraclides Ponticus and Dionysius Metathemenus (or
Spintharus) wrote plays which they ascribed, the former[1] to
Thespis, the latter to Sophocles (D.L. v. 92). Yet such was not
common practice at that time, as we are told it was at the end of
the sixth and in the early fifth centuries, when Onomacritus and
the early Pythagoreans are charged with having perpetrated many
forgeries: Onomacritus in the name of Orpheus and of Musaeus;
Lysis and Hippasus in the name of Pythagoras; Pythagoras himself in the name of Orpheus (Suid. *s.* ’Ορφεὺς Λειβήθρων; Clem.
Strom. i. 131; D.L. viii. 7–8). Whatever we think of these charges
and the many others like them, compositions passing as those of
Orpheus were certainly current in the fifth century (cf. Eur.
Hipp. 953 f.; *Alc.* 966 ff.; *I.A.* 796 ff.), and must have been
written by someone. But the heyday of literary forgery dawned
with the Hellenistic era, when the eagerness of the Ptolemies and
the Attalids to acquire books for their new libraries led to a spate
of fakes.[2]

Literary forgeries can be divided into three classes: (i) Works
ascribed to fictitious or legendary or even divine characters,
such as Sanchuniathon, Chlonthachonthlus (Rohdeii 235),
Orpheus, and Hermes Trismegistus, some so-called but probably

imaginary 'early Pythagoreans', and oracles purporting to ema-
nate from such figures as Abaris, Bacis, or a Sibyl. (ii) Works
ascribed to historical personages, but with new titles—new,
in the sense that there is no independent reason to suppose
that the people to whom they were ascribed ever in fact wrote
works thus entitled. These are very common. The motive for the
false ascription might be convention or respect, as when poems by
Homeridae or Hesiodei, or treatises by members of the philosophical schools, were allowed to pass under the name of the
founder ('forgery' is hardly the proper word for these); or it
might be a desire to obtain a better reception and closer attention
for the work by giving it the *cachet* of a venerable name (this was
presumably always the motive for those in class (i)); or financial,
as in the cheating of the Hellenistic kings; or sometimes perhaps
even sheer devilment (Hippasus was said to have written the
μυστικὸς λόγος in order to bring its supposed author, Pythagoras,
into disrepute, and Dionysius seems to have passed his *Partheno-
paeus* off as Sophoclean for a joke. Heraclides himself when he
forged Thespis—perhaps only 'quotations' from him—must
have been either inventing evidence for his theories or hoping
to indulge in that purely aesthetic pleasure, found at times
among antiquaries as elsewhere, of 'getting away with it').
(iii) Works ascribed to historical personages, bearing titles known
to have belonged to actual works by those personages. This is
the category germane to our present study, but examples of it
are extremely rare—not surprisingly, as a forger would have to
feel sure, before embarking on his task, that the genuine work
was utterly lost, so that there was no danger of its turning up
again. As a natural corollary of this most forgeries of this type
are relatively modern productions, e.g. that of Cicero's *Consolatio*, and the Φοινικικά of Philo Byblius.[3] In fact, I cannot
adduce an ancient example. If Hecataeus' Γῆς περίοδος, in the
fragments we possess, were a forgery of the third century B.C.,
as J. Wells argued, it would provide one; but this view is not
now generally accepted (Pearson 31 ff.).

The chances are, therefore, that an *Arimaspea* was never forged
in a complete form: the most that is likely to have happened is

that some fourth-century author forged 'quotations' from it for his own purposes, in the way I have suggested that Heraclides may have forged 'quotations' from Thespis. This consideration indicates another way to the solution of the question whether the fragments are genuine; for if the *Arimaspea* can be shown to have been still extant in the Hellenistic era or later, that will be a strong argument for accepting their authenticity.

Clearly the first task here is to consider the contexts in which the quotations are preserved, to see if 'Longinus' or Tzetzes indicates whether his source is the poem itself. The answer of the latter is explicit: they were merely a few lines of Aristeas that he had happened to come across [T. 3: οὗπερ αὐτὸς μὲν ἔπεσιν ἐνέτυχον ὀλίγοις]. Yet even if Tzetzes himself had not told us this, we should have been able to deduce it by means of a touchstone which can be applied elsewhere too with significant results.

In the passage of the *Chiliades* in which the lines from the *Arimaspea* appear Tzetzes is speaking of the Hyperboreans. They are mentioned, he says, by Zenothemis and Pherenicus as well as by Aristeas, and he quotes from these authors in support of his statement verses which in fact do not appear to substantiate it: in the lines of Pherenicus Hyperboreans do occur, in those of Zenothemis and Aristeas they do not, though Issedonians and Arimaspi do. The reason for this apparent anomaly is that Tzetzes thought that the Arimaspi *were* Hyperboreans, following a tradition that was long-standing but not derived from Aristeas —for *his* Hyperboreans, as we know from Herodotus, were separated from the Arimaspi by the griffins (and also, as will be seen, by the Rhipaean mountains [39]).

This passage of Pherenicus (a poet of uncertain date, but earlier than Athenaeus, who quotes him) appears again at greater length in a scholiast on Pindar (*Ol.* iii. 28):

> ἀμφί θ᾽ Ὑπερβορέων, οἵ τ᾽ ἔσχατα ναιετάουσιν
> νηῷ ὑπ᾽ Ἀπόλλωνος, ἀπείρητοι πολέμοιο.
> τοὺς μὲν ἄρα προτέρων ἐξ αἵματος ὑμνείουσιν
> Τιτήνων βλάστοντας ὑπὲρ (Voss: ὑπὸ) δρόμον αἰθρήεντα
> νάσσασθαι Βορέαο γύην Ἀρίμασπον ἄνακτα

' . . . and about the Hyperboreans, who inhabit the edge of the world close by the temple of Apollo, and know not war. They, poets sing, sprung from the blood of the Titans of old settled beyond the limpid course of Boreas, [?begging] their acres of king Arimaspus . . .'. However the sense is to be completed (with λισσομένους v.s.?), here Hyperboreans and Arimaspi are closely conjoined (a *Scythian* king Arimaspus is mentioned by Diodorus Siculus (ii. 43); he is clearly a creature of poetic fancy). Stephanus Byzantius calls the Arimaspi a 'Hyperborean tribe', but far earlier than this they are Hyperboreans for Callimachus: those who first carried the corn offerings to Delos (Hyperboreans, according to Hdt. iv. 33) brought them 'from the fair-haired Arimaspi' (*H.* iv. 291)—called ἔθνος τῶν Ὑπερβορέων by the scholiast:

πρῶταί τοι τάδ' ἔνεικαν ἀπὸ ξανθῶν Ἀριμασπῶν
Οὖπίς τε Λοξώ τε καὶ εὐαίων Ἑκαέργη,
θυγατέρες Βορέαο.

So too in *Aetia*, fr. 186. 8 'the sons of the Hyperboreans escort' these offerings 'from the Rhipaean mount', and the men of Dodona 'are the first of the Greeks to receive them from their Arimaspian convoy':

υἷες Ὑπερβορέων
Ῥιπαίου πέμπουσιν ἀπ' οὔρεος, ἧχι μάλιστα
τέρπουσιν λιπαραὶ Φοῖβον ὀνοσφαγίαι.
Ἑλλήνων τάγε πρῶτα Πελασγικο[ὶ Ἑλλοπιῆες⁴
ἐξ Ἀριμα]σπείης δειδέχαται κο[μ]ι[δῆς.

Though Callimachus is the earliest author who we can be certain[5] made the identification, Stephanus (*s.* Ὑπερβόρεοι) asserts that it was made by Antimachus. If we accept Stephanus' text— and there is no adequate reason for emending to Καλλίμαχος with Ruhnken—we still cannot tell which Antimachus is meant. The poet of Colophon is perhaps the likeliest candidate, which would take the confusion back another century and a half. The 'Homeric' *Epigoni*, in which the Hyperboreans were indeed mentioned (Hdt. iv. 32), was said to be by an Antimachus; but if this were he of Teos[6] and he were really contemporary with the foundation of Rome, he would, of course, be too early to know about Arimaspi. Yet that the blurring of the distinction between the

Hyperboreans and their horse-keeping, nomadic neighbours began very soon after the appearance of the *Arimaspea* is shown by a fragment of the Hesiodic *Catalogus*, where they are called 'the well-horsed Hyperboreans' ([῾Υ]περβορέων εὐίππων: fr. 49 T. = *Pap. Ox.* xi. 1358, fr. 2. 21) [189].

The amalgamation of the Arimaspi with the Hyperboreans seems to indicate that men were forgetting the poem that first had introduced the former to the Greeks. The supersession of the tradition of the *Arimaspea* would have been helped by the interest which Utopias held for fourth-century prose writers. The desire to give these ideals a local habitation was one factor in the birth of the 'philosophical romance'; but the Atlantis of Plato and the Meropis of Theopompus (or his source) had their prototype in the blessed Hyperboreans, whose location had long been fixed. It is not therefore surprising that an author of this period wrote an entire treatise on them.

This was Hecataeus of Abdera (*fl.* second half of the fourth century B.C.), who, in his περὶ ῾Υπερβορέων, let his imagination run riot in an exuberance of detail. Not only did he describe the customs of the people, but he added a mass of topographical circumstance to give the ring of truth: the frozen sea of Amalcius; the island of Elixoea inhabited by Hyperboreans called Carambycae after a neighbouring river; another river, Parapanisus, flowing into the northern ocean; the city of Cimmeris. Jacoby (iii, note on 264 F 11) discusses the derivation of these names, and justly remarks that Hecataeus' powers of invention were not great. But it is interesting to find him subdividing the Hyperboreans, and giving names to the subdivisions. The Carambycae constitute the only sample of these names we know from Hecataeus; whether the Arimaspi were for him Hyperboreans cannot be said, but to include their neighbours with the latter would be an easy step in the process of providing a detailed Hyperborean ethnography, which perhaps Hecataeus started and others developed (Hierocles spoke of Hyperboreans called Ταρκυναῖοι—named after τὰ Ἀρκύνια ὄρη (Arist. *Meteor.* i. 13)?— in whose country were the gold-guarding griffins: Steph. Byz. *s.* Ταρκυνία).

These considerations destroy the value of the entry in 'Suidas' [T.11]: 'Aristeas: son of Democharis [204] or Caystrobius, from Proconnesus, epic poet. Author of the hexametric poem called *Arimaspea* (τὰ Ἀριμάσπεια καλούμενα ἔπη); this is an account of the Hyperborean Arimaspians, in three books. . . . He also wrote a prose *Theogony*, running to about a thousand lines (εἰς ἔπη ͵α).' At first sight this would seem to confirm the survival of the *Arimaspea* into the Alexandrian era, its division into books and cataloguing; but the statement that it was 'an account of the Hyperborean Arimaspians' is enough to show the untrustworthiness of the testimony. It is guesswork: τὰ Ἀριμάσπεια καλούμενα ἔπη is an echo of Herodotus (T. 12: τὰ ἔπεα ταῦτα τὰ νῦν ὑπ' Ἑλλήνων Ἀριμάσπεα καλέεται), and the bald summary of the contents a conjecture based on the title by someone to whom the identification of the Arimaspi with the Hyperboreans was the familiar tradition.[7] It may be added that we can discern enough of the actual contents of the poem to be sure that it contained much else besides an account of the Arimaspi; though this account must have caught the imagination of early hearers sufficiently to give a name to the whole work, as the slaying of Dolon gave the name *Dolonea* to what is now the tenth book of the *Iliad*.

Who was responsible for concocting the lie that 'Suidas' has perpetuated? According to W. Crönert, following Hiller, it was Lobon of Argos, an even mistier figure than Aristeas himself. We know of his existence only from two mentions by Diogenes Laertius, and anything that we say about him must be deduced from such fragments as we are prepared to assign to him. He was not, Crönert assures us, the evil-minded forger that Hiller had depicted, peddling false scholarship in the hope that men would take it for true, but a harmless joker, who would have doubled up with laughter had he found later generations taking his inventions seriously (128). Let us call the culprit Lobon, if that is more satisfying than to call him *x*; but I cannot believe that he preceded Callimachus (130: 'adhibuit Lobonem praeter Hermippum nemo Alexandrinorum, quod sciam. aspernatus est ut par est Callimachus', &c.), for such a *jeu d'esprit* as his must presuppose not only the bibliographical activities of the Alexandrian scholars (especially the division of longer works into 'books') but also common knowledge of them. Against this, Crönert's main argument for an earlier date (Lobon's use of ἔπος instead of στίχος to mean a line of prose (127)) does not have sufficient weight.

The importance of the extract of 'Suidas', then, is to prove the opposite of what it appears to prove: it indicates that the *Arimaspea* was not possessed by the cataloguers of the library at Alexandria (at least, not by the earlier ones), thus confirming the conclusion already foreshadowed by Callimachus' identification of Arimaspi with Hyperboreans.

The fact that it was not extant in Alexandria in the third century B.C. would not necessarily mean that it had disappeared from human ken, though in view of the zeal with which the early Ptolemies collected books for their library the probability would be that it had. But the poem might have turned up later. Is there any evidence that it did?

For an answer to this question it is natural to go first to our other source of professed quotation from the *Arimaspea*, 'Longinus', but unfortunately we get little help from it. In the context 'Longinus' is remarking how the great poets pick out the most striking circumstances in the situations they are describing, for example Sappho describing the symptoms of one in love, and Homer the dangers of the storm-tossed. This last is contrasted with the lines from the *Arimaspea* and the climax of a passage of Aratus remarking the hardihood of sailors who brave the rough sea at all seasons of the year (*Phaen.* 299). The comparison of Homer with the others is introduced thus: 'It is, I fancy, much in the same way that the poet in describing storms picks out the most alarming circumstances. The author of the *Arimaspea*, to be sure, thinks these lines awe-inspiring ... ' (trans. Hamilton Fyfe). From this it appears that 'Longinus' imagined all three of his examples to depict sailors in storms. I have already mentioned the difficulties involved in thus interpreting these lines from the *Arimaspea* [9]: if they are in fact about sailors they are probably not genuine; but if they are not about sailors it would seem that 'Longinus' did not know them in their context but only as a quotation.[8]

Why did 'Longinus' not name Aristeas here, but merely speak of 'the author of the Arimaspea'? He could hardly have been ignorant of who the author was reputed to be, for he was well acquainted with his Herodotus: had he forgotten—which would suggest both that he got the lines at second-hand and that Aristeas was not a well-known figure at that time? Or did he use this form of words to express doubt of that authorship (in which case we might rather have expected him to be more explicit, as he is over the Hesiodic authorship of the *Shield* (9. 5))? Or is it just a figure of contempt?

That the *Arimaspea* survived into Roman times seems so unlikely on the evidence so far considered that it comes as something of a shock to hear of a copy of Aristeas being picked up cheap in the second century of our era. The event is related by the purchaser, Aulus Gellius [T. 9]:

We had disembarked, on our way back from Greece to Italy, at Brundisium, and were strolling through that famous port, which Ennius has described by the unusual but exceedingly appropriate epithet 'well-favoured' [*praepetem*: cf. vii. 6. 6], when we espied some bundles of books for sale. I hurried eagerly across to them. They proved to be all Greek books full of tales and marvels, unheard-of things that passed belief, by old writers of no small authority— Aristeas of Proconnesus, Isigonus of Nicaea, Ctesias, Onesicritus, Philostephanus, Hegesias; the very volumes were disfigured with the mould of ages, and as filthy to the touch as they were to the sight. Nevertheless I inquired their price: it was astonishingly low, and as a result I bought a great quantity of books for a tiny outlay.

I spent the next two nights in running quickly through them, excerpting and summarizing a number of curious items which Latin authors have generally neglected; and I have introduced them into this work, that my readers may not, through ignorance, be caught entirely at a disadvantage in discussions about such topics.

Tournier (52), taking this testimony at its face value, thought that Gellius had lighted upon an actual copy of the *Arimaspea*.

Unfortunately it is not so. What manner of work it was is revealed by Pliny (*N.H.* vii. 9–26), who anticipates the extracts of the later writer in a fuller form, and, unlike him, assigns them to their respective authors. I set the two texts side by side, italicizing close similarities of language:

Pliny, *N.H.* vii. 9 ff.

A. Gell. ix. 4. 6 ff.

Esse Scytharum genera et quidem plura, quae *corporibus humanis vescerentur*, indicavimus... (10) sed iuxta eos, *qui sunt ad septentrionem versi*, haut procul ab ipso aquilonis exortu specuque eius dicto, quem locum Ges clithron appellant, produntur *Arimaspi*, quos diximus, *uno oculo in fronte media* insignes. quibus adsidue bellum esse circa metalla cum grypis, ferarum volucri genere, quale vulgo traditur, eruente ex cuniculis aurum, mira cupiditate et feris custodientibus et Arimaspis rapientibus, multi, sed maxime inlustres HERODOTUS et ARISTEAS Proconnesius scribunt. (11) super alios autem *Anthropophagos* Scythas in quadam convalle magna Imavi montis regio est quae vocatur Abarimon, in qua silvestres vivunt homines *aversis post crura plantis, eximiae velocitatis*, passim cum feris vagantes.[9] hos in alio non spirare caelo ideoque ad finitimos reges non pertrahi neque ad Alexandrum Magnum pertractos BAETON itinerum eius mensor prodidit. (12) priores Anthropophagos, quos ad septentrionem esse diximus, decem dierum itinere supra Borysthenen amnem ossibus humanorum capitum bibere cutibusque cum capillo pro mantelibus ante pectora uti ISIGONUS[10] Nicaeensis. idem *in Albania gigni* quosdam glauca oculorum acie,

Scythas illos penitissimos, *qui sub ipsis septentrionibus aetatem agunt, corporibus hominum vesci* eiusque victus alimento vitam ducere et ἀνθρωποφάγους nominari;

item esse homines sub eadem regione caeli *unum oculum in frontis medio* habentes, qui appellantur *Arimaspi*, qua fuisse facie Cyclopas poetae ferunt;

alios item esse homines apud eandem caeli plagam *singulariae velocitatis, vestigia pedum habentes retro porrecta* non, ut ceterorum hominum, prosum spectantia;

praeterea traditum esse memoratumque in ultima quadam terra, quae *Albania* dicitur, *gigni* homines, *a pueritia statim canos, qui noctu plus quam interdiu cernant.*[11] idem itinere dierum XIII *supra Borysthenen Sauromatas tertio die cibum capere semper.*[12]

(16) *in eadem Africa familias quasdam effascinantium* ISIGONUS et NYMPHODORUS, quorum laudatione intereant probata, arescant *arbores, emoriantur infantes,* esse eiusdem generis in Triballis et *Illyris* adicit ISIGONUS, qui *visu quoque effascinent interimantque quos diutius intueantur, iratis* praecipue *oculis,* quod eorum malum facilius sentire puberes; notabilius esse quod *pupillas binas in oculis singulis habeant.*

(22) in monte, cui nomen est Nulo, homines esse aversis plantis octonos digitos in singulis habentes auctor est MEGASTHENES; (23) in multis autem *montibus genus hominum capitibus caninis* ferarum pellibus velari, *pro voce latratum edere,* unguibus armatum *venatu et aucupio vesci*: horum supra centum viginti milia fuisse prodente se CTESIAS scribit, et in quadam gente Indiae feminas semel in vita parere genitosque confestim canescere. idem *hominum* genus, *qui Monocoli vocarentur, singulis cruribus, mirae pernicitatis ad saltum*; eosdem Sciapodas vocari, quod in maiore aestu humi iacentes resupini umbra se pedum protegant.[13] non longe eos a Trogodytis abesse, rursusque ab his occidentem versus *quosdam sine cervice oculos in humeris habentes.* . . .

qui *in pueritia canescant* et *plus cernant oculis per noctem quam interdiu*; item esse compertum et creditum *Sauromatas,* qui *ultra Borysthenen* fluvium longe colunt, *cibum capere semper diebus tertiis,* medio abstinere. (7) id etiam in isdem libris scriptum offendimus, quod postea in libro quoque Plinii Secundi naturalis historiae septimo legi, esse *quasdam in terra Africa hominum familias* voce atque lingua *effascinantium,* (8) qui si *impensius forte laudaverint* pulchras *arbores,* segetes laetiores, *infantes* amoeniores, egregios equos, pecudes pastu atque cultu opimas, *emoriantur* repente haec omnia nulli aliae causae obnoxia. *oculis* quoque exitialem *fascinationem* fieri in isdem libris scriptum est, traditurque esse homines in *Illyriis,* qui *interimant videndo quos diutius irati viderint,* eosque ipsos mares feminasque, qui visu ita nocenti sunt, *pupillas in singulis oculis binas habere.*

(9) item esse in *montibus* terrae Indiae *homines caninis capitibus* et *latrantibus,* eosque *vesci avium et ferarum venatibus*;

atque esse item alia aput ultimas orientis terras miracula *homines, qui 'monocoli' appellantur, singulis cruribus saltuatim* currentes *vivacissimae pernicitatis*;

quosdam etiam esse *nullis cervicibus oculos in humeris habentes.* . . .

(25) MEGASTHENES gentem inter Nomadas Indos narium loco foramina tantum habentem, anguium more loripedem, vocari Sciratas. *ad extremos fines Indiae* ob oriente circa fontem Gangis Astomorum *gentem sine ore, corpore toto hirtam* vestiri frondium lanugine, *halitu tantum viventem et odore,* quem *naribus trahant, nullum illis cibum,* nullumque potum, radicum tantum *florumque varios odores* et silvestrium malorum, quae secum portant longiore itinere, ne desit olfactus; graviore paulo odore haut difficulter exanimari. (26) super hos extrema in parte montium Trispithami *Pygmaeique* narrantur, ternas spithamas longitudine, hoc est *ternos dodrantes, non excedentes.* ...

(10) idem illi scriptores *gentem* esse aiunt *aput extrema Indiae, corporibus hirtis* et avium ritu plumantibus, *nullo cibatu* vescentem, sed *spiritu florum naribus hausto* victitantem;

Pygmaeos quoque haut longe ab his nasci, quorum qui longissimi sint *non longiores esse quam pedes duo et quadrantem.*

Clearly the source for both these passages was the same: the authors named by Gellius in his introduction all appear among those cited by Pliny (Onesicritus in this chapter (28); Philostephanus and Hegesias[14] get a mention much later in the same book (207)); the order in which the items succeed each other is identical, as would be natural if both our authorities were summarizing the same book; and the similarities of language are remarkable—so remarkable as to suggest the suspicion that Gellius was really using Pliny after all. But we have no right to impute such flagrant dishonesty to him, and it is discounted by the fact that he mentions his later discovery of the Plinian passage (7). When he goes on to quote the older writer (13 ff.) he makes proper acknowledgement. There is in fact actual proof to the contrary, which also proves that the common source was not a Latin work of any kind (lest there be those who would thus explain the resemblances of language): in their accounts of that delicate Indian tribe whose sole sustenance is the scent of flowers Pliny and Gellius diverge uniquely on a point of fact, the former saying that they clothe themselves in soft leafage (*vestiri frondium lanugine*[15]), the latter that they are feathered like birds (*avium ritu plumantibus*); a divergence which is most easily explicable on the assumption that one word in a Greek text has been confused with another (e.g. πτίλον with πέταλον). This is reinforced by the consideration that, though there is no disagreement about the height of the Pygmies, it is expressed in different ways (*ternos dodrantes* Pl.: *pedes duo et quadrantem* Gell.—both interpreting τρισπίθαμοι). Finally, there are the Greek proper names, sometimes transliterated, sometimes not—Anthropophagi, Ges clithron, Monocoli, &c.—and the hint of a Graecism in *semper* in the expressions *tertio die cibum capere semper / cibum capere semper diebus tertiis* (for διὰ τρίτης ἡμέρας ἀεὶ σιτοῦνται *v.s.*?).

We may conclude, then, that the source we are seeking was a Greek prose work concerning παραδοξολογούμενα περὶ ἐθνῶν: a mere compilation from various authorities who were named, after the manner of the extant Ἱστορίαι θαυμάσιαι of Apollonius. The terms of its date are Isigonus and Pliny: the latter half of the first century B.C. or first half of the first century A.D.[16] There is clearly no reason to assume that its author excerpted Aristeas at first-hand: he may have owed this information to a succession of previous writers. Whether there is here any testimony independent of Herodotus is a question to be discussed later [64 f.; 93].

That there was in existence in the first century B.C. a prose account of Scythia passing under the name of Aristeas was suggested by Hubmann (Tournier (32) disagrees with this). This view is founded upon a passage of Dionysius of Halicarnassus [T. 10]:

All the historians who preceded Thucydides used some of these stylistic devices. . . . Now what sort of style was affected by the really ancient authors, of whom nothing is known but their names, I am unable to conjecture . . . for in most cases their writings are no longer extant, and those which are are not universally accepted as genuine; instances are those of Cadmus of Miletus, Aristaeus the Proconnesian, and the like.

The *Arimaspea* cannot possibly be meant here: of course Dionysius is speaking of prose authors, as we should expect in one discussing the antecedents of a prose author, and as is confirmed by his mention of Cadmus. But what prose work of Aristeas could he have had in mind? We hear of none such except the *Theogony*, and that solely in the suspicious entry in 'Suidas'. It may never

have existed except as a title. Eudocia's statement [T. 11] that
it was 'a fine piece of work' may be discounted as evidence of its
existence: it is her own editing of her source, Hesychius of
Miletus.[17] If it did exist it was certainly not genuine, for such an
ascription would only have been possible after Aristeas had
acquired the reputation of a θεολόγος, like Abaris, Epimenides,
and Pherecydes, to whom also *Theogonies* were ascribed. If there
was in fact such a work, to which Dionysius is here referring, our
view of Lobon, or whoever he was, will have to be modified
accordingly: he was either an astonishingly industrious writer
if he composed all these forgeries himself, or a more truthful
reporter than has been credited if he found them already in
existence. But in fact Dionysius' meaning is ambiguous: it is not
clear whether he is instancing the writings of Cadmus and
Aristeas as works current at the time but of doubtful authenticity,
or as early prose works that had not survived. If the latter, then
he may have classed Aristeas as an early prose author because he
knew that he had been credited with a *Theogony*.[18]

Strabo, who says that Homer may have had the idea for his
Cyclops from Aristeas' description of the one-eyed Arimaspi,
probably owed this knowledge of the poem to Herodotus, of
whose language there seems to be a reminiscence in a later
reference to Aristeas as 'the poet of the so-called *Arimaspea*',
ὁ ποιητὴς τῶν Ἀριμασπείων καλουμένων ἐπῶν [T. 7; 25].

Only one more author, Pausanias in the second century A.D.,
gives the appearance of using the *Arimaspea* direct. Describing
the statue of Athena in the Parthenon he says that her helmet
had in its centre a representation of the Sphinx, flanked on both
sides with griffins. He goes on [T. 4]:

Aristeas of Proconnesus says in his poem that these griffins fight for
the gold with the Arimaspians who dwell beyond the Issedonians, and
that the gold which the griffins guard is produced by the earth. He
says, too, that the Arimaspians are all one-eyed men from birth, and
that the griffins are beasts like lions, but with the wings and beak of
an eagle. So much for the griffins (trans. Frazer).

These words have a Herodotean ring (especially the last, γρυπῶν
μὲν πέρι τοσαῦτα εἰρήσθω: cf. Hdt. iv. 15. 4 Ἀριστέω μέν νυν

πέρι τοσαῦτα εἰρήσθω; 36. 1 καὶ ταῦτα μὲν Ὑπερβορέων πέρι εἰρήσθω; and cf. μονοφθάλμους πάντας ἐκ γενετῆς with Hdt. iv. 23. 2 πάντες φαλακροὶ ἐκ γενεῆς), and the source of much of the passage could have been Herodotus. But it also comprises matter which is not from him—the statement that the gold is the yield of the earth, and the description of the griffins. However, it is clear from Pausanias' remark in the course of a digression on the Hyperboreans that he was not directly acquainted with the *Arimaspea* [T. 6]: 'Aristaeus of Proconnesus, who also mentions the Hyperboreans, *may perhaps* have learned something more about them from the Issedonians, to whom he says in his epic that he came' (trans. Frazer). The gist of all this is in Herodotus; even the tell-tale guess is suggested by him (iv. 32: Ὑπερβορέων δὲ πέρι ἀνθρώπων οὔτε τι Σκύθαι λέγουσι οὐδὲν οὔτε τινὲς ἄλλοι τῶν ταύτῃ οἰκημένων, εἰ μὴ ἄρα Ἰσσηδόνες. ὡς δ' ἐγὼ δοκέω, οὐδ' οὗτοι λέγουσι οὐδέν. ἔλεγον γὰρ ἂν καὶ Σκύθαι). An author who knew the poem himself would not have served up this jejune rehash of someone else.

Neither Pausanias' present (φησίν, T. 4) nor Strabo's perfect (ἐνδέδωκεν, T. 7) proves the contemporaneous existence of the poem or acquaintance with it. There is a tendency to repeat the tense of one's authority, a tendency that is natural, and sometimes perhaps a little disingenuous. This is illustrated well by Pliny *N.H.* vii. 9 ff., which, as I have shown [30], is not derived at first hand from the authors it quotes, in spite of appearing to be so by the almost invariable use of the present (*Agatharchides scribit* (14), *refert Clitarchus* (30), &c.).

In 1893 C. von Holzinger published, in *Zeitschrift für die österreichischen Gymnasien* (xliv. 394), the text of an idyll by Maximus Planudes, a fellow citizen of John Tzetzes though a century later in date. Humorous in intent, this poem owes its form and much of its phraseology to Theocritus. Thamyras opens by complaining to another bumpkin, Cleodemus, that this is the first time they have seen each other since they met in the house of a mutual friend, Aristaeus, at a festival of Demeter (l. 8):

ἐξότ' ἐνὶ μεγάροισιν Ἀρισταίου θαλίῃσιν
ἥμενοι ἡμέριοι Δημήτερος ἐκρινόμεσθα.

D

Cleodemus then relates a tale of troubles that have befallen him recently. Having lost an ox he went to Aethra, the town of Zeus (ἐς μεγάλου Διὸς Αἴθρην), to buy a replacement. This town was situated on the peak of Olympus, 'near the clouds, veiled from sight by the snow-flakes of Boreas' (l. 66: ἀγχινεφὴς χιόνεσσι καλυπτομένη βορέαο). When he arrived a festival to Zeus was being celebrated with games and music; and in the midst of the celebrations there came an Egyptian magician, a wild man with bestial features, black all over, with straggling beard and long, snaky locks darker than a raven's feathers (l. 78):

> τοῖσι δὲ τερπομένοισιν ἐφίκετο δαιμόνιός τις
> ἄγριος ἀνὴρ θηρὸς ἔχων ὄπα, θηρὸς ὀπωπὴν
> ἀμφιλαφὴς πλοκάμοισιν ἀμαυροτέροισι κοράκων
> οἷον ἐχιδναίῃσι τιταινομένοις πλέον οὐρῆς
> καὶ σκολιῇς ἑλίκεσσι ἑλισσομένοις ὑπὲρ ὤμων,
> μηκεδανὸν τὸ γένειον ἀπὸ στομάτων προϊάλλων
> καὶ μέλας ἅψεα πάντα, πρόσωπα χέρας τε πόδας τε.

With him was a boy carrying a large sack on his back.

The magician addressed the assembled crowd, and said he wanted to know what Zeus was doing at that moment. He then produced from the sack two apples, one of which he threw into the sky so that it disappeared. When it failed to return with news of Zeus he threw its companion after it, and when this too failed to return he threw the boy up. As the boy himself did not re-appear, the magician told the crowd that, on his repute as a sooth-saying seer (l. 144: εἴ τι ἐγὼ ἀψευδὴς τελέθω καὶ μάντις ἀληθής), the gods were celebrating the marriage-feast of Ares and Aphrodite. As he said this the boy returned from heaven with the apples in his pocket and holding a leg of chicken (l. 151: δεξιτερῇ δὲ ὄρνιθος πόδα καλόν), which he said Zeus had given him, together with greetings to the magician, 'the best of Zeus' servants' (l. 173: ἀμφιπόλων τὸν ἄριστον). Thamyras exclaims at the divine powers of the magician: he must be a pupil and a scion of the gods:

> δαιμόνιός τις ἐκεῖνος ἔην καὶ ἐπήβολος ἀνήρ,
> ἀθανάτων παίδευμα δίδαγμά τε οὐρανιώνων,
> ὃς τοιαῦτα τέτευχε· θεῶν νύ τοί ἐστιν ἀπορρώξ.

Cleodemus, however, has personal reasons for dissociating himself from this praise; for when the magician heard what he wanted, he took a mouse, changed it into an ox, and sold it to the bumpkin. But when it had been driven to Cleodemus' farm it turned back into a preternaturally fierce mouse, which slew the cat, invited in a multitude of other mice, at whose head it placed itself, and proceeded to eat Cleodemus out of house and home. To Thamyras' suggestion that they try to find the magician and bring him to book, Cleodemus replies that he never wants to meet him again, lest he turn Cleodemus himself into a beast, or throw him into the sky. Thamyras then promises instead to introduce Cleodemus to a man who will sell him a 'wooden cat'— a mousetrap.

Little notice was taken of this trifle for forty years. Then, in 1936, Th. Nissen pointed out that the original of Planudes' magician appeared to be Aristeas, that 'trickster if ever there was one' (T. 25: ἀνὴρ γόης εἴ τις ἄλλος). That he is called an Egyptian need deceive no one: Egypt was a conventional breeding-ground of magicians. His real identity is betrayed by his bestial appearance and raven-black locks—a reminder that Aristeas himself was a raven as well as a man. So too Aristeas was a great seer, μάντις [157], as is this magician. Again, though Planudes has not told us his wizard's name, he has shown us that the Proconnesian was in his mind as he wrote, for he calls the mutual friend of his two bumpkins *Aristaeus*— a form under which Aristeas himself sometimes appears [205]. More: Aethra, the town of Zeus, hidden beyond the snow-storms of Boreas, the north wind, is no market-town on the top of Mount Olympus, but in fairyland—in the land of the blessed Hyperboreans to be exact, which, as Pindar says, 'cannot be approached by land or sea', but is situated in the Olympian heaven, above the region of rain and snow (cf. *Od*. vi. 42 ff.), accessible only to the disembodied soul. The passage of the boy into the sky, and his return therefrom holding a chicken's leg, which proved he had indeed attended a banquet of the gods, is a parody of a soul-journey into the Beyond; just such a journey in the soul as Aristeas made to the Hyperboreans and related in the *Arimaspea*, which Tzetzes had read not long before Planudes wrote.

That Planudes has here been much influenced by a tradition about Aristeas the miracle-monger, whose soul visited the Hyperboreans [T. 20], is I think very likely. But Nissen goes too far in suggesting that the Byzantine idyll may be a parody of the *Arimaspea*. He was writing in the year following the publication of K. Meuli's widely accepted suggestion that Aristeas was a Greek shaman, who made journeys not in the body but in the spirit, and the *Arimaspea* a 'shamanistic' poem, describing such a journey of Aristeas' own soul. I hope to show that this view of the *Arimaspea* cannot be sustained [132 ff.].[19] There may still have been even in the fourteenth century popular oral traditions lingering on in Byzantium about the old 'magician' from nearby Proconnesus (cf. Nissen 299). Planudes may have known some such, or he may have got his ideas from old literary sources; but there is no cause to suppose that the *Arimaspea* itself figured among the latter. Had it still been extant in the preceding century the case might have been different, but Nissen is wrong is supposing Tzetzes to have read it [22]. The idyll of Planudes preserves a reminiscence of the poet but not of the poem.

There is another sphere besides the literary in which the *Arimaspea* could be expected to have left an impression: that of pictorial art. We have already seen that it probably did do so in the case of the Kelermes grypomachy of the early sixth century [6]. It remains, therefore, to review some other grypomachies of classical art.[20]

(i) Rhyton from Campania. A barbarian, right, clean-shaven, bare-headed, long-haired, with one foot on a small rock and a Scythian bow in one hand, with the other raises a sword to strike a griffin of the classical type [89]. The griffin has sprung on to the back of a horse facing the barbarian, and is burying its beak in the horse's neck (Reinach i. 53). As the same scheme of a griffin leaping on the back of its victim (this time an elk) is found on a leather sheet of the fifth century B.C. from Pazirik in the Altai (Rice 137), the theme is clearly both early and Greek in origin, and may well be owed to the *Arimaspea* in the first place. The barbarian has perhaps dismounted to steal the gold when his horse is attacked (The enmity between the griffin and the horse, which carried the robber to safety, became proverbial—Verg. *E.* viii. 27.)

(ii) Vase from Mylasa in Caria. Mounted barbarian, left, bearded, wearing spotted 'tights', spears half-prancing griffin, right. The terrain appears to be rough; to rear of horse's tail is 'blasted' tree. Above griffin is an amorphous stone-like object (Winter 376). The vase is a so-called pelike, which supplanted the amphora in the fourth century B.C.; Winter takes it to be an Attic export. The barbarian he calls a Scythian, probably rightly. Is the stone-like object meant to be a nugget of the 'guarded gold'?

(iii) Italiote warrior, left, mounted and wearing a helmet with two horns, menaces with poised spear a half-prancing, classical, and somewhat disgruntled-looking griffin, right (Reinach ii. 319). The scheme is that of (ii). There are four odd objects, two round and two square, above and below the combatants: formalized nuggets?

(iv) Aryballus of early fourth century B.C., by the Xenophantus painter, depicting a hunt by the Persian king. Right and left barbarians (some with 'Persian' names superscribed) attack two half-prancing griffins, one classical, the other a strange horned type, not unlike some fourth-century B.C. wooden griffins from Pazirik (Rice, pl. 21). In the background are a date-palm and silphium (Reinach i. 23; Minns 343). The vase comes from Panticapaeum (Kerch), and either it is an Attic export or the painter was an Athenian settler there.

(v) Vase of early fourth century B.C. Three Amazons fight three half-prancing classical griffins (Reinach ii. 295; Tischbein ii, pl. 9). Tischbein thinks (30) that this scene was suggested by some tradition that the Amazons made an expedition against the griffins to win the gold. (For another such fight between Amazons and griffins cf. Reinach i. 492.)

Not a great deal can be surmised from these representations. Just as the Kelermes grypomachy was a revival of a conventional scheme, though the revival was probably caused by the artist's knowledge of the *Arimaspea*, so the later grypomachies, though they differ schematically from that of Kelermes, tend to become conventional. This is illustrated by all the examples I have adduced, with the exception of (iv), which is a mere fantasy of the artist, in which quite different elements, Persian (dress and names), Libyan (silphium plant), and Scythian (griffins), are jumbled together. It is easy to infer that (i) and (ii) are nearer to the inspirational source, the *Arimaspea*, than (iii), but impossible to say *how* near they are. The Amazons are interesting: for though there is no evidence of a tradition such as Tischbein postulates, the first artist to conjoin them with griffins must have had some reason for doing so. The reason was, I suggest, that he knew that some authority placed the Amazons in Scythia—in griffin-country in other words; and we shall see reason to suppose that Amazons were indeed located in Scythia in the *Arimaspea* [50 ff.; 178].

The one considerable testimony that the *Arimaspea* survived into the Hellenistic era is that of 'Longinus'. But even this is not conclusive, and is, in my opinion, outweighed by the evidence to the contrary. Except for a few quotations, and these of doubtful authenticity, it had I think disappeared irrevocably before the foundation of the Alexandrian library. The hope, then, would be vain that we might recover any fragments of it from papyri; but it is reasonable to assume that the poem had debtors who did not always acknowledge their debt, and that borrowings from it were handed down the ages, in literature as in art, after their originator had been forgotten. It is in the identification of these that the only way now lies to a fuller discernment of the contents of the *Arimaspea*.

III

THE POEM'S DEBTORS

OF clues to probable borrowings from the *Arimaspea* our initial supply must be furnished by the information about its contents provided by Herodotus. The Issedonians are crucial. No subsequent author adds anything to his account of them;[1] he himself states that they lay beyond the range of the regular Scythian trade-route, though it was 'certain knowledge' that they inhabited the country to the east of the limit of this (iv. 25). No one save Aristeas ever, as far as we know, claimed to have reached them. Whether they were fact or fancy is at the moment of no importance: if the latter, they were *his* fancy; such account of them as the ancients possessed it is safe to credit to the author of the *Arimaspea*.

But it was the Issedonians who told of the one-eyed Arimaspi living beyond them, who stole the gold from the guardian monsters identified in the poem with griffins. These, then, are our primary clues: Issedonians, Arimaspi, and griffins (if gold-guarding or given a geographical location); mention of any of these will suggest the influence of the *Arimaspea*. Hyperboreans too will merit attention, but here care will be necessary, as the concept of the Hyperboreans may be older than Aristeas; they may be a contribution of his own Greek world to the furniture of the poet's mind, as was perhaps the appearance of the griffin [85 ff.]. Armed with these clues we must try to add to the matter which Herodotus expressly assigns to the poem.

The first addition can be made with confidence. The order in which the peoples succeeded each other according to Aristeas was: Scythians, Issedonians, Arimaspi, griffins, Hyperboreans, sea. Now according to Herodotus' contemporary, Damastes of Sigeum, 'beyond the Scythians dwell the Issedonians, beyond them the Arimaspi, then there are the Rhipaean mountains, from which Boreas blows and where there is always snow. Beyond these mountains the country of the Hyperboreans reaches down to the other sea' (ἄνω Σκυθῶν Ἰσσηδόνας οἰκεῖν, τούτων δ᾽ ἀνωτέρω Ἀριμασπούς, ἄνω δὲ Ἀριμασπῶν τὰ Ῥιπαῖα ὄρη, ἐξ ὧν τὸν βορέαν πνεῖν, χιόνα δὲ μήποτε αὐτὰ ἐκλείπειν. ὑπὲρ δὲ τὰ ὄρη ταῦτα Ὑπερβορέους καθήκειν εἰς τὴν ἑτέραν θάλασσαν, fr. 1: see Jacoby's note). That this is from the *Arimaspea* can hardly be doubted. The griffins are omitted, as palpable fable perhaps; remarkable restraint on Damastes' part in that case, if Strabo's criticism of him as an unreliable romancer is correct (47; cf. 684), which may be explicable by his use of a more sober intermediary— perhaps Hecataeus (cf. Agathem. *Geogr.* i. 1). But we learn something new—that the poem told of the chilly, remote mountain home of Boreas.

For Homer this wind dwells no farther afield than Thrace (*Il.* ix. 5), in a mountain or where is not indicated. But the mountain appears in the beautiful lines of Alcman (fr. 59):

> Ῥίπας ὄρος ἀνθέον ὕλᾳ,
> νυκτὸς μελαίνας στέρνον,

'mountain of Rhipe [*or* of the stormy blast, ῥιπᾶς?], blossoming with woods, breast of black Night'. That this is no Thracian Haemus but a distant range on the edge of the world towards the north is shown by its association with Night: it is the 'Rhipae buried in darkness', ἐννύχιαι Ῥῖπαι, of Sophocles (*O.C.* 1248).[2] Later, mathematical geographers were to deduce that the long arctic darkness must be counterbalanced by equally long daylight,[3] but the northern expanses, which the sun seemed to shun, were at first the special realm of cold, storm, and gloom to the Greeks for that very reason. Undeserved as this reputation was in fact (Minns 4 f.), it would be somewhat confirmed by the bitter winters of the Russian steppes. It was a reputation not fully enjoyed by Thrace, which, though cold, was not characterized as particularly dark.

We have already seen that Alcman knew of the Issedonians, and that it is difficult to escape the conclusion that he owed this knowledge to the *Arimaspea* [5]. It is reasonable to suppose that, just as he took his Issedonians from that poem, so he borrowed another feature from it, the far-off mountain of Boreas, enveloped in black wintry storms.[4]

From the same source as Damastes used appears to derive the reference in Hippocrates' *Airs Waters Places* 19 (a work generally considered authentic): Scythia

lies right close to the north and the Rhipaean mountains, from which blows the north wind (ὅθεν ὁ βορέης πνεῖ: cf. ἐξ ὧν τὸν βορέαν πνεῖν reported from Damastes). The sun comes nearest to it only at the end of its course, when it reaches the summer solstice, and then it warms it but slightly and for a short time. The winds blowing from hot regions do not reach it, save rarely, and with little force; but from the north there are constantly blowing winds that are chilled by snow, ice, and many waters [*or* heavy rains], which, never leaving the mountains (οὐδέποτε τὰ ὄρεα ἐκλείπει: cf. χιόνα μήποτε αὐτὰ ἐκλείπειν Damastes, and Eustath. *ad* Dion. P. 311), render them uninhabitable. A thick fog envelops by day the plains upon which the Scythians live, so that winter is perennial, while summer, which is but feeble, lasts only a few days (trans. W. H. S. Jones, very slightly changed).

And so the tradition continued. Near the Arimaspi

lie the Rhipaean mountains and the region which, from the likeness to feathers of the snow which is perpetually falling there, is called Pterophoros; a part of the world which Nature has written off (*pars mundi damnata* [cf. Luc. ix. 858] *a rerum natura*); it is buried in thick murk, is unproductive except of cold, and holds the icy womb where the north wind is conceived (*neque in alio quam rigoris opere gelidisque Aquilonis conceptaculis*).

So Pliny (*N.H.* iv. 88); and Lucan (iv. 106 ff.) likens to conditions at the pole an unbroken pall of rain-clouds which obliterated the Spanish day and joined night to night:

> sic mundi pars ima iacet, quam zona nivalis
> perpetuaeque premunt hiemes: non sidera caelo
> ulla videt, sterili non quicquam frigore gignit
> sed glacie medios signorum temperat ignes.[5]

It is in the *Airs Waters Places* that we first meet the adjective Ῥιπαῖος at first hand, later to be used by the Alexandrians and to become more familiar to us through the Latin form. It was

probably used too by Hecataeus of Abdera (Ael. *N.A.* xi. 1),
and possibly by Damastes and Hecataeus of Miletus; but the
lines of Alcman and Sophocles indicate that the mountain was not
so called by Aristeas. To him it was perhaps 'the mountain of the
storm gusts' (ῥιπῶν ὄρος *v.s.*) of Boreas—cf. *Il.* xv. 171; xix.
358 (ῥιπὴ Βορέαο); if he gave it a more specific name I shall
suggest that it was other than τὰ 'Ριπαῖα ὄρη [118].

The earlier usage makes its last appearance in Aristotle, who
records two further opinions about this range: it was incredibly high, and it was the source of a number of large rivers:
'Beneath the Bear itself beyond the farthest part of Scythia is
a range of mountains called the Rhipae: the stories told of their
size are too fanciful for credence, but they say that from them
the greatest number and, after the Istrus, the largest of
European rivers flow' (ὑπ' αὐτὴν δὲ τὴν ἄρκτον ὑπὲρ τῆς ἐσχάτης
Σκυθίας αἱ καλούμεναι 'Ρῖπαι, περὶ ὧν τοῦ μεγέθους λίαν εἰσὶν
οἱ λεγόμενοι λόγοι μυθώδεις· ῥέουσι δ' οὖν οἱ πλεῖστοι καὶ
μέγιστοι μετὰ τὸν "Ιστρον τῶν ἄλλων ποταμῶν ἐντεῦθεν, ὥς φασιν:
Arist. *Meteor.* i. 13. 350ᵇ7 (trans. H. D. P. Lee, very slightly
changed)). The immense height of this range was to provide
the sixth-century physicist Anaximenes with a screen to account
for the obscuration of the heavenly bodies as they moved laterally
about the earth from their setting to their rising.[6]

Though Herodotus nowhere names the Rhipaean mountains,
he does speak of mountains which might well be these. At the
limit of the northern trade-route dwell the Argippaei, in the foothills of a range lofty and impassable; it is inhabited, so these
people say, by goat-footed men, and beyond it are others who
sleep for six months of the year (iv. 23. 2; 25. 1). Now Herodotus
must have conceived of this range as lying to the north of the
Argippaei, for to the east of them were the Issedonians; if extended, it would then lie to the north of the latter too, exactly where
geographers located the Rhipaean chain [117; 181 f.]; while its
great height would befit the fabulous Rhipae.

From the feathery snow that perpetually fell there the Rhipaean region was dubbed by someone *Pterophoros* (Pliny, l.c.).
The unmetrical form of this name is sufficient to show that Pliny

was not here using Aristeas direct; and the author of it (Hecataeus of Abdera?) may have been inspired by no remoter source than Herodotus, who says (iv. 7): 'Above, to the northward of the farthest dwellers in Scythia,[7] the country is said to be concealed from sight and made impassable by reason of the feathers which are shed abroad[8] abundantly. The earth and air are alike full of them, and it is this which prevents the eye from obtaining any view of the region.'

Herodotus ascribes this information to the Scythians themselves, but it has that touch of the bizarre that suggests the *Arimaspea*, and the suspicion that it may have originated there finds some confirmation. First, its context: it occurs at the end of what Herodotus calls the Scythians' own account of their origin—they (or rather the so-called Royal Scyths, who regarded themselves as pre-eminent, cf. iv. 20. 1; 5. 4) were descended from one Colaxais. This name does not occur elsewhere, but an adjective Κολαξαῖος applied to a horse by Alcman (fr. 1. 59) is apparently coined from it to mean 'Scythian'. It seems not improbable that Alcman got his knowledge of this name, as of the Issedonians and the Rhipaean mountains, from the *Arimaspea*;[9] which need not, however, have contained all the genealogy and outlandish proper names given in Hdt. iv. 5–7, but merely the statement in 7. 2 that Colaxais divided his kingdom into three among his sons. This statement is part of a tradition which differs only slightly from that given by Herodotus immediately before, in 5 ff. They are doublets, in fact: in the first version the whole Scythian nation originates from Targitaus through his three sons; the Royal Scyths, descended from the youngest son, Colaxais, preserve the sacred gold which gave him his pre-eminence. In the second version Colaxais divides the whole of Scythia among his three sons; the sacred gold is preserved in the largest of these three kingdoms. It is noteworthy that Herodotus remarks (iv. 13. 2) that Aristeas does not agree with the Scythians in his account of the country (he means in his account of how its inhabitants came to be there). This must mean that the first version, in 5 ff., is not from the *Arimaspea* (for it treats the Scythians as aboriginals, whereas the *Arimaspea* said they were immigrants), but need not preclude mention in the poem of threefold rule among the Scyths by the descendants of their common progenitor, Colaxais (as in the second version).

A second pointer to the *Arimaspea* is in iv. 31. There Herodotus expresses the opinion that by these feathers the Scythians *and their neighbours* mean snow. So others beyond the Scythians spoke of the 'feathers': but how could Herodotus know this? From Scythian report heard in a Black Sea mart? Possibly; but it is also possible that these others are the Issedonians, and that the feathers are another bit of Issedonian lore retailed by Aristeas. If that is the case, Herodotus would be here making a tacit assumption similar to the open assertion in iv. 27, where he says that the Greeks got their knowledge of the Arimaspi from the Issedonians by way of Scythian intermediaries (not, he implies, by way of Aristeas).

Thirdly: when Herodotus, with a noteworthy fussiness, equates the feathers with snow-flakes, he may seem to us to be labouring the obvious. Yet strangely enough it does not seem to have been a similitude that readily presented itself to the Greek mind, or we might expect to meet it more often in the poets; but the only place where I recall having met it is in the *Prometheus Vinctus* (993 λευκόπτερος νιφάς)—significantly, I think, as there is evidence that Aeschylus made use of the *Arimaspea* in this play. It is possible that it did not occur to Hippocrates (l.c.), or his source, and that the thick fog (ἠὴρ πολύς) in which he says the Scythians live— puzzling, as the truth is rather the reverse (cf. Minns 5)—is another rationalization of the feathers which fill the air and obscure the sight.

In the region of the falling feathers, then, are the Rhipaean mountains and what Pliny calls the *Aquilonis conceptacula*, 'the womb in which the north wind is conceived' [41]. The nature of this *conceptaculum* is specified elsewhere by Pliny, in a passage already discussed in another context [28; T. 8]:

That there are Scythian tribes, and those quite numerous, who are cannibals I have already indicated. . . . Near those in the north, and not far from the very starting-point of the north wind and the cavern which is called 'the North Wind's Cave (*haut procu ab ipso aquilonis exortu specuque eius dicto*)—the place named *Ges clithron*—are said to be the Arimaspi, remarkable for having a single eye in the middle of the forehead. They are always fighting for precious ore with the griffins, winged animals whose appearance is well known, which throw up gold when they make their holes [cf. xi. 111]. . . . Many writers relate this, but the most famous are Herodotus and Aristeas of Proconnesus.

'The North Wind's Cave so-called' occurs again in [Plut.] *fluv.* 14. 5: the herb called Phrixa, to be found by the Tanais, is particularly abundant near 'the cave of Boreas', παρὰ τὸ Βορέου προσαγορευόμενον ἄντρον. Little reliance can be placed on the writer of this treatise, who gives as his authority here 'Agathon of Samos in the second book of the *Scythica*', an author and work otherwise unknown; but at least the Cave of Boreas is not his own invention, and its situation 'by the Tanais' need not surprise us when we recall that this river was thought by some to flow from the Rhipaean mountains (e.g. Mela i. 115; schol. *ad* Dion. P. 10). The other name mentioned by Pliny, *Ges clithron*, presumably means 'the entrance to the Earth's windpipe'—a sense of κλεῖθρον for which the earliest testimony is the Hippocratic corpus, and so it is perhaps not directly from the *Arimaspea*;[10] though anatomical metaphors applied to geographical locations are old enough (*Od.* i. 50 νήσῳ ἐν ἀμφιρύτῃ, ὅθι τ' ὀμφαλός ἐστι θαλάσσης). The actual name may have been coined by the same brain that produced *Pterophoros*, and like that may have summarized some statement in the *Arimaspea*.

I have said that Aeschylus knew the *Arimaspea*. At least he shows two of the primary symptoms—mention of griffins in a geographical location, and of Arimaspi; gold too is associated with the latter. Io, instructed in the future course of her wanderings by Prometheus, is told to avoid the griffins and the host of one-eyed Arimaspi who dwell about 'the spring of Pluton's stream that flows with gold' (*P.V.* 803 ff.):

ὀξυστόμους γὰρ Ζηνὸς ἀκραγεῖς κύνας
γρῦπας φύλαξαι, τόν τε μουνῶπα στρατὸν
Ἀριμασπὸν ἱπποβάμον', οἳ χρυσόρρυτον
οἰκοῦσιν ἀμφὶ νᾶμα Πλούτωνος πόρου.

The four words μουνῶπα στρατὸν Ἀριμασπὸν ἱπποβάμονα are almost a summary of frr. 4. 2 f. and 5. 1 of the *Arimaspea*—or the latter might be an expansion of Aeschylus!

Because of this, and because Aeschylus' sketch of Io's route is the earliest account of any length that we possess concerning the Greek geography of the northerly parts of the world, I propose to examine it in detail: if Aeschylus borrowed his griffins and Arimaspi from Aristeas he may have borrowed other things too. It is indeed not easy to discern any rational scheme underlying this account at all: it seems at first to be a mere jumble of geographical and mythological names, fitted together not only capriciously but incoherently. Nevertheless I believe that sense can be made out of it, and in the exposition that follows I give my own interpretation [Map I]. The clarification of Aeschylus' geography is, of course, only half the present task: we have also to identify borrowings if possible—always a difficult matter in the case of genius, which does not copy but digests its sources.[11]

In the *P.V.* Prometheus is fettered to a craggy mountain somewhere to the west of Scythia and to the north of Greece. Aeschylus does not, in this play at least, call this mountain the Caucasus; it is called so by one Hypothesis, in accordance with the usual tradition, but the warning later appended to the same Hypothesis should be heeded: 'Aeschylus does not say that the scene of Prometheus' binding is the Caucasus, as it is in the common account, but near the European margin of Ocean, as we can infer from the speech with Io.' The question need not concern us now whether the Caucasus was the scene of the *Prometheus Solutus*, or whether Cicero in his translation of a portion of it (fr. 193. 28) and Strabo (183) have been led into error by their acceptance of the traditional scene of Prometheus' sufferings: our present starting-point is sufficiently fixed by two bearings— Io has reached Prometheus (829–41) by way of Dodona, along the Ionian sea (the Adriatic), and then has changed her north-westerly course for an easterly one (παλιμπλάγκτοις δρόμοις 838); when she leaves him she will approach the Palus Maeotis from the west (707; 729–35). The first part of this agrees well enough with the account of Io's wanderings in Apollodorus (ii. 1. 3): she reached the Adriatic (*'Ιόνιος κόλπος*), then travelled through Illyria and crossed the Haemus range; but Apollodorus now takes her over the Thracian, not the Cimmerian, Bosporus, adding vaguely that she then 'went off into Scythia and the Cimmerian land'. He appears to be conflating two separate versions of the legend here.

When Io leaves Prometheus she will go east, and first come to the Nomad Scyths, far-shooting archers who live in caravans, whom she is to avoid by going along the shore (707–13):

> πρῶτον μὲν ἐνθένδ᾿ ἡλίου πρὸς ἀντολὰς
> στρέψασα σαυτὴν στεῖχ᾿ ἀνηρότους γύας·
> Σκύθας δ᾿ ἀφίξῃ νομάδας, οἳ πλεκτὰς στέγας
> πεδάρσιοι ναίουσ᾿ ἐπ᾿ εὐκύκλοις ὄχοις,   710
> ἐκηβόλοις τόξοισιν ἐξηρτυμένοι·
> οἷς μὴ πελάζειν, ἀλλ᾿ ἁλιστόνοις πόδας
> χρίμπτουσα ῥαχίαισιν ἐκπερᾶν χθόνα.

We hear of these wagon-dwelling Scyths as early as the Hesiodic *Catalogus*, where Phineus is driven by the Harpies *Γλακτοφάγων ἐς γαῖαν ἀπήνας οἰκί᾿ ἐχόντων* (fr. 54 R. = fr. 48 T.). Their position calls for little comment, except that Herodotus (iv. 19) puts them nearer the Palus Maeotis, east of the Borysthenes. So does Aeschylus himself in another passage (417 ff.); here they are separated from the Palus Maeotis by the river Hybristes.

It is with the next people that Io will have on her left, the inhospitable Chalybes, workers of iron (714), that a difficulty arises:

> λαιᾶς δὲ χειρὸς οἱ σιδηροτέκτονες
> οἰκοῦσι Χάλυβες, οὓς φυλάξασθαί σε χρή,   715
> ἀνήμεροι γὰρ οὐδὲ πρόσπλατοι ξένοις.

Hecataeus (fr. 203) puts them on the southern shore of the Euxine, north of Armenia, and this was the position assigned to them by e.g. Herodotus (i. 28), Xenophon (*Anab.* iv. 5. 34; v. 5. 1), 'Scylax' (88), and Apollonius Rhodius (ii. 1001). I know of no other author who puts them on the north side of the Black Sea, though curiously they are called *ἔθνος Σκυθικόν* by Hesychius, and by the scholiast on Apollonius Rhodius in several places (*ad* i. 1321, 1323; ii. 375—where they are put by the Thermodon;

and 378—where their neighbours the Tibareni are also called ἔθνος Σκυθικόν; yet both the Thermodon and the Tibareni are on the south shore of the Euxine).

Io's connexion with the Chalybes here may be a reminiscence of the earlier version of her wanderings already mentioned, whereby she crossed from Europe into Asia by the *Thracian* Bosporus, and travelled through Asia Minor on her way to Egypt, when she would have the Chalybes on her left. This earlier version is recounted by Aeschylus himself in the *Supplices* (538 ff.), where Io's route is through Phrygia, Mysia, Lydia, Cilicia, and Pamphylia. There is no mention of the Chalybes, however, and they would indeed be a considerable way off her path.

Another explanation is possible. In several places Aeschylus connects Scythia with iron: at *P.V.* 301 it is called 'the mother of iron', σιδηρομήτωρ; at *Sept.* 818 iron is called 'Scythian', at 728 'an emigrant from Scythia' (Χάλυβος Σκυθῶν ἄποικος). Was this collocation merely a poetic one (it is appropriate that the source of the metal of war should be a fierce people)? It would then be appropriate too to transfer the traditional iron-workers, the Chalybes, to Scythia. Or was it not poetic fancy but hard fact that Scythia was 'the mother of iron'? The description would be grounded on fact today, for Krivoy Rog and Kerch are among the most important producers of iron ore; but I do not know that we ever hear of exports of Scythian iron, and in antiquity the discovery of bronze rather than of iron was normally credited to the Scythians. A papyrus fragment (189) of Hellanicus is thus restored by Wilamowitz: [σιδηρ]ᾶ δὲ ὅπλα πρῶτος Ἑλλάνικος κατασκευάσασθαί φησιν Σάνευνον Σκυθῶν ὄντα βασιλέα, 'Hellanicus is the first to say that a Scythian king Saneunus discovered how to forge iron';[12] and Hesychius has this gloss on *Chalcidice*: 'Scythian; iron-mines were first discovered there' (Χαλκιδική· Σκυθική· τὰ μέταλλα τοῦ σιδήρου ἐκεῖ πρῶτον εὑρεθέντα). It is unfortunate that in the former every letter of the crucial word except the last should be conjectural; while in the latter σιδήρου may be a slip for χαλκοῦ— if Χαλκιδική has not been confused with Χαλυβική.

There is yet another possibility. The Chalybes, in their usual position south of the Pontus, are the neighbours of the Amazons who dwell around the Thermodon; and when Aeschylus put his Amazons about the Palus Maeotis (731) he may have transferred their neighbours the Chalybes as well to keep them company.

Having passed the Chalybes Io will come to a river which Aeschylus calls Hybristes.[13] This she must not try to cross but must follow to its source in the Caucasus, where, climbing the lofty peaks, she will round it and head southwards. She will now be in the country of the man-hating Amazons, who will be glad to lead another woman to the next landmark, the Cimmerian Bosporus:

ἥξεις δ' Ὑβρίστην ποταμὸν οὐ ψευδώνυμον,
ὃν μὴ περάσῃς, οὐ γὰρ εὔβατος περᾶν,
πρὶν ἂν πρὸς αὐτὸν Καύκασον μόλῃς, ὀρῶν
ὕψιστον, ἔνθα ποταμὸς ἐκφυσᾷ μένος   720
κροτάφων ἀπ' αὐτῶν. ἀστρογείτονας δὲ χρὴ
κορυφὰς ὑπερβάλλουσαν ἐς μεσημβρινὴν
βῆναι κέλευθον, ἔνθ' Ἀμαζόνων στρατὸν
ἥξεις στυγάνορ', αἳ Θεμίσκυράν ποτε
κατοικιοῦσιν ἀμφὶ Θερμώδονθ', ἵνα   725
τραχεῖα πόντου Σαλμυδησσία γνάθος,
ἐχθρόξενος ναύτῃσι, μητρυιὰ νεῶν·
αὗταί σ' ὁδηγήσουσι καὶ μάλ' ἀσμένως.
ἰσθμὸν δ' ἐπ' αὐταῖς στενοπόροις λίμνης πύλαις
Κιμμερικὸν ἥξεις, ὃν θρασυσπλάγχνως σε χρὴ   730
λιποῦσαν αὐλῶν' ἐκπερᾶν Μαιωτικόν.
ἔσται δὲ θνητοῖς εἰσαεὶ λόγος μέγας
τῆς σῆς πορείας, Βόσπορος δ' ἐπώνυμος
κεκλήσεται. λιποῦσα δ' Εὐρώπης πέδον
ἤπειρον ἥξεις Ἀσιάδα.   735

You will come to the river Hybristes, which does not belie its name: this do not cross—for its crossing is not easy—until you reach the Caucasus—none other—, loftiest of ranges, where the river spouts forth its might from the very brows of the mountain. In traversing those peaks which neighbour the stars you must bend your path southwards, when you will come to the host of man-hating Amazons, who one day will settle at Themiscyra by the Thermodon, where the step-mother of ships, Salmydessus, arms the sea with jagged fangs and gives evil entertainment to sailors. These Amazons will guide you on your way, and gladly, to where, right by the narrow gateway of the salt-mere [the Palus Maeotis], is the Cimmerian isthmus. This you must be bold to leave, and cross the Maeotian channel; far flung and ever-lasting will be the fame of your crossing, and from it men will call the strait *Oxford* [*Bosporus*]. Now, having left the plains of Europe, you will enter the Asian continent.

Here we are faced with the central problem of Aeschylus' geography: where is his Caucasus? If the Hybristes rises in the conventional Caucasus, and Io heads south after surmounting its peaks (721 ff.), then the Palus Maeotis and Cimmerian Bosporus which she next has to cross will be on the east or even on the south side of the Euxine—and she will cross from north to south (or east to west), instead of from west to east as it appears she does in 790 f.:

> ὅταν περάσῃς ῥεῖθρον ἠπείροιν ὅρον,
> πρὸς ἀντολὰς φλογῶπας ἡλιοστιβεῖς . . . .

Kiessling (210) solves the problem ingeniously: Aeschylus' Hybristes is a confusion of the Hypanis-Bug, which flows into the Euxine to the west of the Palus Maeotis, with the Hypanis-Kuban (or Anticites—Strabo 494), which rises in the Caucasus and empties into the eastern side of the Palus Maeotis [Map I], north of Colchis, where Aeschylus locates the Amazons (415). This confusion has caused him to shift the Amazons west, and place them on the far, or western, side of the Palus Maeotis.

For me this explanation lacks conviction because it is the sort of mistake a scholar might make, as Alexander Polyhistor and Pliny actually appear to do (Steph. Byz. *s.* Ὕπανις; *N.H.* iv. 84), but hardly a likely one for a poet who does not seem to have briefed himself with up-to-date information: it postulates too much topographical knowledge on the part of Aeschylus. It is also perhaps worth remarking that the earliest extant reference to the Hypanis-Kuban is in Aristotle (*Hist. An.* v. 552[b] 17). The river is not mentioned by Herodotus, though the Hypanis-Bug is.

There is in fact no need to suppose that Aeschylus has trans-ferred the Amazons at all, for there were Amazons to hand in the place in which he puts them, about the Palus Maeotis; and it is these that are meant here. They are the Σαυρομάται γυναικο-κρατούμενοι of Ephorus ('Scymnus' 878–85), the Amazons of Mela (i. 116; cf. Plin. *N.H.* vi. 19), whose presence in this district Herodotus (iv. 110 ff.) explains thus. After the Greeks had defeated the Amazons in the battle of the Thermodon they put their prisoners on three of their ships, and sailed for home. But the Amazons rose and slaughtered their captors; then, having no knowledge of seamanship, they were carried by wind and wave to the west shore of the Palus Maeotis. Here they disembarked, and soon made friends with some Scythian youths, who became their husbands. The Amazons refused to join the Scythians' families, on the ground that they would never get on with the women-folk; instead they persuaded their husbands to migrate with them.

Crossing the Tanais [says Herodotus (iv. 116)] they journeyed eastwards a distance of three days' march from that stream, and again northward a distance of three days' march from the Palus Maeotis. Here they came to the country where they now live, and took up their abode in it. The women of the Sauromatae have continued from that day to the present to observe their ancient customs, frequently hunting on horseback with their husbands, sometimes even unaccompanied; in war taking the field; and wearing the very same dress as the men.

This is clearly a Greek aetiological myth, to account for certain sociological characteristics of the Sauromatae, or perhaps more properly of the southern neighbours of the Sauromatae by the mouth of the Tanais and the eastern shore of the Palus Maeotis, Iazamatae or Maeotians (Rostovtzeff[11] 100 f.): they must be evidence of kinship with the Amazons of Greek legend, who dwelt on the south side of the Euxine (cf. Ebert 340). But Aeschylus, it should be noted, knows nothing of the myth as it is given in Herodotus; at least, he says the opposite: his Amazons will *later* make their home by the Thermodon (724 f.; cf. Sall. *Hist.* iii 73). It seems as if Aeschylus were here drawing on someone who had noticed the equality of the sexes in these tribes, and the similarity of their women with the Amazons of Greek legend, but who had preceded the time when the Greeks had worked up the aetiological story given by Herodotus. These tribes are considered to have been indigenous remnants, who survived the Cimmerian and Scythian migrations (Vernadsky 54); they would then have been in much the same position in the seventh century B.C. as in the fifth.

These northern Amazons are mentioned by Euripides (*H.F.* 408), and seem to be meant by Pindar: 'With this clear and gratifying prophecy Apollo quickly drove away to Xanthus, the well-horsed Amazons and the Ister' (*Ol.* viii. 46: ὡς ἦρα θεὸς σάφα εἴπαις Ξάνθον ἤπειγεν καὶ Ἀμαζόνας εὐίππους καὶ ἐς Ἴστρον ἐλαύνων). The Amazons of the Thermodon were not a favourite haunt of Apollo; these must be the northern Amazons, and be taken closely with the Ister—by which Pindar refers to that place beloved of Phoebus, the land of the Hyperboreans, where were the sources of the Ister (*Ol.* iii. 13 ff.).[14] Finally, these are the Amazons who are the antagonists of the griffins in classical art [37].

If Aeschylus' Amazons are Sauromatae or kindred Maeotian tribes, and Io approaches them from the north (722 ff.), then the course of the Hybristes must be from north to south, and the Caucasus, in which it has its source, cannot be the conventional Caucasus. Its situation fits perfectly the traditional location of the Rhipaean mountains, and if this identification is made the worst stumbling-block to the introduction of some order into Aeschylus' geography is removed.

Aeschylus' Caucasus shares another feature with the Rhipaean mountains besides geographical position: immense height. It is ὀρῶν ὕψιστος, 'loftiest of ranges'; its peaks 'neighbour the stars'— compare the fabulous height of the Rhipaeans [42]. In the passage of the *Meteorologica* there quoted, Aristotle says that the largest European rivers are reputed to have their source in the Rhipaean range: Aeschylus puts the source of the Ister there, as does Apollonius (Aesch., fr. 197 *ap.* schol. *ad* Ap. Rhod. iv. 284); so too does Pindar, as I have just stated. The Tanais rises in the Rhipaean mountains, according to Mela (i. 115), Pliny (*N.H.*

iv. 78), Lucan (iii. 272 f.), and Orosius (i. 2. 4) ; in the Rhipaean
Caucasus, according to Dionysius Periegetes (663 ff.) :

> τοῦ δ' ἤτοι πηγαὶ μὲν ἐν οὔρεσι Καυκασίοισι
> τηλόθι μορμύρουσιν· ὁ δὲ πλατὺς ἔνθα καὶ ἔνθα
> ἐσσύμενος Σκυθικοῖσιν ἐπιτροχάει πεδίοισιν

—on which comments Eustathius 'we must understand at this
point that the Caucasus [or the Caucasus in this context] is one
of (τι) the most northerly sections of the Taurus, reaching down
to the neighbourhood of the Cronian sea [the Arctic Ocean], of
which a part is also the afore-mentioned [l. 315] Rhipaean
range'.[15] The scholiast on l. 10 of Dionysius, quoting l. 663 on the
Tanais rising in the Caucasus, says (what might, however, be a
mere guess) ⟨'i.e.⟩ the Rhipaeans ; for some locate its source there'.
Those who thought that the Caucasus where the Tanais rose was
the conventional Caucasus had to postulate a course for the river
at first south to north from its rising, then turning south again to
the Palus Maeotis (Strabo 493)—though Herodotus had long before put its source somewhere in the far north (iv. 123; cf. 57).
Eustathius says that this northern Caucasus is the scene of
Prometheus' punishment (not true of the *P.V.* [46]), and is not to
be found in the map of the *periegesis*: τὸν δὲ τοιοῦτον Καύκασον,
περὶ ὃν καὶ ὁ τοῦ Προμηθέως πλάττεται ἀνασκολοπισμός, οἱ παλαιοὶ
μὴ ἐγκεῖσθαί φασι τῷ τῆς περιηγήσεως πίνακι (ad Dion. P. 663).
Whatever this means exactly (a map once attached to the
periegesis of Dionysius? or just 'the map of the world'?), it cannot
mean the conventional Caucasus. There appears to be a reference
to this Rhipaean Caucasus in [Plut.] *fluv.* 5. 3, where Cronus is
said to have fled from Zeus to the Caucasus, which till then had
been called 'the lair of the North Wind' (Βορέου κοίτη) (and so
Cronus gave his name to the Arctic sea adjoining, τὸ Κρόνιον
πέλαγος?).[16]

A grave difficulty is the association of Arabians with the Caucasus in *P.V.* 420 :

> Ἀραβίας τ' ἄρειον ἄνθος,
> ὑψίκρημνον οἳ πόλισμα
> Καυκάσου πέλας νέμονται

'and the warlike flower of Arabia, holders of the high-perched fortress near the Caucasus'. It is a difficulty which has not yet been satisfactorily resolved. The text as it stands is most improbable; yet no convincing emendation has been proposed. The codices' ὑψίκρημνόν θ' is unmetrical, and was not the reading before the eyes of the Medicean scholiast (λείπει ὁ καί). Of attempts to emend Ἀραβίας[17] Burges's Ἀβάριες most humours my theory; but unfortunately Avars are not heard of until nine centuries after Aeschylus, and in classical times Abaris is only the name of an individual Hyperborean. I suppose that it is not impossible that Aeschylus coined a tribe on the analogy of this name[18] (the Hyperborean Abaris was known to Pindar, fr. 283), but it would be very ill-chosen, as the Hyperboreans were the reverse of warlike. Oddly enough Ovid (*Met.* v. 86) has a *Caucasius Abaris* (again a personal name), but this is probably a mere coincidence.

If, in spite of this difficulty, my location of the Caucasus of the *P.V.* is correct, poor Io, as she wends her way up the western bank of the Hybristes, will be marching straight into the teeth of the north wind. Now there is a passage quoted by Galen as from the *P.V.*, though, as it is not found in our texts, Galen is thought to have written ἐν Προμηθεῖ δεσμώτῃ in error for ἐν Προμηθεῖ λυομένῳ (fr. 195):

> εὐθεῖαν ἕρπε τήνδε· καὶ πρώτιστα μὲν
> βορεάδας ἥξεις πρὸς πνοάς, ἵν' εὐλαβοῦ
> βρόμον καταιγίζοντα, μή σ' ἀναρπάσῃ
> δυσχειμέρῳ πέμφιγι συστρέψας ἄνω.

Paley tentatively inserted the passage in the *P.V.* between 791 and 792, to fill what appears to be a lacuna; there are, however, three objections to such a context—(i) πρώτιστα μέν of the fragment has no answering δέ (though of course the lacuna may have contained more than these four lines); (ii) Io will hardly avoid the harrying northern blasts simply by coasting along in the sea (792)—as if the sea were immune from winds; (iii) it implies that the north wind blows across south Russia only in a narrow corridor—why should Io, if she is travelling west to east, have to

take precautions against it at only one point? This last is a serious
difficulty for any interpretation except one—that Io is actually
nearing the birthplace of the north wind; and the fragment does
fit excellently between 720 and 721:

> ἥξεις δ' Ὑβρίστην ποταμὸν οὐ ψευδώνυμον,
> ὃν μὴ περάσῃς, οὐ γὰρ εὔβατος περᾶν,
> πρὶν ἂν πρὸς αὐτὸν Καύκασον μόλῃς, ὁρῶν
> ὕψιστον, ἔνθα ποταμὸς ἐκφυσᾷ μένος·   720
> εὐθεῖαν ἕρπε τήνδε· καὶ πρώτιστα μὲν   720a
> βορεάδας ἥξεις πρὸς πνοάς, ἵν' εὐλαβοῦ   720b
> βρόμον καταιγίζοντα, μή σ' ἀναρπάσῃ   720c
> δυσχειμέρῳ πέμφιγι σύστρεψας ἄνω   720d
> κροτάφων ἀπ' αὐτῶν. ἀστρογείτονας δὲ χρὴ   721
> κορυφὰς ὑπερβάλλουσαν ἐς μεσημβρινὴν
> βῆναι κέλευθον . . . .

Do not cross the Hybristes [says Prometheus] until you reach its
source, in the Caucasus. Keep to this course [i.e. following the course
of the Hybristes, as implied in 718 f.] without wavering, and first of
all you will come to the blasts of the North Wind's breath, where
mind its hurtling roar, lest with its stormy whirl it spins you round
and sweeps you from the very brow of the mountain [i.e. in the very
act of accomplishing your goal of turning the river]. Then as you are
crossing those peaks that neighbour the stars [i.e. in order to round the
source of the Hybristes; note the present participle—Groeneboom's
ὑπερβαλοῦσαν is misconceived] you must bend your way south . . . .

The μέν of the first line of the fragment has its answering δέ in 721
(there would, of course, be no more adversative force here than
between πρῶτον μέν and Σκύθας δ' ἀφίξῃ in 707 and 709); and
there would be considerable point in telling Io to be particularly
careful when she is approaching the cavern in the mountain
whence Boreas issued, where his full force would be felt.

Now, under the guidance of the Amazons, Io will come to the
Cimmerian Bosporus, and must cross from Europe into Asia
(729–35). Herodotus states that some made the Tanais and the
Cimmerian Bosporus the boundary between the continents,
others the Colchian river Phasis; and expresses surprise at the
arbitrary division of a world naturally one (iv. 45). We may
share Herodotus' surprise on one score at least: the choice of the

Phasis as a boundary. This, to Herodotus and subsequently, was the river known in modern times as the Rion, a third-rate stream flowing into the easternmost recess of the Euxine. Yet it was an older boundary-line than the Tanais, according to Agathemerus (i. 3).

This seems very odd. Yet even odder is an author who names *both* the Cimmerian Bosporus *and* the Phasis as the boundary of Europe and Asia, and this not in separate works written at widely different times but almost in the same breath: for Aeschylus himself at the beginning of the *Prometheus Solutus* says (fr. 191)

$$\pi\hat{\eta} \; \mu\grave{\epsilon}\nu \; \delta\acute{\iota}\delta\upsilon\mu\omicron\nu \; \chi\theta\omicron\nu\grave{\omicron}\varsigma \; E\mathring{\upsilon}\rho\acute{\omega}\pi\eta\varsigma$$
$$\mu\acute{\epsilon}\gamma\alpha\nu \; \mathring{\eta}\delta' \; \mathring{A}\sigma\acute{\iota}\alpha\varsigma \; \tau\acute{\epsilon}\rho\mu\omicron\nu\alpha \; \Phi\hat{\alpha}\sigma\iota\nu \ldots$$

'where great Phasis, forming a double boundary, to Europe and to Asia . . . '. How is this to be accounted for? Is it just another example of Aeschylus' wondrous ignorance of, or disregard for, geography, or is it rather that our own ideas about the Phasis need an overhaul?

It is obvious that the ideal dividing-line of continent from continent is a strait connecting sea and sea, such as the Hellespont, Propontis, and Thracian Bosporus; or, even better, connecting sea and Ocean, such as the Straits of Gibraltar. These were, of course, well-known and accepted boundaries. When the Greeks in their exploration to the north of the Euxine came upon the Cimmerian Bosporus, it would seem clear to them that here was another natural boundary between Europe and Asia, like the Thracian Bosporus they knew. Then it would be discovered that the Palus Maeotis was not a bay of Ocean, but a sea in its own right. Enclosed, yes, but in the far north-eastern corner there was a large channel (of what was later to be called the Tanais[19]): was this a river, or did it lead through into Ocean, to complete the division of the continents? Might this not be the Phasis, famous in Argonautic legend? For in the earliest form of this story the Argonauts sailed through the Phasis to the Ocean: in other words, Phasis was less a river than a strait. Hesiod took his Argonauts on their return journey through Phasis into Ocean, and in this he was followed by Hecataeus of Miletus (schol.

ad Ap. Rhod. iv. 284; 259).[20] Indeed, Mimnermus in the seventh century B.C. put the city of Aeetes, the goal of the Argonauts, on the brink of the eastern Ocean (fr. 11. 5 ff.):

Αἰήταο πόλιν, τόθι τ᾽ ὠκέος Ἠελίοιο
ἀκτῖνες χρυσέῳ κείαται ἐν θαλάμῳ
Ὠκεανοῦ παρὰ χεῖλος, ἵν᾽ ᾤχετο θεῖος Ἰήσων

'the city of Aeetes, where the rays of the swift Sun rest in a golden store-room, by the lip of Ocean, whither god-like Jason went'. He presumably went through the Phasis to get there.

So the original Phasis, the legendary strait, would make an ideal intercontinental boundary, and it can be seen how it might at first have been thought of as an extension of the Palus Maeotis. Later, after it had been discovered that the Phasis-Tanais was only a river after all and when the Milesians had penetrated to the easternmost corner of the Euxine and could sail no farther, they considered that they had really come ἐς Φᾶσιν, ἔνθα ναυσὶν ἔσχατος δρόμος, 'to the Phasis, the farthest point a ship can reach', and here was to be the permanent location of the Phasis, still with its legendary reputation, which it could now ill support. So later geographers, feeling the inadequacy of the Phasis-Rion as an intercontinental boundary, sometimes spoke of this boundary as 'the Phasis *and* the isthmus between the Pontus and the Caspian'.

But the Phasis of Aeschylus, or of his authority, was not this historic Phasis-Rion, but the older strait, conceived of as adjacent to the Cimmerian Bosporus and continuing the latter's function of cleaving the continents: so Aeschylus would be no more inconsistent in speaking of both Phasis and Cimmerian Bosporus as the boundary of Asia and Europe than he is when he speaks of the Cimmerian and Thracian Bosporus as the boundary (cf. *Suppl.* 544 ff.).

I suggest, therefore, that there were three stages in the history of the Phasis: (i) it was a legendary strait towards the east connecting the inner sea with Ocean; (ii) it was identified with the river which came to be called Tanais; (iii) it was later identified with the most easterly river flowing into the Euxine, the Rion.

(i) would account for its ever being selected as an intercontinental boundary at all; (ii) for the Tanais being selected as an intercontinental boundary; (iii) for the tiny Rion assuming such disproportionate importance. When Agathemerus says that the Phasis was an older boundary than the Tanais he is referring to stages (i) and (ii), not to stage (iii)—though without knowing it: for him the Phasis was the Phasis-Rion. If Aeschylus, or his authority here, were at stage (ii) it could also account for his speaking of the Tanais as well as the Phasis as the boundary of Europe and Asia in the *P. Sol.* (schol. *ad* Dion. P. 10; though we cannot certainly infer from this that Aeschylus specified the Tanais here by name).[21]

If this view is correct we should expect the Tanais sometimes to exhibit another trace of its former identification with the Phasis: that is, to have the character of a strait connecting the Palus Maeotis with Ocean. And so it does. According to the scholiast on Ap. Rhod. iv. 284 Scymnus stated that the Argonauts sailed by way of the Tanais to Ocean and thence back into the Mediterranean, adding by way of explanation (παρεκβολεύεται) that they manhandled the Argo at some point overland until they reached the sea. This sea is presumably the outer sea or Ocean, and Scymnus may have felt that it was necessary to explain how the Argonauts could proceed by ship from the source of the Tanais to the Ocean (cf. Timaeus *ap.* Diod. Sic. iv. 56); but I suspect that no explanation was necessary in the original version, in which the Tanais-Phasis actually debouched into the Ocean. This would accord not only with the earliest (Hesiodic) form of the legend known to us, but also with the latest: for in the *Argonautica* of 'Orpheus' the heroes sail right through into the Arctic Ocean by way of a river whose continuations or branches are the Araxes, Phasis, Tanais, Thermodon, and Saranges (749 f.; 1036–82)![22]

Again, Eratosthenes spoke of those who represented the continents as islands divided from each other by the Tanais and the Nile (Strabo 65; Hecataeus seems to have joined the Nile to the Ocean (fr. 302)). These, then, conceived of the Tanais as a strait (and that such a conception was current is confirmed by the fact

that the strait of the Cimmerian Bosporus was sometimes called
Tanais [note 21]); one such was presumably Pytheas of Marseilles,
for it is the obvious explanation of his claim to have explored the
whole ocean seaboard from Gades to the Tanais—which would
be a way of claiming to have explored the whole northern coastline of Europe (Strabo 104: πᾶσαν ἐπέλθοι τὴν παρωκεανῖτιν τῆς
Εὐρώπης ἀπὸ Γαδείρων ἕως Τανάιδος)—whatever river it was whose
mouth he took to be the northern outlet of the Don (cf. Thomson
146).

Finally, this same idea appears to underlie the opinion that
the Palus Maeotis was an inlet of Ocean: cf. Lucan iii. 277 (and
other passages quoted by Housman ad loc.):

> quaque, fretum torrens, Maeotidos egerit undas
> Pontus, et Herculeis aufertur gloria metis,
> Oceanumque negant solas admittere Gades

and where the Euxine drains the rushing waters of the Maeotian
Mere through the strait; and thus men deny that Gades alone lets
in the Ocean, and the Pillars of Hercules are robbed of their boast
(trans. J. D. Duff).

This is perhaps the place to mention another topic which,
while not germane to Aeschylus and Io's wanderings, may be
germane to the main inquiry. I have just said that 'Orpheus' connects up the Araxes, Phasis, Tanais, and Ocean. The Tanais is
said to be a branch of the Araxes by Hecataeus (of Abdera, probably [note 21]) and by Aristotle; the latter states that the Araxes
itself flows into the Hyrcanian (i.e. Caspian) sea (*Meteor.* i. 13).
According to Strabo (512 f.) the Araxes flows by one outlet into
the Caspian, and by several into the northern ocean; and Mela
says that the Caspian intrudes itself into the land at first like
a river through a long and narrow strait (iii. 38: 'mare Caspium
ut angusto ita longo etiam freto primum terras quasi fluvius
inrumpit'). Now wonder has often been expressed at the lack of
notice of the great river Volga before Ptolemy (who calls it
Rha); on the other hand, there are two passages in Herodotus
where the Volga is probably meant by the Araxes. In iv. 11 the
nomad Scyths, formerly dwelling in Asia, are said under warlike
pressure from the Massagetae to have moved across the Araxes

into the Cimmerian land, their present home. Here the Araxes is very plausibly identified as the Volga (Ebert 82); and in i. 201 f., where the Massagetae are placed 'towards the east, beyond the Araxes, facing the Issedonian folk' (ἀντίον δὲ ᾿Ισσηδόνων ἀνδρῶν), a description of the river is given which is in fact a conflation of at least two, one of which may well be the Volga (How and Wells i. 152), while Herodotus' 'towards the east, beyond the Araxes' suggests a river with a north–south orientation. Mention of the Issedonians is noteworthy, and How and Wells remark the poetic language (᾿Ισσηδόνες ἄνδρες), and think of the *Arimaspea* as a possible source (which would carry with it the corollary that the Massagetae were mentioned in the poem).

It seems to me that if in the beginning the Araxes-Volga was held to be an offshoot of the Phasis-Tanais we may have the germ of two later stories: (i) that the Araxes bifurcated into the Caspian and, through the Tanais, into the Palus Maeotis; (ii) that the Araxes flowed both into the Caspian and into the northern ocean. We may also have the germ of the persistent theory of Hellenistic and Roman times that the Caspian was an inlet of the outer sea (cf. Mela, l.c.). Herodotus perhaps says nothing on this head because of his scepticism respecting an encircling Ocean or an outer sea in the northern hemisphere (cf. ii. 23; iv. 45. 1; iii. 115. 2. Outer sea in the southern hemisphere: i. 202. 4). To illustrate my point I have shown the Araxes-Volga on Map I.

To return to Aeschylus. Where the Phasis was, there would be Colchians; hence the Colchis of the *P.V.* neighbours upon the Palus Maeotis, and the Amazons can be called 'inhabitants of the Colchian land', Κολχίδος γᾶς ἔνοικοι (415).

When Io has crossed into Asia her course will still be east (791); east too—towards the eastern Ethiopians (807 ff.)—after a lacuna of unknown length before 792, where she is swimming again: through what sea it is perhaps vain to ask, but the Caspian springs to the mind. Apollodorus is not specific: 'After travelling to Scythia and the Cimmerian land, after covering vast tracts of land and swimming wide stretches of sea in Europe and Asia, Io reached Egypt' (ii. 1. 3).

Now she will come to the plain of Cisthene, the country of the Gorgons, where dwell in darkness the Gorgons' aged sisters, the three Graeae with their single communal eye and tooth. These are to be avoided, as also are the griffins and the Arimaspians who dwell by the stream of Pluton:

> ὅταν περάσῃς ῥεῖθρον ἠπείροιν ὅρον,   790
> πρὸς ἀντολὰς φλογῶπας ἡλιοστιβεῖς
>
> .   .   .   .
>
> πόντου περῶσα φλοῖσβον, ἔστ᾽ ἂν ἐξίκῃ
> πρὸς Γοργόνεια πεδία Κισθήνης, ἵνα
> αἱ Φορκίδες ναίουσι, δηναιαὶ κόραι
> τρεῖς κυκνόμορφοι, κοινὸν ὄμμ᾽ ἐκτημέναι,   795
> μονόδοντες, ἃς οὔθ᾽ ἥλιος προσδέρκεται
> ἀκτῖσιν οὔθ᾽ ἡ νύκτερος μήνη ποτέ.
> πέλας δ᾽ ἀδελφαὶ τῶνδε τρεῖς κατάπτεροι,
> δρακοντόμαλλοι Γοργόνες βροτοστυγεῖς,
> ἃς θνητὸς οὐδεὶς εἰσιδὼν ἕξει πνοάς·   800
> τοιοῦτο μέν σοι τοῦτο φρούριον λέγω.
> ἄλλην δ᾽ ἄκουσον δυσχερῆ θεωρίαν·
> ὀξυστόμους γὰρ Ζηνὸς ἀκραγεῖς κύνας
> γρῦπας φύλαξαι, τόν τε μουνῶπα στρατὸν
> Ἀριμασπὸν ἱπποβάμον᾽, οἳ χρυσόρρυτον   805
> οἰκοῦσιν ἀμφὶ νᾶμα Πλούτωνος πόρου.
> τούτοις σὺ μὴ πέλαζε.

When you cross the current which divides the continents, towards the fiery-faced, sun-trod Levant . . . crossing the sea-surge, till you reach the plain of Cisthene, home of the Gorgons, where dwell the three daughters of Phorcys, aged swan-shaped maids, possessing one eye in common and one tooth; them the sun never gazes upon with his rays, nor the moon by night. Nearby are their three sisters, the winged Gorgons with snaky hair, bane of men, whom no mortal may look upon and still draw breath. Such are they that beset this place. And hear of another sight that you will see with woe: beware the sharp-beaked griffins, hounds of Zeus that bark not, and the host of one-eyed Arimaspians, the horsemen who live about the spring of Pluton's stream that flows with gold. Go not near them.

Where was Cisthene? A Thracian mountain ('Suidas' and

Harpocration, incorrectly glossing Isocr. *Paneg.* 153) will not do here; and the Medicean scholiast, who says it is 'a city of Libya or Ethiopia', is probably guessing, from the traditional location of the Gorgons in the west of Libya. That Cisthene on the farthest edge of the earth, which Cratinus mentions, is probably ours (fr. 309: κἀνθένδ' ἐπὶ τέρματα γῆς ἥξεις καὶ Κισθήνης ὄρος ὄψει). More information is lacking. To Aeschylus it was in the east, and that is all that can be said.

But what were the Gorgons doing here? The ancients usually placed them in the west—with one notable exception. Pindar says 'under the guidance of Athena, the son of Danae once came to the throng of the Blessed Folk [the Hyperboreans]; and he killed the Gorgon' (*Pyth.* x. 45); on which the scholiast exclaims rather pettishly:

What was Perseus doing, going to the Hyperboreans to behead the Gorgon? The Hyperboreans live in the southern (πρὸς τοῖς Ἐρυθραίοις μέρεσι [these are rather Hypernotians—cf. Hdt. iv. 36!]) and northern parts, but the Gorgons either in Ethiopia, that is, towards the south-east (πρὸς ἀνατολὴν καὶ μεσημβρίαν), according to some authorities [who probably meant the *western* Ethiopians, in fact], or, as others have it, on the western limits of Libya. That there are no Gorgons in the north is clear: for no one says there are.

There is a further oddity about the Gorgons' sisters, the Phorcides or Graeae, inasmuch as Aeschylus characterizes them uniquely as 'swan-shaped' (κυκνόμορφοι). The answers to these two problems may be related, and the consideration of them must be postponed for the present [101 f.]. Here I would merely say that the location of the Gorgons in the north-east is compatible both with Perseus' slaughter of Medusa during his visit to the Hyperboreans and with Prometheus' warning to Io to avoid them on her way to the eastern Ethiopians; for we need not suppose that Aeschylus thought of the disk of the earth as very large.[23]

This last point makes me think also that perhaps too much has sometimes been made of the position of the griffins here. By moving them from Apollo's Hyperboreans and posting them before Zeus' Ethiopians, and by calling these Apolline beasts 'hounds of Zeus', Aeschylus, it has been suggested, is deliberately extolling Zeus at the expense of Apollo (cf. Meuli 154). In fact, they need be no nearer to the Ethiopians than they are to the Hyperboreans; not on Io's route, but near enough to demand caution lest she deviate from it. I do not feel well qualified to judge whether the title 'hounds of Zeus' is religious propaganda or not; but I do feel that this phrase is dramatically effective in the context, whereas 'hounds of Phoebus' would have smacked of pedantry. Anyway, Zeus has some proprietary interest in griffins, which are half eagle—which is also called a 'hound of Zeus' in this same play (1021 f.: $\Delta\iota\dot{o}s$ $\kappa\acute{v}\omega\nu$)!

Of the Arimaspi[24] I merely note now that we have early confirmation of their equestrian habits ($\iota\pi\pi o\beta\acute{a}\mu o\nu a$), which are not mentioned by either Herodotus or the fragments (fr. 4. 3 need mean no more than that they *owned* horses) [198].

The final lap of Io's journey (807–15), alongside the river Aethiops to the Papyrus mountains, thence by the banks of the Nile to Egypt, does not concern us; but it is noteworthy how briefly Aeschylus dismisses it, and with what jejuneness of detail compared with the preceding narrative. This may be significant: however much or little it had fed his imagination up to this point, the *Arimaspea* would certainly not have helped him here.

Aeschylus' use of some authority, and that an early one, for his northern geography seems indicated by several things. There is enough system, and enough accuracy, to argue a fairly good source of information; yet the overall vagueness, the intrusion of mythological elements, the dearth of geographical names suggest that this source was earlier than the Ionian scientists. This dearth seems to be a defect which Aeschylus attempts to repair by his invention of descriptive names for his rivers Hybristes and Pluton; as though his source had merely referred to the one as a turbulent river hard to cross,[25] to the other as a gold-bearing river. The Sauromatae/Maeotian-Amazons have not yet been snugly accommodated to the Amazons of Greek legend, as they have in Herodotus (whose disembarkation of his Amazons on the western side of the Palus Maeotis in the first instance may be a sop to this earlier account). The strange situation of the

Caucasus and the Phasis points to a time before the eastern
Euxine had been properly explored and those features discovered which were finally to receive and keep these names.
(So far from being the first regions of the Black Sea coast to
become known to the Greeks, as might be inferred from the
common interpretation of the Argonautic legend, the east and
the north-east seem in fact to have been the last.[26]) Finally, the
identification of this early authority as the *Arimaspea* is suggested
by Aeschylus' mention of Arimaspians, griffins, and the lair of
the North Wind (for wherever fr. 195 should be placed I have no
doubt that it refers to this); also perhaps by the expression
λευκόπτερος νιφάς.

Aeschylus makes no direct mention of the griffins' role of
guardians of gold, though there seems to be a side-glance at this
in his gold-bearing river about which the Arimaspi live. On the
way this gold is obtained Herodotus is non-committal: 'Evidently
by far the greatest quantity of gold is to be found in the northerly
parts of Europe. Its provenance I cannot confidently declare:
but the story is that the one-eyed Arimaspians filch it away from
the guardianship of the griffins' (iii. 116: πρὸς δὲ ἄρκτου τῆς
Εὐρώπης πολλῷ τι πλεῖστος χρυσὸς φαίνεται ἐών. ὅκως μὲν γινόμενος,
οὐκ ἔχω οὐδὲ τοῦτο ἀτρεκέως εἶπαι, λέγεται δὲ ὑπὲκ τῶν γρυπῶν
ἁρπάζειν Ἀριμασποὺς ἄνδρας μουνοφθάλμους). This is clearly from
the *Arimaspea*, and adds something to Herodotus' statement in his
summary of its contents that the griffins were the guardians of
the gold: the Arimaspians were the thieves; and the phrase ὑπὲκ
τῶν γρυπῶν ἁρπάζειν shows that in the *Arimaspea* the Arimaspi
stole the gold and did not win it by doing battle with the griffins
(this is confirmed by the 'doublet' of the gold-guarding ants
shortly to be considered, and later authors who imply otherwise
(Pausanias' μάχεσθαι and Pliny's *bellum* [T. 4; 8]) are inexact and
were perhaps misled by the grypomachies of artists). But if we
want more details of Aristeas' account we must search later
authorities.

The paradoxographer excerpted by Pliny, whose date was
about the turn of the era, states that the griffins throw up the gold
when they make their burrows (*eruente ex cuniculis aurum*); the

authorities for this passage are said to be Aristeas, Herodotus, and many other writers [28]. In spite of this plurality, we have seen reason, from the mention of the starting-point of the North Wind, and of the feather-filled region in the related passage of Pliny [41], to accept the *Arimaspea* provisionally as the fountain-head of all that we are told in this paragraph [T. 8]. Pausanias reports Aristeas (though not at first hand) as saying that the gold which the griffins guard is 'produced by the earth' (τὸν δὲ χρυσόν, ὃν φυλάσσουσιν οἱ γρῦπες, ἀνιέναι τὴν γῆν) [32]. This phrase, with its undertone of spontaneous production—as if the gold sprang up from the earth like a crop—at first appears to contradict the Plinian account; yet that it is not obligatory to assume any such contradiction may be shown by Plato, *Crat.* 403a: the god of the underworld gets his name Pluto from his bestowal of wealth upon us, 'inasmuch as wealth is extruded from the depths of the earth' (ὅτι ἐκ τῆς γῆς κάτωθεν ἀνίεται ὁ πλοῦτος) —though here not mineral but cereal wealth may be meant (cf. Nilsson[i] 32). I think that all that Pausanias' expression is intended to convey is that, where the griffins live, the gold is near the surface of the earth—the topsoil is χρυσῖτις.

That the gold was dug up by the griffins is also the assertion of Aelian, using Ctesias (*fl.* end of the fifth century B.C.), in a most detailed and colourful description of the creatures and their antagonists.

I hear [writes Aelian] that the griffin of India has four legs like a lion, with claws as strong as strong can be, themselves very like lion's claws. It is winged, and the plumage on its back is reputed to be black, on its breast red, while its wings are neither of these colours, but white. Ctesias relates that its neck is bedecked with dark-blue feathers, that it has the beak of an eagle, and a head such as the artists and sculptors portray. Its eyes, he says, are fiery. It makes its nest in the mountains, and, though it is quite impossible to take a fully-grown griffin, they do sometimes capture the chicks. The Bactrians who are the Indians' neighbours say that they guard the gold of those parts, which, when they have dug it up, they weave into their nests, while the Indians take the residue. The Indians themselves, however, deny that the creatures intentionally guard the stuff: for, they say, griffins have no need of gold (and if they do say this they seem to me to be talking sense); the truth being that on the gold-prospectors' approach they take fright for their young, and so give battle to the intruders. They never oppose a lion or an elephant, though they fight and easily overcome any other animal.

The natives, out of respect for the mettle of these beasts, avoid making their gold-hunting expeditions by day. They come in the night-time, when they have most chance of avoiding discovery. Now the place where the griffins live and where the gold is to be found is a howling desert. Into this, waiting for some moonless night, come the treasure-seekers in armed bodies of one or two thousand men, with shovels and sacks, and dig. If the griffins do not notice them, they reap a double reward, for their own lives are preserved and they bring home their cargo, which those who have the peculiar art of the goldsmith purify and render into a rich recompense for the dangers they have undergone; but if they are caught in the act it is all over with them. I am informed that they return home after an absence of two or three years (*N.A.* iv. 27; cf. Ctes. *Ind.* 26 = Phot. *Bibl.* 46b).

This pleasing story looks uncomfortably like that which Herodotus tells, on Persian authority, about the gold-guarding ants (iii. 102 ff.). These inhabited the Bactrian desert, in shape like Greek ants, but in size intermediate between foxes and dogs. They had their homes in burrows, and in the process of making these they extruded sand which contained gold. This the Indians who bordered on the desert would gather in the following manner. They would yoke together camels in groups of three, two males with one female who had recently foaled; then, choosing the heat of the day, when the ants retire underground for a nap, they would approach, pack the sand into the saddlebags of the male camels, and make off at top speed. The ants, smelling the thieves, would emerge and give chase; and so fleet-footed were the insects that were it not for the start the Indians gained while their enemies were mustering, and the eagerness of the female camels to get back to their young, not a man would reach home. A similar tale is told by Megasthenes about a century and a half later, perhaps from an Indian source, though his account has reminiscences of, as well as additions to and sometimes disagreements with, Herodotus (fr. 23 = Strabo 706; Arrian, *Ind.* 15).[27] Clearly then it is Ctesias' griffins that are the interlopers, and we need suppose no more than that their author has let his imagination (aided by some pictures of griffins?) work upon a conflation of three adjacent passages of Herodotus—iii. 102 ff. on the gold-guarding ants and the Indians; iii. 116 on the gold-guarding griffins and the Arimaspi; and iii. 111 on the roc-like birds who used cinnamon, coveted by the local Arabians, to build their nests, which were plastered by means of mud against mountain precipices (νεοσσιὰς προσπεπλασμένας ἐκ πηλοῦ πρὸς ἀποκρήμνοισι ὄρεσι: cf. Ael., l.c. νεοττιὰς δὲ ἐπὶ τῶν ὀρῶν ποιεῖται . . . καὶ ἐκ τούτου [sc. τοῦ χρυσοῦ] τὰς καλιὰς ὑποπλέκει(ν); and xvii. 21).

The ripples of the ant–griffin confusion spread down antiquity. Nearchus said that the skins of these ants were like those of leopards in appearance (Strabo 705 *fin.*); Pausanias reproves those who say that *griffins* have spots like leopards (viii. 2. 7). According to comm. Bern. *ad* Luc. vii. 756 the ants dwell near the Arimaspians: 'ARIMASPUS Scythiae populus. aput quos μύρμηκες sunt quaedam animalia formicis similia quae terras eradunt et repertum aurum egerunt.' For Aelian they dwell near the Arimaspians' neighbours, the Issedonians, and while carrying out their duty of guarding the gold will go no farther than a certain river: 'The ants of India in guarding the gold will not cross the river Campylinus. The neighbours of these ants are called, and are, Issedonians' (*N.A.* iii. 4: οἱ μύρμηκες οἱ Ἰνδικοὶ τὸν χρυσὸν φυλάττοντες οὐκ ἂν διέλθοιεν τὸν καλούμενον Καμπύλινον ποταμόν. Ἰσσηδόνες δὲ ⟨οἱ⟩ τούτοις συνοικοῦντες τοῖς μύρμηξι καλοῦνταί τε καί εἰσιν[28]). I take it that here the Issedonians are the robbers, and that if they can pass the river with their spoils the ants give up the chase (cf. the Gallic serpents who pursue the mounted robber of their magic egg 'donec arceantur amnis alicuius interventu' (Plin. *N.H.* xxix. 52). Is it relevant that supernatural beings often cannot cross water?).[29]

If this is so, Aelian is, of course, carrying the confusion a stage farther with his *Issedonian* gold-thieves. Yet the mention of the nearby river is interesting, and may actually be a remote echo of something in the *Arimaspea* itself. The Hellenistic writer Zenothemis, in a couplet of his *Periplus* preserved by Tzetzes (*Chil.*

vii. 683) says: 'Marching with the Arimaspians is the great tribe of the Issedonians belonging to Scythia (?), by the springs of the river. . . . ':

σύγχορτον δ' Ἀριμασποῖσι⟨ν⟩ ναίει μέγα φῦλον
Ἰσσηδῶν Σκυθίης νάμασι πὰρ ποταμοῦ. . . .

The form Ἰσσηδοί is notable: though vouched for by Stephanus, it only otherwise survives in fr. 3 of the Arimaspea [8 f.]; also νάμασι: in the P.V. the Arimaspi dwell about the νᾶμα of the river Pluton [61]. Zenothemis probably gave the name of his river in the next line. Aelian's Campylinus is a possible candidate; or is this name only a distortion of another Asiatic river, the Campasus?

This latter features in a fragment of the Apollo of Simias (fl. early third century B.C.), which is of such interest that I quote it in full (Tz. Chil. vii. 695; Powell, Collectanea Alexandrina 109):

τηλυγέτων δ' ἀφνειὸν Ὑπερβορέων ἀνὰ δῆμον,
τοῖς δὴ καί ποτ' ἄναξ ἥρως παρεδαίσατο Περσεύς,
ἔνθα δὲ Μασσαγέται ⟨τε⟩ θοῶν ἐπιβήτορες ἵππων
ναίουσι⟨ν⟩ τόξοισι πεποιθότες ὠκυβόλοισι⟨ν⟩,
θεσπέσιόν τε περὶ ρόον ἤλυθον ἀενάοιο   5
Καμπάσου, ὃς ⟨θ'⟩ ἅλα δῖαν ἐς ἀθανάτην φέρει ὕδωρ.
ἐκ δ' ἱκόμην ἐλάταισι περὶ χλωρῇσιν ἐρεμνὰς
νήσους, ὑψικόμοισιν ἐπηρεφέας δονάκεσσιν.
ἡμικύνων τ' ἐνόησα γένος περιώσιον ἀνδρῶν,
τοῖς ὤμων καθύπερθεν ἐυστρεφέων κύνεος κρὰς   10
τέτροφε γαμφηλῇσι περικρατέεσσιν ἐρυμνός.
τῶν μέν θ' ὥστε κυνῶν ὑλακὴ πέλει, οὐδέ τι τοίγε
ἄλλων ἀγνώσσουσι βροτῶν ὀνομάκλυτον αὐδήν.

And passing through the rich land of the far-off Hyperboreans, who once feasted the princely hero Perseus and where dwell the Massagetae, riders of fleet steeds, whose trusty weapon is the swift-sped arrow, I approached the wondrous stream of ever-flowing Campasus, which rolls its waters to the divine immortal sea. And my way lay by islands dark with green firs,[30] overgrown with lofty reeds; and I remarked the monstrous race of men who are half dog, upon whose supple necks is set a canine head armed with powerful jaws. Like dogs too they bark, yet comprehend the articulate(?) speech of other men.

This combines the marvels of the paradoxographer with the orderly progress of the guide-book: we pass from the Hyperboreans by way of the Massagetae to the giant reeds and Dogmen (of India?).[31] But the effect of speed is remarkable, as also the apparent disregard of water-obstacles in reaching the islands of l. 8: who is this traveller who speaks in the first person, and how was he travelling?

Antoninus Liberalis (*Met.* 20) tells the story of the Babylonian Cleinis, who was so friendly with Apollo that he often accompanied the god on his visits to his temple among the Hyperboreans and witnessed the ass-sacrifices there (ὁμοῦ τοῖς θεοῖς τούτοις [Apollo and Artemis] ἀφίκετο πρὸς τὸν ναὸν τοῦ Ἀπόλλωνος τὸν[32] ἐν Ὑπερβορέοις καὶ εἶδεν ἱερουργουμένας αὐτῷ τὰς θυσίας τῶν ὄνων). Later, however, he got into trouble by trying to sacrifice asses at home on his own account, and Apollo finally turned the whole family into birds. The scholiast says that the story is told by Boeus in the second book (of his *Ornithogonia*), and by Simias in the *Apollo*. How much of it was related by Simias we do not know, but we may guess fairly confidently at the friendship with Apollo and the visit to the Hyperboreans, for the ass-sacrifice, which is only welcome to the god when performed by the Hyperboreans, is fundamental to the story. It comes, of course, from Pind. *Pyth.* x. 33 ff., and the second line of Simias' fragment is inspired by the line almost preceding this (31: παρ' οἷς ποτε Περσεὺς ἐδαίσατο λαγέτας). I approve, therefore, of the view that Cleinis is the speaker here (cf. Powell), and believe that he is giving an account of a ride in the god's chariot[33] on the way back from the Hyperboreans. That the tale is not mythology but fourth-century or Alexandrian romantic invention is shown by the fact that there is no mention of Cleinis in earlier literature, and that he is a Babylonian; but the inventor, in depicting his hero as 'seized by Apollo', φοιβόληπτος (in a literal sense—as carried to and from the Hyperboreans *through the air* in the god's chariot[34]), and as describing the peoples and marvels on his route, was following a tradition about Aristeas [121 f.].

The Campasus, then, is situated in the north-east near the Massagetae, and is no doubt to be identified with the river called

by Pliny Caspasus, which flows through the country of the Asiatic
Scyths, who comprise the Sacae, Massagetae, Essedonians [184],
Arimaspi, and others (*N.H.* vi. 51). I do not, however, think that
the alteration of Καμπάσου in l. 6 here to Κασπάσου (cf. Powell)
on this account is justified, and would prefer to emend the text
of Pliny, if emendation is needed and it is not just a mistake of
Pliny or his authority (by analogy with *Caspius*?). For the form
given by Tzetzes is supported by *Campesus* in Valerius Flaccus
(v. 593 *al.*). There it is the name of a hero, an ally of Aeetes, but
it is taken from the river in the way Valerius coins names for
a number of his barbarians.[35]

There is something wrong with the text of the remainder of
l. 6, ὃς ἅλα δῖαν ἐς ἀθανάτην φέρει ὕδωρ (ὃς ῥ’ Brunck, ὃς θ’ ego;
δῖον Harberton), but we hardly need to follow Powell so far as to
adopt Bergk's εἰς ἅλα δῖαν ὃς ἀθάνατον φέρει ὕδωρ. The alteration
of ἀθανάτην to ἀθάνατον anyway introduces a difficulty of sense.
Most rivers flow into the sea, and we could guess for ourselves
that the Campasus does without being told so. But we should be
grateful for the information, which sea. And this information
ἀθανάτην supplies: the immortal Ocean is meant.[36]

For this reason I have tentatively shown Aeschylus' Pluton as
flowing into the Ocean [Map I]; the river about whose upper
reaches the Arimaspi dwell may be the same as that about whose
upper reaches their Issedonian neighbours dwell (Zenothemis):
the river which Aeschylus calls Pluton and some later writers
Campylinus or Campasus [but cf. 115 and 118].

I turn now to a contemporary of Aeschylus. It may be that
Pindar knew something about Aristeas himself [127 ff.], but it is not
clear whether he knew the *Arimaspea*. In his extant work there is
no mention of griffins, Arimaspians, or Rhipaean mountains. Of
the customs of the Scythians there are two curiously intimate little
pictures: one, of the social ostracism incurred among the nomad
Scyths by him who has no wagon-borne home (fr. 94. 4: νομάδεσσι
γὰρ ἐν Σκύθαις ἀλᾶται στρατῶν ὃς ἀμαξοφόρητον οἶκον οὐ πέπαται);
the other the grotesque fragment 192, about people who by daylight profess a distaste for dead horseflesh but by night sneak out
and devour it avidly. But the only real indication of knowledge of

the *Arimaspea* is Pindar's location of the Gorgons in the region of the Hyperboreans [62]. Whether he had the journey of Aristeas in mind when he wrote that one cannot reach the Hyperboreans 'by ship or by foot' (*Pyth.* x. 29) is a question interesting but unanswerable.

In spite of thus placing them firmly in another world, Pindar has quite a lot to say about the Hyperboreans. Theirs is an idyllic life (*Pyth.* x. 31 ff.; fr. 272), passed in song and dance, feasting and worship of their god Apollo. They know not disease or old age, though their span of life is a thousand years [but cf. 99]. Toil, war, and Nemesis are strangers to this holy race:

> νόσοι δ' οὔτε γῆρας οὐλόμενον κέκραται
> ἱερᾷ γενεᾷ· πόνων δὲ καὶ μαχᾶν ἄτερ
> οἰκέοισι φυγόντες
> ὑπέρδικον Νέμεσιν.

There is no need to suppose any other source than his own genius for Pindar's details; but it is worth remarking a similarity of the just and sacrosanct Hyperboreans with the northern Argippaei of Herodotus [42]: they too are unwarlike, inviolate, and under divine protection (τούτους οὐδεὶς ἀδικέει ἀνθρώπων (ἱροὶ γὰρ λέγονται εἶναι), οὐδέ τι ἀρήιον ὅπλον ἐκτέαται), arbiters in their neighbours' quarrels and a safe asylum for fugitives; trees provide their food, trees their shelter (iv. 23. They appear in Latin writers as Aremphaei or Arimphaei: Mela i. 117; Pliny, *N.H.* vi. 34 f.).

In fact, the two characteristics of justice and vegetarianism are ascribed to the northern barbarians by Homer (*Il.* xiii. 5: ἀγαυῶν Ἱππημόλγων γλακτοφάγων, Ἀβίων τε δικαιοτάτων ἀνθρώπων). Probably for Homer they were just because they were communists, as Strabo suggests (300 f.), not because they were vegetarians;[37] but by the time of Aeschylus their justice seems to be associated causally with their abstention from flesh: 'The Scythians, eaters of mare's-milk cheese, ⟨? are⟩ a well-ordered people' (fr. 198: ἀλλ' ἱππάκης βρωτῆρες εὔνομοι Σκύθαι. Cf. Ephorus *ap.* Strab. 302). Hellanicus, a contemporary of Herodotus, makes this connexion explicit in a claim for the Hyperboreans themselves, that 'they practise righteousness by abstaining from meat and living on fruit'; and this shows a sign of deriving from Aristeas, as Hellanicus also says that the Hyperboreans 'live beyond the Rhipaean mountains' (fr. 187b: τοὺς δὲ Ὑπερβορέους Ἑλλάνικος ὑπὲρ τὰ Ῥιπαῖα ὄρη οἰκεῖν ἱστορεῖ· διδάσκεσθαι δὲ αὐτοὺς δικαιοσύνην μὴ κρεοφαγοῦντας, ἀλλ᾽ ἀκροδρύοις χρωμένους).[38]

The review of passages which by their dependence, direct or indirect, on the *Arimaspea* may help to throw light upon its contents is now almost complete. In the second chapter of Book I of Dionysius' *Ornithiaca* we are told that the author 'has nothing firm to report about the griffins, which they say live in the water-meadows of the wealthy Arimaspae and dig up and collect gold from the earth; the Arimaspae, so it is said, have one eye each instead of two' (μηδὲν ὑπὲρ γρυπῶν σαφές ἐστιν εἰπεῖν, οὕς φασιν ἐν τοῖς τῶν πλουσίων Ἀριμασπῶν ἔλεσι τρεφομένους χρυσὸν ἐκ τῆς γῆς ἀγείρειν ὀρύσσοντας, τοὺς Ἀριμάσπας δὲ τούτους οὐχὶ δύο τοὺς ὀφθαλμούς, ἀλλ᾽ ἕνα ἕκαστον ἔχειν φασίν). We possess this poem only in a prose Byzantine paraphrase; the poet has been thought with some reason to have been Dionysius Periegetes,[39] which would date him to the early second century A.D. From his scant knowledge about the griffins and his use of the phrase 'they say' it would seem that Dionysius did not know the *Arimaspea* at first hand (the form Ἀριμάσπης may be an inference by the paraphraser from the accent of the genitive plural; but cf. Orph. *Arg.* 1063); but the words ὀφθαλμούς ... ἕνα ἕκαστον ἔχειν are so like Aristeas' ὀφθαλμὸν δ᾽ ἕν᾽ ἕκαστος ἔχει that one wonders if Dionysius had not come upon the same fragment as Tzetzes (fr. 5. 1). This would mean that what was only a quotation in the twelfth century was still no more than a quotation in the second. As for the little Dionysius tells us, we have heard most of it before, but the statement that the Arimaspi lived in ἕλη, 'water-meadows', is interesting. The only other authority to say that the Arimaspi dwelt by a river is Aeschylus [61], and he was using the *Arimaspea* apparently. It looks, then, as if Dionysius, albeit indirectly, is preserving some genuine lore from that poem. If so, and if fr. 5. 1 was associated with it in Dionysius' source, weight will have been added to the view that the fragments are authentic.

It remains to mention that griffins occurred in some Hesiodic poem, perhaps the third book of the *Catalogus* (see fr. 49 T., and F. Gisinger in *R.M.* lxxviii (1929), 319); anyway, the Medicean scholiast on *P.V.* 830 claims that 'Hesiod was the first to portray the monstrous griffins' (πρῶτος Ἡσίοδος ἐτερατεύσατο τοὺς γρῦπας). Nothing can be built upon this claim. The scholiast may have had his own views on the relative dating of 'Hesiod' and Aristeas, or, more probably, have been ignorant of the *Arimaspea*.

Though Hyperboreans, Rhipaean mountains, griffins, and Arimaspi (and even Essedonians [184], in Lucan and Valerius Flaccus) are known to Latin poets, they are no more than learned stock-in-trade, and throw no further light on their ultimate source. There are two possible exceptions, both early and isolated references to the Rhipaean mountains as gold-bearing. The slave of Lyconides in Plautus' *Aulularia*, when he has stolen the miser's hoard, jubilantly cries out that he is wealthier than the griffins who inhabit the golden mountains (701: 'picis[40] divitiis, qui aureos montes colunt, ego solus supero'); and again Ennius speaks of nuggets *v.s.* 'which ten one-eyed men dug up on the Rhipaean peaks' ('⟨massas⟩ . . . decem coclites quas montibus summis Ripaeis fodere' Varro, *L.L.* vii. 71[41]). There is perhaps nothing more in the Plautine passage than hyperbole (Wagner compares *Stich.* 30 'neque ille sibi mereat Persarum montis, qui esse aurei perhibentur'), or in the Ennian than inexactitude; but there will be cause to recall these later [97; 100].

It is quite uncertain—and indeed at present unknowable—how far Hecataeus of Abdera, in the fourth century B.C., was using, or imitating, the *Arimaspea* in his book on the Hyperboreans. The fragments of this work deal mainly with the Hyperboreans themselves, their customs and their country, whither the author of the *Arimaspea* did not come. It is a pity that we do not know how Hecataeus professed to have gained his information. Jacoby says that we shall hardly be unfair to him in seeing him as a direct successor to Aristeas.[42] It is possible that Hecataeus had in mind a certain tradition about Aristeas, as I conjectured Simias may have done [69]; but that we may be unfair to Aristeas by classing him with a mere romancer like Hecataeus of Abdera will be suggested by what follows.

IV

TALES OF A TRAVELLER

IT is now time to make a tentative reconstruction of the contents of the *Arimaspea*. The author stated in his poem that, possessed by Apollo, he journeyed beyond the Scyths to a neighbouring people, the long-haired Issedonians dwelling by a river. This was the farthest point he reached, but the Issedonians (with whom he presumably spent some time, if it is correct that he was absent from home for six years) gave him an account of the regions beyond. Therein was an immensely high mountain-range, covered in darkness and snow (and wooded?), where was the home of a wind in a cavern, a wind identified by Aristeas as Boreas, which at home would have been the North Wind, but perhaps described by his informants merely as a cold and powerful wind. Visibility in these parts was further reduced by a rain of feathers which perpetually filled the air. This mountain-range was not called 'Rhipaean' until a later date; the Issedonians may have given it a name which Aristeas rendered as 'Caucasus'. Beyond it lived righteous vegetarians, whose domain extended to the outer sea; this folk Aristeas took to be the Hyperboreans, the apparent goal of his journey.

The area between the mountains and the Issedonians was rich in gold (or possibly the gold-bearing region was in the mountains themselves). This was guarded, having been thrown up in the process of making their lairs, by monsters, called by the poet griffins, from which it was stolen by certain warlike neighbours of the Issedonians, the Arimaspi. These were one-eyed, hairy savages, equestrian nomads with a wealth of cattle, sheep, and goats. They lived now about a gold-bearing river (perhaps flowing into the northern ocean, and perhaps the same as the river about which the Issedonians lived—though these are little more than guesses), but they were not stationary, and the Issedonians themselves were compelled to shift their abode under the hostile pressure of the Arimaspi. So it happened that the Issedonians in their turn drove their neighbours on the other side, the Scyths, from their territory; and this Scythian migration caused the departure of the Cimmerians from their home on the northern shores of the Black Sea.

The Issedonians may have told Aristeas other stories too: of cannibals; of another kind of monster inhabiting the region of darkness, which the poet equated with the Gorgons and Phorcides of Greek legend; of giant reeds, and of dog-headed men who understood the human tongue though they had not the use of it; perhaps also of some kind of mermen. And Aristeas must have included in his work first-hand observations of the peoples through whom he passed: possibly he told of the Scyths' working iron, living in horse-drawn wagons, eating horse-flesh and mares'-milk cheese, and how they claimed to be three nations descended from the three sons of the patriarch Colaxes; of a nation whose women were so manly that he took them for Amazons; of the difficulties of river-crossings, and of one broad river which he thought was the Phasis of the Argonautic story, joining the inner to the outer sea.

Was all this fact, or was it really nothing more than the workings of some stay-at-home Greek's fancy? Were the very fantasies mere creations of one poetic imagination, or were they genuine bits of foreign folk-lore, obtained from a far-off people either at first hand (as the poet professed), or at second hand through some itinerant intermediary? I have anticipated my answer by the phraseology of the above summary: I believe that the *Arimaspea* comprised someone's first-hand observations of the Eurasian hinterland, and items of Asiatic folk-lore interpreted, not unnaturally, in terms that a Greek would understand.

At the outset one is predisposed in favour of Aristeas' good faith by his confession that he got no farther than the Issedonians, and that all he had to say of the parts beyond he owed to their report. This is a mark either of extreme honesty or of cunning both extraordinary and unnecessary: for why should a poet trouble to disarm his audience thus? This favourable first impression is fortified by Aristeas' account of how the Scyths came to possess their country to the north of the Black Sea: his description of the migratory pressures of the nomads of the Eurasian steppes is historically correct, and stands out in sharp contrast to what might be called the official Greek and Scythian accounts of the same thing, with their trappings of the marvellous and their genealogy of the Scyths traced from Heracles or some mythical royal ancestor (Hdt. iv. 5–10).

I have already said that Aristeas seems to have been the only Greek who ever claimed to have reached the Issedonians. Herodotus locates them beyond the terminus of the regular trade route, yet he is able to give some account of their customs. It is reasonable, therefore, to suppose that he owes this account to the *Arimaspea*. This is what he says of them (iv. 26):

The Issedonians are said to have the following customs. When a man's father dies, all the near relatives bring sheep; which are sacrificed, and their flesh cut in pieces, while the body of their host's father undergoes the like treatment. The two sorts of flesh are afterwards mixed together, and the whole is served up at a banquet. The head of the dead man is stripped bare, cleansed, and coated with gold (καταχρυσοῦσι: 'set in gold' *Rawlinson*). This they treat as something precious and holy, to which they make important sacrifices every year (ἅτε ἀγάλματι χρέωνται, θυσίας μεγάλας ἐπετείους ἐπιτελέοντες: 'it then becomes an ornament on which they pride themselves, and is brought out year by year at the great festival which sons keep in honour of their fathers' death' *Rawlinson*, which I think blunts the point). A son performs this duty for his father, just as the Greeks observe the Genesia [probably an aside by Herodotus himself]. In other respects the Issedonians are reputed to be observers of justice, and their women to have equal authority with the men.

The customs of the Issedonians, then, included the ceremonial eating of the deceased father; the preservation of his skull by his family; and equality of the sexes. It is as well to be clear about the true significance of these, as the commentators are sometimes misleading.

In the first place we must be careful to distinguish the cannibalism practised upon the bodies of enemies or executed criminals, ascribed by various authors to the Tibetans, the Tatars, and the

Chinese (Yule i. 301, 311 ff.), from the cannibalism practised by a man's kin upon him as an act of piety, as here. Such a custom, sometimes anticipating nature by the slaying of the sick or aged victim, was referred to the Massagetae, to their near neighbours the Derbices, to the Indian Callatiae and Padaei, and even to the Irish (Hdt. i. 216, cf. Strabo 513; Strabo 520, cf. Ael. *V.H.* iv. 1; Hdt. iii. 38, 99; Strabo 201). In more modern times it is attested for tribes in India, the Arakan, Sumatra, Australia, and South America, as well as for the Samoyeds and Ostiaks (*E.R.E.* iii. 202 f.; ix. 465); so we cannot, with Hermann (2246), see here a possible indication that the Issedonians were of Indo-Germanic stock. Thirteenth-century travellers said that it had been a Tibetan custom:

These people haue a strange or rather a miserable kinde of custome. For when anie mans father deceaseth, he assembleth all his kindred, and they eate him (Carpini). . . . Men which were wont to eate the carkases of their deceased parents: that for pities sake, they might make no other sepulchre for them, then their owne bowels. Howbeit of late they haue left off this custome, because that thereby they became abominable and odious vnto al other nations. Notwithstanding vnto this day they make fine cups of the skuls of their parents, to the ende that when they drinke out of them, they may amidst all their iollities and delights call their dead parents to remembrance. This was tolde mee by one that saw it (Rubruquis) (Beazley 118, 232).

Ceremonial eating of the dead by Tibetan lamas is reported as a fact even for the end of the last century by A. H. S. Landor, who adds that if there are insufficient lamas available to perform the rite the relatives expose the body to be devoured by animals or time, having first themselves partaken of a morsel of the flesh (ii. 68 ff.);[1] in this last we might perhaps see the atrophied token of an earlier practice when the entire corpse was consumed.

It will be noticed that Rubruquis says that the Tibetans made the skulls of their parents into drinking-cups. Their use of human skulls for this purpose is vouched for elsewhere (cf. Yule i. 312), and Landor saw and sketched such a cup, which he says were to be found in all the monasteries (ii. 71 f.). These were not family possessions, but were used by the lamas in magical ceremonies, and it may have been such a ceremony that Rubruquis's informant witnessed—and misunderstood.

Herodotus states that the Scythians were wont to make drinking-cups of human skulls, but they were the skulls of enemies, or of kinsmen with whom they had quarrelled. They sawed off the cranium, lined the outside with leather and the inside (if they could afford it) with gold (ἔσωθεν καταχρυσώσας); it was then produced at parties, and evoked suitable reminiscences from the proud host (iv. 65). It is this custom of the Scythians to which Plato refers in the *Euthydemus* (299). It is reported also of the Boii, the Lombards, and other primitive peoples (*E.R.E.* vi. 535). But there is no hint in Herodotus that this was the purpose for which the *Issedonians* preserved their fathers' skulls, and I believe Rawlinson, How and Wells, and Hermann (2246) to be mistaken in thinking that it was. J. A. MacCulloch is surely right in seeing it as an example of the early and widespread practice of preserving the heads of ancestors in order to maintain communion with them or to retain their protection and good offices in return for the honour paid them (*E.R.E.*, l.c.). The skulls become cult objects, the focus of annual sacrifices. The Issedonians, then, went in for ancestor-worship, of which the respect shown to the skull was one expression and the ceremonial eating of the body another.

The Issedonian treatment of these skulls finds, I think, a remarkable illustration in a recent discovery on the site of pre-pottery neolithic Jericho. The inhabitants of this place often detached the skulls of their dead; and a number of such skulls has been recovered which had had the features restored in an overcoat of plaster. The care with which this had been done, and the fact that headless burials were found in successive levels of excavation, indicate that the skulls were not mere trophies but were those of venerated ancestors used for cult purposes. The sex of these portrait-skulls was probably male in all cases; the radiocarbon age of two samples comparatively high up in the pre-pottery sequence was given as *c.* 6250 B.C. and *c.* 5850 B.C. (Kathleen M. Kenyon and others in *Antiquity* xxvii (1953), 105 f.; xxviii (1954), 198; xxx (1956), 196 f., 187). We can perhaps see here a clue to the meaning of Herodotus' καταχρυσοῦσι: the inhabitants of Jericho reproduced the features of their dead in plaster, with which they coated the outside of the skull; the Issedonians did the same, but their medium was gold.

It remains to note on the third characteristic of the Issedonians recorded by Herodotus, the equality of their women with the men, that Rawlinson goes too far in seeing in it a hint of matriarchy. Such would be extraordinary in a society which treated its dead fathers with religious veneration; Herodotus says only that the women were ἰσοκρατέες τοῖσι ἀνδράσι; and How and Wells are probably correct in seeing here no more than an allusion to the sharing by the women of activities which in other societies are usually a masculine prerogative. The Issedonian ladies may have been like those of the Hazaras of north Afghanistan, a pastoral and agricultural Mongol tribe, of whom Josiah Harlan had the following to say in 1840 (150; cf. 148):

The wife and husband amongst the Hazarrahs are inseparable in public affairs. She sits with her husband, in the *divan*, dressed like him and booted, ready for the chase or even a military foray! They would not go upon a distant expedition, but in civil dissentions and in border difficulties, to which their excursions are mostly confined, they generally participate. In the chase both sexes use the fire-lock expertly and accurately. They will gallop their unshod horses over a precipitous deer path, regardless of danger, and bring down the game at full speed. Females of the poor manage the household duties, assist in tending flocks, bringing in thorns, carrying water, and all the hard, laborious work.[2]

These customs, though so far from being fantastic as to find parallels in many ages and in many parts of the world, would yet be so foreign to the mind of a seventh-century Greek that it is easier to ascribe them to first-hand observation and to regard them as the historical fact that they were supposed to be than as the inventions of their recorder's imagination. They will then be a further vindication of Aristeas' veracity.

The Issedonians were sheep-rearers; but it would be rash for us, having in mind the example of the Budini [104], to conclude from this that they were nomads of the steppes. I defer further consideration of their possible location to the next chapter, and turn now from the people themselves to an examination of the tales Aristeas said they told him about the regions beyond them.

Were the griffins and the one-eyed Arimaspi who filched the gold from them the creations of Aristeas' own fancy, or did the Issedonians really tell him about them? The reader will recall Herodotus' story about the outsize ants of the Bactrian desert, how they cast up gold as they made their burrows, and how the neighbouring Indians made forays to collect this [66]. The gold-guarding ants and the Indian robbers must be doublets of the gold-guarding griffins and the Arimaspian robbers, and this would seem to prove that it was the same basic story, of monsters who guarded and of men who stole the gold, that the Persians, whom Herodotus names as his authorities for the ant version, heard in the south and Aristeas heard farther north. The possibility suggests itself, however, that the ant–Indian story is really a *Greek* invention inspired by the griffin–Arimaspian story in the *Arimaspea*; but fortunately this possibility can be ruled out. Herodotus says that in order to evade the ants' pursuit the Indians would take their camels yoked in groups of three, one member of each trio being a female which had recently foaled; her eagerness to get back to her young would give just that extra turn of speed that was needed to out-distance the angry ants. Now if the basic story were a genuine piece of folk-lore originating from some central point and as it spread in different directions assuming different locations and different actors appropriate to the location, we should expect that the newly-foaled camels in the southerly version would be answered by newly-foaled mares in the northerly one. We are lucky in having the bit of independent evidence needed to fulfil this expectation.

Speaking of the far north of Asia, Marco Polo says:

Still further north . . . there is a region which bears the name of DARKNESS, because neither sun nor moon nor stars appear, but it is always as dark as with us in the twilight. The people have no king of their own, nor are they subject to any foreigner, and live like beasts. The Tartars however sometimes visit the country, and they do it in this way. They enter the region riding mares that have foals, and these foals they leave behind. After taking all the plunder that they can get they find their way back by help of the mares, which are all eager to get back to their foals, and find the way much better than their riders could do (Yule, ii. 484).

In his note on this passage Yule thinks that the story is probably of great antiquity, as in a tale given by Rashiduddin the ruse is said to have been used by the patriarch of the Turco-Tatars in an incursion into the Kingdom of Darkness.[3]

That the story of the gold-guarding ants was not a Greek or a Persian invention is further confirmed. It was known to ancient India, for the *Mahabharata* calls gold paid as tribute 'ant-gold' (Tarn 107). The tale did not, however, originate in India but in central Asia and came in with the gold, as has been shown by Laufer, who ingeniously conjectured that it arose from a confusion between the name of a Mongolian tribe (*Shiraighol*) and the Mongolian word for ant (*shirgol*). This suggestion is treated with reserve by Tarn, who states, however, that Laufer's view, that the story travelled from Mongolia to India rather than the other way about, has been proved by Darius' Susa inscription.

Laufer notes the mention of monstrous ants in the Mongolian region by certain ancient Chinese authorities, and it is worth expatiating on these.[4] They occur in two works, *Ch'u Tz'u* and *Shan Hai Ching*, both embodying the shamanistic lore of the 'Yangtze Valley culture'. From the former, *Chao Hun* ('The Summons of the Soul') is probably to be dated to the mid-third century B.C.:

Oh soul come back! for the west holds many perils:
The Shifting Sands stretch on for a hundred leagues.
You will be swept into the Thunder's Chasm, and dashed into pieces, unable to help yourself;
And even should you chance to escape from that, beyond is the empty desert,
And red ants as huge as elephants, and wasps as big as gourds.[5]

The second book, *Shan Hai Ching*, is syncretic and did not emerge in its present form much before the end of the first century B.C. There is, however, good reason to believe that the parts to be cited now and later were in existence two centuries before this; and the matter they contain, being in the nature of folk-lore, was presumably much earlier.

Hai Nei Pei Ching ('Within the Sea, north'). . . . To the north of the K'un Lun Mountain is a man called Ta Hsing Po who holds a halberd

in his hand. East of him is the land of Ch'üan Feng. The body of
Erh Fu is to the east of Ta Hsing Po. The land of Ch'üan Feng is
also called the land of the Dog Jung. The appearance of these people
is like dogs. . . . The land of the Kuei[6] is to the north of the body of
Erh Fu. These people have the faces of men but only one eye. . . . The
Ch'iung-ch'i is like a tiger with wings. . . . To the east of the Ch'iung-
ch'i are the giant wasps which look like wasps and the giant ants which
look like ants.[7]

It looks, then, as if central Asia is the starting-point for a story
which sent out radiations to China by an easterly, to India and
Persia by a southerly, and to Greece, through Aristeas, by a
westerly route.

Though *Shan Hai Ching* does not associate the ants with them,
it will be noticed that it lists in the same area men with one eye.
Such appear again in another passage, though this time located
beyond the northern sea.[8]

Hai Wei Pei Ching ('Beyond the Sea, north'). These are the things
from the north-east corner to the north-west corner.[9] The land of the
Shankless is to the east of the Long-legged. The people there have no
shanks. The Spirit of Chung Mountain is called Torch Dark. When
he opens his eyes it is day and when he shuts them it is night. When
he blows hard it is winter; when he blows soft it is summer. He neither
drinks nor eats nor rests. His breath makes the wind. His body is a
thousand *li* [three hundred miles] long. He lies to the east of the Shankless. He has a man's face and a serpent's body, red in colour. He dwells
at the foot of Chung Mountain. The land of the One-eyed is to the
east. The people there have one eye set in the midst of their faces. The
land of Jou-li is to the east of the One-eyed. These people have one
hand and one foot. . . . [10]

The One-eyed appear again in the same location in the encyclo-
pedia called *Huai Nan Tzu*, compiled at the court of Liu An,
king of Huai Nan, who died in 122 B.C. 'There are thirty-six
lands beyond the seas. . . . From the north-east to the north-west
are the Tip-toes, the Kou Ying, the Sunken-eyed, the No-bellies,
the Jou-li, the One-eyed. . . . '[11]

These strange peoples may be largely the product of Chinese
imagination; but some of them at least may be derived from the
folk-lore of Inner Asia, as the monstrous ants must have been. The

Siberian Buriats in the region of Lake Baykal say that the Ruler of the Dead has (like Odin) one eye in the middle of his forehead; and the wealthy one-eyed Forest man of the Votiaks just west of the Urals is said by Holmberg to have been borrowed from the Tatars (479; 179. Cf. 181, 182).[12] Much more remarkable is the following from A. N. Athanasiev (260) :

> Herodotus speaks of a whole race of one-eyed people. The Ukranians to this day preserve memories of that race; according to their stories the *edinookie* dwell somewhere far away over the seas [cf. *Shan Hai Ching* and *Huai Nan Tzu*]; the Tatars when campaigning used to sack towns and villages, slay the old people and children, but carry off the young men and women and sell the plumper ones to one-eyed people who drove them off like sheep to their territory, fattened them up, killed them and ate them (*Lud. Ukrainski* i. 352). The legend also lives on with the Ural peoples (*The Ural Peoples, the Life of the Ural Peoples and the Kossaks*, by I. Zheleznov, i. 87–89).[13]

Here we have a blend of Arimaspians and Anthropophagi.

Just as Aristeas' gold-guarding griffins had their counterparts in the gold-guarding ants on the borders of India, so did his one-eyed Arimaspi have their counterparts in an Indian people, also emanating, I suggest, from that common centre whence had originated the guardians of the gold. These were described by Megasthenes as having the ears of dogs, the eye in the centre of the forehead, hair stiff like bristles, and shaggy breasts (Strabo 711: μονομμάτους τε ἄλλους ὦτα μὲν ἔχοντας κυνὸς ἐν μέσῳ δὲ τῷ μετώπῳ τὸν ὀφθαλμόν, ὀρθοχαίτας, λασίους τὰ στήθη). A characteristic of the Dog-heads has clearly been grafted on to them, but otherwise the similarity of this description with the fifth fragment of Aristeas is striking. Whether there is any significance in the fact that Megasthenes also mentioned in his account of India Hyperboreans 'who lived for a thousand years' (Strabo, l.c.) will be discussed later [98 ff.].[14]

Various theories have from time to time been put forward as to the originals of the griffins and the Arimaspi. The most ridiculous (cf. Tournier 12) are those that see in the latter a real tribe whose other eye had become atrophied from being constantly closed to aim a bow, or a mining people whose single eye was in fact a lamp strapped to the forehead. Hardly more plausible is the view that the authentic griffin is the mild little *baibak*, a relation of the jerboa inhabiting the steppe (Minns, Hennig). Far more impressive is the explanation offered by Adolph Erman (ii. 87):

By comparing numbers of the bones of antediluvian pachyderms, which are thrown up in such quantities on the shores of the Polar Sea, all these people [the Samoyeds; Erman is dealing especially with the Samoyeds in the region of the mouth of the Ob] have got so distinct a notion of a colossal bird, that the compressed and sword-shaped horns, for example, of the *Rhinoceros teichorinus*, are never called, among the Russian promuishleniks and merchants, by any other name than that of 'birds' claws'. The indigenous tribes, however, and the Yuka-girs in particular, go much further, for they conceive that they find the head of this mysterious bird, in the peculiarly vaulted cranium of the same rhinoceros; its quills in the leg-bones of other pachyderms, of which they usually make their quivers; but as to the bird itself, they plainly state that their forefathers saw it and fought wondrous battles with it: just as the mountain Samoyedes preserve to this day the tradi-tion, that the mammoth still haunts the sea-shore, dwelling in the recesses of the mountain and feeding on the dead.

These birds, then, are for Erman the original of Aristeas' griffins; the Arimaspians he refers to the pre- or non-Samoyeds who lived in subterranean dwellings and worked metal (the Samoyeds had stories of how they had ventured to approach the entrances to these caverns and had heard them within speaking an un-intelligible language). Yet for all its attractiveness Erman's theory must be discarded, if we are right in placing the starting-point of the story in central Asia, among Turco-Tatars rather than Samoyeds.

Scholars recently have followed a different tendency—to see in the griffins and the Arimaspians figures from another world, a world of the spirit, to which the shaman makes his journeys in the soul. The former are to be identified with the dragons which defend the Golden Mountain where God dwells, the latter with evil one-eyed infernal beings; both known to the mythology of Turco-Mongol Altaic peoples. This was the suggestion of Alföldi, followed by Meuli and Phillips.[15] Though primitive men naturally tend to locate their spiritual world somewhere in this one, on the edges of the earth or beneath it, there is yet an important distinction between this view and the earlier ones: for if we accept it, and think that here Aristeas misunder-stood his Issedonian informants, taking for fact some religious myth, we are wasting our time if we try to equate the Arimaspi with some historical tribe. Yet the Issedonians could hardly have been forced to migrate by the pressure of infernal beings, and I think that for them the Arimaspi were a real, flesh-and-blood people, as real as were the Dog Jung and the Kuei of the Chinese in spite of the prodigious shape ascribed to them. How they came by their reputation of having only a single eye, whether this feature was dubbed on to them by analogy with mythical demons or was chance fancy born of that revulsion for the stranger of alien race which lends him non-human characteristics,[16] cannot be decided and does not matter.

If the Arimaspi were not entirely creations of the imagina-tion, their enemies from whom they were supposed to steal the gold were. They were monsters of some sort, monsters described in one version of the tradition as enormous ants, in the version of Aristeas as griffins. To a Greek the word γρύψ, 'griffin', would in classical times denote a beast having the body of a lion and the head and wings of an eagle, a very different thing from an ant, however magnified. The attributes of the lion and the eagle are sharp-sightedness, speed, and ferocity. The questions now at issue are: what governed Aristeas' choice of the word γρύψ to denote the creatures of the Issedonian tale? Was the word a translitera-tion of some Issedonian word for the guardians of the gold, or was it a name Aristeas knew already for a certain kind of monster? How did the Issedonians themselves describe the creatures? Actually as half lion and half eagle? Or rather as monsters with the characteristics of speed, ferocity, and vigilance, whose physical appearance was not clear to Aristeas, so leading him to make his own identification with a monster he already knew?

To attempt an answer to these questions a survey must be made of the history of the griffin in ancient art.[17] Three species may be distinguished: the bird-griffin, with the body of a lion and the head of a bird, either winged or wingless; the snake-griffin, with the body of a lion (often covered with scales), snake's head, the forefeet of a lion and the hindfeet bird's legs, with or without wings, generally with a scorpion's tail; and the lion-griffin, with lion's body (often scaly), lion's head and forefeet, bird's legs for hindfeet, and bird's tail, with or without wings. We should not expect a monster the principal component of which is leonine to have originated in the more northerly parts of the world;[18] and the evidence points to the Middle East as its home. Prinz summarizes its development thus: the bird-griffin started in Egypt, whence between 2000 and 1500 B.C. it passed into the art of the Hittites and of other Middle Eastern countries. The Hittite type then in its turn affected certain griffin types of the Egyptian New Kingdom, Assyria, and probably the Mycenaean–Cretan culture; also derived from the Hittite is the Phoenician griffin. Lion- and snake-griffins came from Babylonia, and influenced Hittite, Assyrian, and Persian art. All these cultures regarded the griffin both as a beast of prey and as a supernatural creature, but it might also take on a variety of significances—in Egypt as representing royalty and various gods; in Babylon and its environs and the Mycenaean world as a divine animal.[19]

In Egypt the bird-griffin only appears, and can be traced back to prehistoric times (before 3300 B.C.). He is represented as a real beast of the desert, to be hunted as men hunt the lion, while himself hunting other beasts. From the Middle Kingdom on we find the griffin as a symbol of royalty, with the hawk's head of Horus, and, congruously with this, as a supernatural creature. In the New Kingdom there is a development in the artistic treatment of the griffin which is owed to other Middle Eastern countries, the principal feature of which is the loose curls on the beast's head.

In Babylon the snake-griffin and the lion-griffin are found as supernatural beings associated with various gods. From the time of the dynasty of Ur onwards the lion-griffin is depicted in combat with men and with other creatures; he is simply a fierce beast of prey, and there is nothing symbolical here.

The typical Hittite griffin has the body of a lion, wings and head of a bird, on which is a sort of crest or comb in three sections.

From the head depends a curling lock. It is here perhaps, in the mountains of the Anatolian region, that the bird-griffin acquired its eagle's head, in place of the falcon's or sparrow-hawk's of the earlier Egyptian type (the eagle-headed type first appears in Egypt in the time of the Hyksos: cf. Phillips 172 f.). The Hittite griffin makes its first appearance in the first half of the second millennium before Christ. It is essentially a beast of prey, seizing lions or gazelles; no symbolical meaning can be discerned in it, nor any connexion with the divine.

In the world of Crete and Mycenae only the bird(eagle)-griffin is found. Typical are the curl-like decorations which not only depend from the head but also sometimes surround the base of the wings. The crest or comb also occurs. It is thus a direct relative of the Hittite and later Egyptian griffin (the earliest example is to be dated about 1600 B.C., which would not preclude at least Hittite influence). It plays the part of a divine beast (e.g. held on a lead by a god, or drawing a car in which ride deities, one of whom may be the Magna Mater; and cf. *J.H.S.* xxi (1901), 158, fig. 36), or of a beast of prey. It is on an object of late Mycenaean date, an ivory mirror-handle found at Enkomi in Cyprus, that we come upon the first grypomachy proper, or fight of the bird-griffin with a man [Plate II]. The theme was to become a common one in Assyrian, Phoenician, and Persian art, but on the strength of this mirror-handle Prinz is inclined to look to late-Mycenaean Cyprus as the home of its first formal representation.

This is doubtful. The scene shows the figures in profile. The warrior presents his right side to the viewer, and stabs with downward sword-thrust in the chest the prancing griffin facing him. The vigour of the man and the drooping wings of the dying griffin are effectively portrayed. The beast is indeed of the Mycenaean type, with eagle's head and curling locks which extend along the initial part of the wing; but the equipment of its opponent alines him rather with the Philistines and Shardana, the Peoples of the Sea who were defeated by Rameses III *c.* 1194 B.C., while the upward tilt of his face betrays Syrian influence (cf. Dunbabin 36). The mirror then is probably of Phoenician workmanship, and an import rather than a product of Cyprus itself

(Lorimer 151, 200, 252, 392). In view of this it is perhaps better to place the origin of the grypomachy theme farther east, and to trace its inspiration to the combats of the Babylonian lion-griffin with men.

Assyrian art knows all three types of griffin. Its snake- and lion-griffins are closely related to the Babylonian counterparts, its bird-griffins to the Hittite (the crest-like feature of the latter has now become a proper crest or comb). There are several representations of gods fighting or hunting griffins (mostly lion-headed).

This motif of combat between a god and the monster becomes in Persian art (which confines itself to the type of the lion-griffin) simply a combat between the monster and the Great King; otherwise the griffin's role is purely decorative.

Phoenician representations of the griffin follow closely the lines of the late Mycenaean, and are also like the Hittite in many ways. Egyptian influence is also evident; when for example the griffin is depicted trampling an enemy. Phoenician grypomachies generally follow the lines of the scene on the Enkomi mirror-handle (Perrot–Chipiez iii. 789, fig. 552 (here the monster's head is turned away from its vanquisher, who delivers his blow under-arm to the creature's belly, while grasping its locks; from Curium in Cyprus); cf. 771, fig. 546. On a *patera* from Varvakeion a grypomachy is depicted which is schematically quite different from that on the Enkomi mirror-handle: 783, fig. 550).

In archaic Greek art the griffin is depicted in a calm, watchful attitude, whether walking, sitting, or lying down. Its beak is strongly hooked, occasionally continuing the curve of the skull in an unbroken line, and almost always wide open and menacing. The eagle's head always has long, pointed, upright ears; almost always a lock hanging from the base of the ear to the neck; and frequently an ornament extending back from the head, which may end in stylized leafage or flower-shapes: a sort of crest. It shares these characteristics with Egyptian, Mycenaean, Assyrian, Hittite, and Phoenician types; but a specifically Greek development is the upright knob above the eyes (cf. the horn of the lion- and snake-griffin). Also purely Greek is the upward curve of the wings, a change in the tradition which can be paralleled from Greek representations of Gorgons, Harpies, and Sphinxes. This archaic Greek griffin appears ordinarily alone or in heraldic pairs; if associated with other beasts it displays neither hostility nor friendship towards them. Evidence for an early connexion with Apollo is literary in the first place; the most important example is the old statue of Apollo at Delos, which was flanked by prancing griffins. Later it is associated also with Dionysus, Artemis, and Nemesis; but the oldest and longest association is with Apollo.

Classical Greek art removed all the 'unnatural' features from the griffin—curling locks, ornamented crest and knob—except for the pointed ears; and substituted the fin-like mane running the length of the neck often as far as the beak (this was long to be a regular feature of the griffin in art). The formal upward curve of the wings too gave place to a more realistic representation.

We are now in a position to make a closer inspection of the scenes on the Kelermes mirror [5 ff., and Plate I]. These are a curious mixture of Greek and barbarian. In one panel are two sitting sphinxes, heraldically arranged facing each other; their wings have the typical upward curve of archaic Greek art. Beneath them is a sitting griffin of the archaic Greek type, with tall ears, gaping eagle's beak, upward-curved wings, pendent locks, and knob above the eyes. In the opposite panel are two more sphinxes, heraldically arranged on either side of a thin column surmounted by a pair of Ionic volutes. These sphinxes are prancing, their heads are retorted, their wings lack the upward curve. This motif of the heraldic pair is repeated in another panel where two prancing lions face each other as if in combat, in the panthers held one in each hand by the 'Winged Artemis', and in the grypomachy panel. There is nothing particularly Scythian in this motif, which has Mycenaean parallels; any more than there is in the 'Winged Artemis', who was represented in the art of Greece and the Mycenaean–Cretan world long before the date of this mirror (Thompson 286 ff.; Nilsson[i] 19, 28; Childe 30). A theme popular in Scythian art, however—the slaying of

a herbivorous animal by a carnivore—appears in the panel
showing a lion biting through the backbone of a bull. Even so,
the Scythians borrowed this theme from their more southerly
neighbours—the steppe is not prolific of carnivores (on a Phoenician silver plate from Caere in Etruria two lions attack a bull
with head retorted; a bird flies above, and there are palm-trees:
Perrot–Chipiez iii. 769, fig. 544; and here the head of the bull
is not retorted in the way often favoured by the Scythian 'animal
style' (on the other hand the heads of the ibex and the wolf are,
as is the head of the griffin—but so is that of his Phoenician fore-
bear [88])). Much more extraordinary are the two panels containing as their principal features in the one case a lion in front of a
tree, in the other a bear just above whose back is a flying eagle.
These animals are 'non-heraldic', standing and presenting their
left side to the viewer, and are strongly reminiscent in their
attitude of a lion and other animals on one of the vases from
nearby Maikop on the north-western fringe of the Caucasus
(Rostovtzeff[i] 23 and his pl. III; Minns 144). This impression is
enhanced by the representation of the tree on the Kelermes
mirror, which looks like an imitation of the trees on the Maikop
vase, and by the fact that on the latter a bird is perched upon the
lion's back in remarkable correspondence with the eagle above
the bear's back on the Kelermes mirror. Yet the Maikop vase is
to be dated in the third millennium B.C.! Some of its features may
have been embodied in an artistic tradition that long endured
in the neighbourhood, and were known to the engraver of the
mirror (yet it is also possible that the ancestry of the latter in some
of its components may rather have been Phoenician).

The heraldic treatment is cleverly applied to the grypomachy
panel. The griffin is the archaic Greek type like his fellow on the
sphinx panel (the knob above the eyes is clear), though the
wings lack the upward curvature. He is prancing; his body faces
towards one of his opponents, while his head is retorted to face
the other, thus giving cohesion to the group. The prancing body
and the retorted head recall the Phoenician grypomachy already
mentioned [88]. The griffin's human adversaries face each other
across him, and appear to grapple with him with their bare

hands. That they are savages of a primitive sort, hirsute 'wild men', is clearly shown by their long, unkempt hair and beards and the stippling that covers their bodies; they answer admirably the description in fr. 5. 2 of Aristeas, 'shaggy with hairs, toughest of all men'.[20] It is interesting that the lower part of this panel, unlike all the others except that containing Artemis, is not filled in with some other beast but, as it were the ground on which the actors tread, with close-packed uniform squiggles: perhaps to represent the desert habitat of the griffin.

It would appear, then, from the admixture of Greek and south Russian features in the scenes depicted on the Kelermes mirror that it must be the work of a Greek craftsman living in one of the colonies on the northern Black Sea littoral.[21] That he included a grypomachy not simply because it was one conventional form of decoration but because he considered it particularly appropriate to the destination of his work is, I think, proved by his substitution of savages for the usual warrior antagonist of the griffin; though he did not so far break with the artistic tradition of the grypomachy as to make them one-eyed.

The date of this mirror is about 575 B.C. It is not the only archaeological evidence that the Greeks already connected the griffin with Scythia; for also at Kelermes, in a burial dated by Rostovtzeff to probably the second half of the sixth century, but by other Russian authorities to the seventh (Rostovtzeff[ii] 279; Rice 154), was discovered an iron rattle surmounted by the head of a griffin of the true archaic Greek type exemplified by a seventh-century bronze found at Olympia (ill. Roscher i. 1766; cf. Dunbabin 43). It has long upstanding ears, gaping beak strongly hooked and continuing the curve of the skull in an unbroken line, while above the eyes an atrophied knob can just be discerned in the photographs [Plate III]. If Rostovtzeff's date for the burial is right, this object must have been manufactured long before, and even if it is itself Scythian work it is proof that the Greek griffin had been introduced into Scythia very early in the sixth century at the latest.

Once established there the griffin became a popular ornament of the art of the European steppe (not true of the grypomachy,

a fact which may indicate that it meant nothing to the natives;
on the other hand, the motif of man against beast was not favoured
by Scythian artists). It remains to note its appearance also far
to the east, in the Altai mountains. There, at Pazirik (lat. 50 N.,
long. 86 E.), in burials dated from the fifth to the third centuries
B.C., both bird-griffins and lion-griffins have been found. The
latter no doubt made their way from Persia, but very remarkable
is a bird-griffin on a Persian pile carpet of the fifth century B.C.
from Pazirik (ill. Rice 138). It has the gaping beak and tall ears of
the Greek griffin, but is in an unusual attitude, standing looking
back over its shoulder. As the bird-griffin was not a Persian type
the carpet may have been home-made rather than imported,
and its maker may have owed this motif to Scythian influence.
The bird-griffin (though in this case with a bird's tail) is also
shown attacking an elk on a carpet from a site yet farther east,
a grave of the first century A.D. at Noin Ula in northern Mongolia
(Rice, pl. 29).

If one were to plot the incidence of the bird-griffin in its earliest-
known artistic examples one would get a roughly parabolic arc
on the map, starting in prehistoric Egypt, extending through
Mycenaean and pre-classical Greece to south European Russia,
thence to western Siberia and ending in Mongolia in the first
century of our era. It appeared in Greece long before Aristeas, in
south Russia soon after him, in Siberia long after him. It is hard to
escape the conclusion that Aristeas did *not* hear the description
of the physical shape of the griffin from the Issedonians, but took
the concept with him on his travels and dubbed it on to the gold-
guarding monsters of his Issedonian informants. His account of it
in the *Arimaspea* on his return home would then underlie its projection into Scythian art, in the first place through the mediation
of Greek craftsmen who knew the poem, and thence farther east
by a drift of artistic tradition across the steppe.

Though the Greeks of Aristeas' time certainly knew and often
used the griffin shape in art, and so presumably had a name for it,
we cannot unfortunately be sure at present that that name was
γρύψ. Ziegler finds the explanations of the word so far proposed
unconvincing—for instance, its derivation from the Indo-

germanic root *grabh (etymologically unsound), or from γρυπός (first in Xenophon:[22] putting the cart before the horse?). He is more sympathetic with those who would relate it to the Hebrew *kerub*, though he maintains a proper scholarly reserve about this in view of our ignorance of the nature of the original cherubim. He sensibly remarks that, as the concept of the griffin was primarily non-Greek, we should probably look for a non-Greek etymology of the name. That it *might* be a transliteration by Aristeas into Greek of an Issedonian word for their monsters, which he defined in the terms of a monster already known to himself and his compatriots, is not to be precluded; obviously if he was introducing a common noun unknown to his Greek public he would have to define it, and this consideration might make us give the evidence of Pausanias more weight than we should otherwise attach to it [32; T. 4]. And it must not be forgotten that some early author thought it necessary to give a description of the appearance of a griffin [72 f.].

To sum up: I am inclined to believe that Aristeas heard from the Issedonians of some sort of swift, fierce, and vigilant monster which guarded the local gold; that the name they gave to this sounded to him like γρύψ; that its attributes of speed, ferocity, and vigilance reminded him of the lion-eagle monsters he had seen in artistic representations at home; and that he accordingly defined the word γρύψ in his poem in terms of this lion-eagle monster.

The grounds are substantial for believing that the originals of the one-eyed Arimaspi and their monstrous adversaries are to be sought in the folk-lore of central Asia. Is the same true of the mountain that neighboured them, where the wind Boreas had his home in a cavern?

We must recall that in the *Odyssey* all the winds are gathered together in a floating island under their ruler Aeolus, who restrains the adverse ones for Odysseus by tying them up in a bag (x. 1 ff.). For Homer, then, they are not confined within a cavernous prison, as they are for Virgil (*Aen.* i. 50 ff.), who is influenced by the later tradition about the Cave of Boreas. This tradition was certainly known in the fifth century B.C. to Sophocles, who says that Cleopatra, the daughter of Boreas, was brought up in her father's cave (*Ant.* 983):

> τηλεπόροις δ' ἐν ἄντροις
> τράφη θυέλλησιν ἐν πατρῴαις
> Βορεὰς ἄμιππος ὀρθόποδος ὑπὲρ πάγου.

Whatever the exact interpretation of this passage, the reference to the North Wind's cave is plain enough; and it is tempting to see in the 'sheer steep' of l. 985 the Rhipaean precipices above which that cave was situated.[23] Though we possess no earlier first-hand mention of this cave, we have had good reason to infer that it occurred in the *Arimaspea* [44 f.], so that it may quite well have been Aristeas who first broke with the Homeric tradition of the island of the winds, and located one of them in a cave on the edge of the world.[24]

The Issedonians again may have been his authorities for this. The notion that winds have their habitation in caves is not only originally un-Greek but unusual. Holmberg notes what he calls a strange idea among the peoples of central Asia and Siberia: that mountains are the home of the winds (457). The Yakuts about the river Lena speak of the winds 'sleeping' in the mountains; the Mongols call days of storm 'running-days', because then the Mountain-spirit runs from mountain to mountain; 'the Goldes believe the winds to come from caves in the mountains, where the Wind spirit holds them captive'. These last dwell in the far east of Siberia, but Holmberg quotes a similar belief among the Lapps (and perhaps the Finns), that winds originate from chasms in the fells. The inhabitants of a mountainous district would note the force with which the wind blows down these natural funnels, and this may be the germ of the idea.[25]

However valuable their witness, Lapps and Goldes are far removed from any possible location of the Issedonians. But the belief is strikingly confirmed for the Altaic region of the Russian steppe by Carpini:

Departing from hence, wee founde a certaine small sea, vpon the shore whereof stands a little mountaine. In which mountaine is reported to be a hole (*quoddam foramen*), from whence, in winter time such vehement tempests of winds doe issue, that traveilers can scarcely, and with great danger passe by the same way. In summer time, the noise indeede of the winde is heard there, but it proceedeth gently out of the hole (Beazley 134; 98).

The 'sea' here mentioned appears to be the lake called Ala Kul. What Douglas Carruthers has to say about the tempestuous gales of this vicinity is of such interest that I take the liberty of quoting him extensively (411) [Map II]:

We had frequently heard of the terrors, dangers, and winds of the Dzungarian Gate. We had read the records of such early travellers as Carpini and Rubruck, both of whom[26] mentioned that 'there blows nearly continuously such a wind through this valley, that persons cross it with great danger, lest the wind should carry them into the sea'. We therefore approached this remarkable geological phenomenon both with interest and a certain amount of anxiety, for the weather was unusually unsettled. . . .

Even at a distance, with the Dzungarian Gate lying before us— unseen, we instinctively became aware of its presence; for when we came within sight of Ala Kul, whilst crossing the open foothills of the Barlik Range some twenty miles from the lake shore and some 2,000 ft. above it, we were in absolute stillness; and yet, strangely enough, the waters of Ala Kul were tossed into waves—the white crests being clearly seen with a glass, while even with the naked eye breakers could be distinguished dashing on to the southern shore of an island in the middle of the lake. Although we were becalmed, there was evidently a gale blowing through the 'Gate', and as we approached nearer we became at every step more keenly alive to the action of this wind-trough. At night we heard a distant roar as the imprisoned winds of the Dzungarian deserts escaped though this narrow defile. The only night we camped on the very shore of the straits, the wind increased to such a violence that our tents, though well protected in a valley, were by the morning all blown away, for the wind swept in great gusts over the hills, and the back eddies tore them down; the noise was terrific, and sleep out of the question. . . .

Fortunately we succeeded in crossing the depression in a nine hours' trek without mishap, a strong head-wind being the only cause for annoyance. Had there been rain or snow falling, travelling would have been impossible, but the wind was luckily from the south, and comparatively warm, the temperature at night only just touching freezing-point. Only just in time did we escape from this home of the

winds, for the day after crossing the valley . . . the wind swung round
to the north and swept cruelly through the gap, bringing with it hail
and snow. Had we then been journeying northwards the making of any
headway would have been out of the question, for neither man nor
beast could have faced the elements. . . . A bleak, inhospitable land-
scape now surrounded us, mountains, clad in fresh snow, showed up
here and there through breaks in the blurred atmosphere, and great
cloud-banks swept through the 'straits', as if rushing through some
gigantic funnel. . . .

The natives relate the usual traditions as to the origin of the winds
in this locality. In the myths of Central Asia a 'hole in the mountain',
or 'an iron gate in a lake' is the usual explanation of the origin of
winds. In the case of which I am writing the island called Ala-tyube—
a small extinct volcano[27] in Ala Kul—is made responsible for the
furious winds which sweep through the depression. . . . From autumn
to spring the prevailing wind is from the south-east. I think, however,
that the wind which causes havoc amongst the nomads, and kills
off men and flocks when caught unprotected, is this north wind when
it attains the velocity of what is called a 'buran'.

Humboldt also preserves the tradition, gleaned from Tatar
sources, not only of the violent winds issuing from the island in
Ala Kul, but of another 'Cave of the Winds' in this same region
of the Dzungarian Gate, some thirty miles south-south-east of Ala
Kul (ii. 84 ff.; 491 ff.). This latter was a very terrible place, of
unknown depth, from which issued, especially in winter, wind
storms of such force that they would tumble everything in their
path and hurl it into the lake.

That Carruthers, Humboldt, and Carpini are recording virtually the same tradition there can be no doubt. Six hundred and
fifty years separate Carruthers from Carpini; it is still a long step
to carry it back another two thousand years before the latter, yet,
in view of the extraordinary persistence of folk-beliefs among
unsophisticated peoples, not impossible.[28] The tale of the wind
that irresistibly snatches away all before it recalls that fragment
of Aeschylus about the danger of being swept away by the blasts
of Boreas [54 f.]. I suggest that we have found, if not the original
Rhipaean Mountain with its Cave of Boreas, yet at least a near
relation; and the general area, if not the precise spot, where it
was situated.

There is indeed a notable difference between the home of the wind in the accounts of Carpini and Carruthers and the Rhipaean range of the ancients: the former is a 'little mountaine' or a 'small volcano', the latter is immensely high. If, therefore, the former is indeed the original of the latter it may have gained altitude by conflation with some other mountain; and there is a candidate for this last whose claims must be considered.

There is a comparatively early Altaic belief that the sky is supported by a pillar at the north pole; and the majority of Central Asiatic peoples tell of a mighty 'world-mountain', whose summit, unattainable to man, is at the North Star, where dwells the supreme god on his golden throne. Everywhere in Asia it is assumed that this mountain is in the north of the world; the Mongols call it Sumur or Sumer, the Buriats Sumbur. An Altaic tale relates how at the creation God sat upon a 'golden mountain' where sun and moon ever shone, which afterwards descended to cover the earth. The underside of this (hollow?) mountain therefore forms our sky (the edges of which do not quite reach down to the earth—thus allowing ingress and egress to the sun and moon, presumably) (Holmberg 333; 341 ff.).

This mountain exemplifies certain traditions we have met concerning the Rhipaean mountains: it is in the far north; it could hardly be higher (most appropriate to it would be Aeschylus' ἀστρογείτων and Aristotle's περὶ ὧν τοῦ μεγέθους λίαν εἰσὶν οἱ λεγόμενοι λόγοι μυθώδεις [49; 42]); and it is golden [73]. There are, however, factors which prompt wariness in accepting that it has contaminated the Rhipaean legend.

Three distinguishable conceptions underlie this 'world-mountain' of Asiatic lore: (i) it is a giant mountain at the centre of the earth's disk (i.e. at the terrestrial pole), whose summit touches the sky; (ii) the mountain is in the sky; (iii) the mountain itself forms the sky. The two latter conceptions are probably developments from the first, and the first is obviously related to the 'world-mountain' of ancient Hindu cosmology; a relationship which is confirmed by the names Sumer, &c., by which the mountain is called. The idea looks, then, not to be native to central Asia, but to be an importation from India; though it is difficult to say for certain that India was its original home (Holmberg 342). An obvious vehicle for its importation would have been that lamaist Buddhism which is widespread among Siberian and Mongolian peoples today, but was of course non-existent in the seventh century B.C. It did not reach the Ili (a river flowing into Lake Balkhash) until the fourth century of our era (Humboldt i. 396).

If this were all, the 'world-mountain' need detain us no longer; but unfortunately the 'blessed Hyperboreans', who dwell beyond the Rhipaean mountains, and whose first appearance in Greek legend cannot be dated by other evidence before Aristeas, demand otherwise: for a people very like them dwelt to the north of the Indian mountain.

According to the geography of the Puranas, our earth is an enormous continent surrounded by an ocean, beyond which are six other continents, each surrounded by its ocean, arranged in concentric rings about ours. In the centre of our earth (and so in the centre of the whole system) rises to an immense height Mount Meru, the seat of the gods. To the south and north of this the continent is divided by six parallel mountain chains, three on each side of Meru, the southernmost being the Himalaya. The land mass to the south of the Himalaya is inhabited by the Indians, among others, that to the north of the northernmost range by the Uttarakurus. According to an alternative account in the *Mahabharata* these last inhabit the northernmost continent of four which extend towards the four cardinal points from the central Mount Meru; but the crucial feature, that they are to the north of the mountain, remains.

The classical descriptions of the Uttarakurus are in the *Ramayana* (iv. 43) and the *Mahabharata* (vi. 7). Their climate is temperate, their land rich in precious stones and metals; they need not labour, for trees provide their every desire—food, drink, clothes, ornaments, and maidens. They are a pious and loving people, who pass their lives in gaiety free from sickness and old age, until they die at the age of 11,000 years (or one thousand, according to the more modest Buddhist estimate).[29]

This account is much like Pindar's of the Hyperboreans [71], but there is no need to postulate any common source to explain a similarity of ideal bliss, which is so conceived pretty universally among mankind. It is a pity that a detail which might be significant, the thousand-year life-span of the Hyperboreans, cannot be certainly claimed as Pindaric; for when Strabo (711) says that Megasthenes in his account of India 'agrees with Pindar, Simonides, and other story-tellers in his account of the Hyperboreans who live for a thousand years', the agreement may have only been about their way, not their length, of life—it may only have been Megasthenes who mentioned the latter. For Megasthenes undoubtedly means the Uttarakurus here by 'Hyperboreans'; it was perhaps he who introduced the knowledge of them to the Mediterranean world. He may have reported their Indian name, for Pliny knows of 'Attacori' in the north of Asia who lead a life like that of the Hyperboreans (N.H. iv. 90; vi. 55, where he says that a certain Amometus[30] wrote a book about them); they are the Ὀττοροκόρραι of Ptolemy (Geog. vi. 16. 5; cf. vi. 16. 8; viii. 24. 7; oros. i.2.45). Some knowledge of Mount Meru itself (Μῆρος) had reached Greece as early as c. 300 B.C., undoubtedly through Megasthenes or some companion of Alexander (Theophr. H.P. iv. 4. 1; cf. Strabo 687).

Pliny and Ptolemy took the Uttarakurus for a real people: were they entirely creatures of fantasy, or were the Indian stories about them based upon a memory of an actual tribe? H. Jacobi inclines to the latter view: their prototypes were a real people living in the Himalaya (E.R.E. ii. 700a; cf. 699a). If this is true it is decisive for our present investigation, for it would mean that the Indian belief in a blessed people living to their north beyond a lofty mountain was not an importation from central Asia but had grown up in India itself—whencesoever they derived their belief in the lofty Mount Meru. Indeed, it is safer to assume that central Asiatic lore owes to India its cosmic mountain, together with the cosmic ocean associated with it; for the idea of such an ocean would not be likely to originate with an inland people (Holmberg 345; 331). It is noteworthy that there seems to be no trace of a northern Asiatic belief in a blessed people in the far north, which here is rather the gloomy abode of the dead

(Holmberg 486); just as the Scythians knew nothing of any 'blessed Hyperboreans', according to Herodotus (iv. 32).

It appears, then, that it would be mistaken to identify the Rhipaean mountains in any way with Mount Meru, or the Hyperboreans of the *Arimaspea* with the Uttarakurus. The original of the Rhipaeans might be, quite generally, the western outliers of the central Asiatic massif; or, if we must look for something more specific, one of the high mountains in the region of the Dzungarian Gate, such as the Altai, whose name means 'golden' [73], and whose summit touches the Milky Way according to a (modern) Chinese source (Humboldt i. 241; 230). It is worth remarking that the Goldes of eastern Siberia, who believe that the winds blow from mountain caves, are a branch of a race which seems originally to have dwelt near the Altai, but is now widespread over central and north Asia, the Middle East and east Europe (Holmberg 299 f.).

I think that it is now safe to assume that Aristeas took with him from Greece ready-made the concept of the happy race of Hyperboreans, the favourites of Apollo, and that they were the goal of his journey, which otherwise seems motiveless; just as he took with him the concept of the griffin, which he attached to monsters described to him by the Issedonians. But, such is the respect that his veracity should now command, we must infer that the Issedonians told him of a distant people with whom his pre-conception of the Hyperboreans was not incongruous. That they did tell him of such, and that he did not himself, having heard of the starting-point of Boreas from them, simply assume that the Hyperboreans must dwell beyond it, is proved by the information that this people 'reached to the sea': the idea of an outer sea would be foreign to a seventh-century Greek, for whom the earth would be bounded by the *river* Oceanus. I incline strongly to the opinion of those who hold that Aristeas heard from the Issedonians something of the civilization of China.[31] To semi-savages living hard and dangerously the ordered society of China might well appear a model of peace, justice, and luxury; and to men whose staple food was meat the agricultural Chinese, whose staple food was cereal, could well appear as vegetarians. The claim of the

Chinese to be Aristeas' Hyperboreans is, I think, to be preferred to that of the Argippaei [71], whose territory did not extend to the sea, and for whom a place in the *Arimaspea* is not confirmed by other evidence.

If I am correct, though the 'Hyperboreans' of whom Aristeas heard from the Issedonians were the Chinese, the original Hyperboreans of the Greeks could, of course, have been nothing of the sort. The origin of this fabled people has been the subject of much dispute, into which there is fortunately no need to enter here at length. It is sufficient to say that, if the interpretation of 'Hyperborean' as 'beyond Boreas' is mistaken, it was a mistake already current in Aristeas' day, who almost certainly located the Hyperboreans beyond Boreas. Personally, though I know that the ancients were often wildly wrong in their etymologies, I see no reason why they should be wrong in this case.[32]

So strong evidence has now been produced that the *Arimaspea* preserved genuine central Asiatic folk-lore that I think we are entitled to reverse the process, and now to confirm for the poem with some confidence our tentative claim to two items which are not expressly attributed to it: the 'feathers' which the inhabitants of the regions beyond Scythia said filled the air and covered the ground to the north [42 ff.]; and the 'swan-shaped' Phorcides of Aeschylus [62]. In the Chinese 'Annals of the Bamboo Books' we are told that King Mu (?961–?906 B.C.)

in his expeditions to the north, travelled over the country of the moving sands, for 1,000 *le*, and that of 'Heaps of Feathers', for 1,000 *le*. Then he subdued the hordes of the K'euen, and returned to the east, with their five kings as captives. Westwards, he pushed his expeditions to where the green birds cast their feathers (the hill of San-Wei). On these expeditions he travelled over 190,000 *le*.[33]

So too central Asiatic tales tell of swan-maidens, ugly—they have leaden eyes, hempen plaits, and yellow nails—and murderous, who live in darkness. I accept E. R. Dodds's attractive suggestion that these underlie Aeschylus' epithet (never before satisfactorily explained) κυκνόμορφοι, 'swan-shaped', for the Phorcides, through the *Arimaspea*.[34]

I venture to suggest a reason why Aristeas may have been led to place the Phorcides and their sisters and neighbours, the Gorgons, where he did. If he heard from the Issedonians tales of creatures ugly, malevolent, and endowed with the power of flight, his thoughts might well have turned to the Greek Gorgons. But there is another feature, common in Mongol and allied folk-lore, which may have played its part: the ability of supernatural beings to doff parts of their body. So swan-maidens can put aside their skins; so too we hear of ogres who can take out their hearts and secrete them elsewhere. If a Greek heard some such story of a swan-maiden, of what would he be reminded more strongly than the Phorcides, with their detachable and transferable eye and tooth? That same process of Hellenizing barbarian story which I have postulated in the case of griffins and Hyperboreans may then have taken place here also, with the resultant location in the *Arimaspea* of Gorgons and Phorcides in the north-east of the world, which had its effect later on both Aeschylus and Pindar [62].

That Herodotus' Androphagi or Cannibals also had a place in Aristeas' poem I have little doubt. They appear in Pliny in association with Nomads (i.e. Scyths), Sauromatae, Issedonians, Arimaspi, the Rhipaean mountains, and the region of 'feathers'; again, with the cave of Boreas, Arimaspi, and griffins (*N.H.* iv. 88; vii. 9 f.); and with Arimaspi and Melanchlaeni (Hdt. iv. 20 *al.*) in a rather curious entry in Pollux, where we are told that 'the Scythians, and of these especially the Androphagi and Melanchlaeni and Arimaspi, use the bones of eagles and vultures as flutes' (iv. 76: Σκύθαι δέ, καὶ μάλιστα τούτων Ἀνδροφάγοι καὶ Μελάγχλαινοι καὶ Ἀριμασποί, ἀετῶν καὶ γυπῶν ὀστοῖς αὐλητικῶς ἐμπνέουσιν). They are of the same order as the one-eyed Arimaspi, with whom indeed we have found them blending in popular tradition [83].

Further than this I am not prepared to venture. The goat-footed people who inhabit the mountains to the north of the Argippaei, and those others beyond them who sleep for six months of the year (Hdt. iv. 25), have the flavour of Aristeas (the latter are perhaps heard of again, as people who 'die' for six months of the year, in the sixteenth century—Hakluyt ii. 330), but as I have said, I see no evidence that the Argippaei, said to be the authors of these stories and at the end of the regular trade-route, were mentioned in the *Arimaspea*. How dangerous it could be to assert the authorship of Aristeas for a Scythian tale just because it is quaint is illustrated by the Neuri, who became wolves once a year and were driven out of their country by an incursion of snakes. This is certainly quaint enough, but the latter event is said to have happened only a generation before the invasion of Darius (Hdt. iv. 105)!

So too with the giant reeds and Dog-men [69]: though the former are actually found, growing to a height of ten to fifteen feet, in Dzungaria (Carruthers 437), and though the latter are vouched for by the same ancient Chinese source that mentions the One-eyed men and the giant ants [82], I am chary of accepting them for the *Arimaspea* without further corroboration. It is true that the Dog-men were known early in Greece, to 'Hesiod', though where he put them is not certain; but Herodotus locates them in the west of Libya: if the *Arimaspea* put them in the opposite part of the world it is strange that he says nothing of it [192].

V

THE TRAVELLER'S ROUTE

WHERE were the Issedonians of Aristeas? The question is a peculiarly difficult one to answer, not only because of the scanty information we have about them, but also because of the constant movement and intermingling of the peoples of Russia since his day. Before giving the views of some modern scholars I shall survey such ancient testimony as we possess.

Aristeas himself placed them next to the Scyths, in the direction of Boreas. His term 'Scyth' probably had a wider connotation than that allowed to it by Herodotus, and he may have included in it peoples whom the later author denies to be Scythian; for instance the Androphagi and the Melanchlaeni (for the former, compare Pliny, *N.H.* vii. 9 with Hdt. iv. 18; the latter were called Scythian by Hecataeus of Miletus,[1] an appellation contradicted by Herodotus (fr. 185; Hdt. iv. 20)). In Aristeas' day, too, the Scythians may have extended over a wider area, being still in the act of migrating. His Scythia, then, may have covered much more than the Scythia of Herodotus. Aristeas too may have been responsible for the statement that the Issedonians 'faced' the Massagetae [60]; a statement so important for our present purpose that it is a pity that we cannot be sure what it means. As it is, it provides some sort of a check, inasmuch as any localization of the Issedonians must take account of it and suggest how it is to be interpreted.

In his fourth book Herodotus gives the following account. East of the Tanais we leave Scythia and enter the country of the Sauromatae, extending northward for approximately 350 miles (fifteen days' journey; in iv. 101 he estimates a day's journey as 200 stades). It is entirely devoid of trees. Beyond this is a well-wooded region inhabited by the lice-eating[2] Budini (21), a large nomadic nation having red hair and blue eyes; also by the Geloni, agriculturalists after whom is named a wooden town,

Gelonus. In the most thickly wooded part is a large lake bordered by marsh, where are taken otters (ἐνύδριες), beavers, and 'animals with square faces'³ (108 f.).

Herodotus does not define the extent of this territory, but says that beyond it (presumably still in a northerly sense) the traveller will pass through uninhabited country for about 160 miles, after which, taking a more easterly course (ἀποκλίνοντι μᾶλλον πρὸς ἀπηλιώτην ἄνεμον), he will reach the Thyssagetae and the Iyrcae. Both these are hunting peoples, the latter firing their arrows from hideouts in trees, then chasing their (wounded) prey on horseback accompanied by their hounds. Inclining east yet again (ὑπὲρ δὲ τούτων τὸ πρὸς τὴν ἠῶ ἀποκλίνοντι) you come upon a group of Scyths. These Herodotus says seceded from the rest and settled there (22); they may in fact have remained behind when the main horde moved into the Pontic area (How and Wells).

So far the way will have lain through rich plains, but henceforth the character of the ground becomes rough and stony (μέχρι μὲν δὴ τῆς τούτων τῶν Σκυθέων χώρης ἐστὶ ἡ καταλεχθεῖσα πᾶσα πεδιάς τε γῆ καὶ βαθύγαιος, τὸ δ' ἀπὸ τούτου λιθώδης τ' ἐστὶ καὶ τρηχέα) for some distance. Beyond this rough tract are the Argippaei at the foot of lofty mountains. These Herodotus describes as large-chinned, snub-nosed, and bald from birth irrespective of sex. Though dressed like the Scythians they speak a different language and have a different diet; for a tree grows there about the size of a fig tree, called *ponticum*, producing fruit like a bean, with a stone inside. The juice of this, which they call *aschy*, they lap or mix with milk; the lees they make into cakes. Their use of milk indicates partial nomadism, but they have not many flocks because the pasturage is poor. They make their homes under trees, which in winter they cover with white felt. They are an unwarlike people, regarded as sacrosanct by their neighbours, in whose quarrels they arbitrate and to whose refugees they offer safe asylum (23).

So far the country is well known through Greek and Scythian traders, who have to transact their business through interpreters in seven languages (though Herodotus has only enumerated six non-Scythian peoples on the route; perhaps the dialect of the separate Scythian group also needed interpretation) (24). Of the region to the north, which is cut off by an impassable mountain range, nothing is known except wild stories told by the Argippaei of men with goats' feet in the mountains themselves, and of men beyond who sleep for six months of the year. But it is known for certain that the territory to the east of the Argippaei is inhabited by the Issedonians (25).

Our next informants are Mela and Pliny, writing 500 years after Herodotus. The former repeats the Herodotean account of the Issedonians' customs, but places them in Europe, west of the Tanais between the Palus Maeotis and the Arimaspi, north of whom are the griffins and the Rhipaean mountains where the perpetual snowfall denies sight or passage (ii. 1 f.; 9; 13). Pliny also places them in the vicinity of the Palus Maeotis in one passage; but in another near the Colchians, and in yet another north of the Jaxartes, where he well adds 'nec in alia parte maior auctorum inconstantia, credo propter innumeras vagasque gentes' (*N.H.* iv. 88; vi. 21; 50).

Ptolemy, in the second century of our era, mentions two towns called Issedon in eastern Asia, which he distinguishes by the epithets *Scythica* and *Serica*; he places the Issedonians themselves about the latter (*Geog.* vi. 16. 5 and 7; viii. 24. 3 and 5; cf. Amm. Marc. xxiii. 6.66). Both towns are due north of the Himalaya on his map, apparently in Chinese Turkestan (Sinkiang); modern authorities differ about their exact situation (Thomson 310).

This completes the ancient testimony. I now propose to summarize the views of some[4] modern scholars [Map II].

1. Humboldt (i. 389 ff.): Moving in a generally northeasterly direction from the Palus Maeotis, we shall pass according to Herodotus through the Melanchlaeni, the Budini, the Thyssagetae, and the Iyrcae (who have been mistaken for a Turkish people by some scholars), and reach, towards the east, an isolated colony of Scyths (perhaps middlemen in the gold and fur trade). Here the plains end and we enter an extensive rough tract, rising into high mountains at the foot of which are the Argippaei. Their physiognomy has led a number of people to identify them as Mongols (Kalmuks), but the Mongols did not penetrate so far west until the thirteenth century;

they may have been Finnish. The name they gave to the juice of the fruit produced by the *ponticum* (thought to be the bird-cherry, *Prunus padus*) has suggested to Erman that they were the Bashkirs, a Turkish [Turco-Tatar]-speaking people of Finnish stock who now inhabit the southern Urals [for the Bashkirs use the juice of the bird-cherry as the Argippaei did their *aschy*, and call it *atchui*[5]]. But we have no historical notice of the presence of the Bashkirs in western Asia until the tenth century of our era.

The regions beyond the Argippaei are unexplored because of high mountains which bar the way. Now Herodotus in these chapters is speaking not of one mountain range but two: this impassable range, which clearly has a west–east orientation, is the Altai; but that in the foothills of which live the Argippaei is the Ural. The route then crosses the Urals from west to east; the Argippaei are to be placed on the eastern slopes of these, and the Issedonians east of the Sea of Aral and the upper Ishim, and north of the Jaxartes-Araxes (Syr), across which they face the Massagetae to the south; perhaps between Karkaralinsk and Semipalatinsk. The Arimaspi would be on the northern slopes of the Altai (the home of the goat-footed men), round the northwestern projection of which they would communicate with the Issedonians; the griffins' gold would be the mineral resources of that area, particularly rich in the Kuznetsk mountains. These considerations put out of court a suggested location of the Issedonians about the little river Iset in the Urals, or of the Arimaspi in the south of that chain, rich though it is in gold.

It is strange that Herodotus appears to make no mention of the Volga in his itinerary. This may be because he thought of it as a continuation of the Don (which he says rises in the country of the Thyssagetae, iv. 123), across the narrow strip separating them [they are now joined together here by a canal in lat. 48.5 N].

The weakest point in this reconstruction is undoubtedly the attempt to force a reference to the Urals out of the ὄρεα ὑψηλά of Hdt. iv. 23, and to a crossing of them in διεξελθόντι τῆς τρηχέης χῶρον πολλόν (such appears to be Humboldt's idea). The 'rough and stony tract', being opposed to πεδιάς τε γῆ καὶ βαθύγαιος, conveys the meaning of barrenness, not at all applicable to the Urals. Also, no one would describe these inconsiderable hills as 'lofty': much of the chain consists of low plateaux, only occasionally rising to peaks over 4,000 feet. It would be very odd too for

Herodotus not to mention them specifically until after they had been crossed; in fact, I do not think that his language can have any other sense than that these 'lofty mountains' are distinct from the 'rough and stony tract' he has just mentioned. Again, the outliers of the Altai are some 700 miles from the Urals: it is incredible that the Argippaei in the latter, with their stories of goat-footed men and so on, could have been referring to the former. The ὄρεα ὑψηλά of c. 23 are clearly the same as the ὄρεα ὑψηλὰ ἄβατα of c. 25, which Herodotus conceives as running from west to east to the north of both Argippaei and Issedonians.

2. Minns (104 ff., mainly following Tomaschek): The Sauromatae stretched up the Don and Volga nearly to Saratov and the forest region; the territory of the Budini probably covered the lower reaches of the Belaya and Kama. The Budini may be represented today by the grey-eyed and reddish-haired Permiaks (and Ibn Fadhlan said of the Bashkirs that they ate lice). The town of Gelonus perhaps stood on the site of the modern Kazan, a trading-post of great antiquity. The Thyssagetae would occupy the western slopes of the Urals from Ufa to Orenburg; a hilly country would be consistent with the fact that several rivers have their source there (iv. 123), and one of these, the Chussovaya, may have the same root as *Thyssagetae*. Tomaschek identifies them with the Voguls [and extends their territory to the junction of the Iset and the Tobol]. Herodotus disregards the Urals, whose incline is so gentle that they do not appear to the traveller as mountains. The method of hunting of the Iyrcae (the name is a Sarmatian form of *Jugra*) requires a country full but not over-full of trees; the basins of the Tobol, Ishim, and Irtysh would fit. The 'separated' Scyths [whom Tomaschek places from the Kulunda steppe north of Semipalatinsk across the upper Irtysh to the Ob] were perhaps remnants left behind in the original home of the Scyths (who were Ugrian?). The rugged tract after passing these is the outliers of the Altai, and the Argippaei (pure Mongols) would be in Dzungaria, between the Altai and the Tien Shan. Their *ponticum* may be the birdcherry, but many other steppe berries are treated similarly by various tribes. The 'trees' covered with felt under which they lived are a description of the felt tent on a light wooden framework now universally used by Asian nomads. The Issedonians east, or rather southeast, of the Argippaei could be Tibetans in the Tarim and Bulunggir basin, where Ptolemy puts them (his *Issedon Scythica* is Ak-Su?), 'opposite' the Massagetae to the west across the Pamir. The Arimaspi

are Huns in Mongolia, of whom the Argippaei would be a western out-
post. The Issedonians may have got gold from them, or perhaps from
the mountains to the south, above India. The Hyperboreans are either
purely imaginary, or may be an inkling of the Chinese; while the
Rhipaean mountains might be any of the many ranges in central Asia.

The 'separate' Scyths are very difficult in this location. Also
Herodotus quite definitely says that the Argippaei got their *aschy*
from the fruit of a *tree*, and there are few trees in the barren plains
of Dzungaria. He also says that they did without the felt covering
on their trees in summer; but at no season of the year do the
Asiatic nomads dispense with the covering of their yurts and
live in the framework! And the explanation of how the Issedonians are 'opposite' the Massagetae is very forced.

3. Westberg (183–7; 189–92): (a) *Position of the Issedonians
according to Herodotus.* The Sauromatae extend from just above the
mouth of the Don to Kamyshin. Herodotus says nothing of the extent
of the territory of the Budini, but it must have been considerable, as he
tells us that they were a large tribe. His account of its features excludes
the treeless left bank of the Volga; but the right bank in olden times
was wooded farther south than today—cf. the testimony of Ibn
Rosteh in the tenth century, who also speaks of open fields here (such
as the Geloni worked), but says that the principal products of the
locality were honey and furs; the extent of this region he puts at
seventeen days' journey both in breadth and length. This would
extend the domain of the Budini from Kamyshin to the north of
Syzran. The 'desert' to the north of the Budini which takes seven days
to cross corresponds to the Zhigulev hills, which extend along the
right bank of the Volga to near its junction with the Kama, up which
the route is deflected eastwards. Here are to be located, in the bend of
the Volga and the lower reaches of the Kama, the Thyssagetae (not
farther east in the Urals—cf. the πεδιὰς γῆ of c. 23). The account of
the Iyrcae's method of hunting shows that they lived almost in the
steppe. To the east of them were the 'separated' Scyths. This proves
that the trade-route did not follow the Kama to the middle Urals, but
kept an easterly direction along the Belaya to the high and thickly
wooded southern Urals, which is the rough, stony tract leading to the
Argippaei (Bashkirs?) at their tip. (Herodotus thought of the Urals as
running west to east because he identified them with the Rhipaeans.)
East of the Argippaei are the Issedonians, opposite the Massagetae

across the Araxes-Jaxartes (Syr); whether Herodotus was right in so placing them is another matter, but Tomaschek does too much violence to his account in putting them in the Tarim basin in an attempt to reconcile him with Ptolemy.

(b) *Position of the Issedonians according to Aristeas.* Herodotus' information concerning the peoples along this trade-route was derived from oral reports; but that about the Issedonians (except perhaps for their location east of the Argippaei), Arimaspians, griffins, and Hyperboreans from a written source—the poem of Aristeas (first half of seventh century)—in spite of the impression given in c. 27 that he may have got this too from the Scythians. Hence too he got the etymology of *Arimaspus* as 'one-eyed', as is shown by [fr. 5] [?] (the etymology of this as 'owners of docile steeds' or 'of wild steeds of the steppe' is dubious; could it be *ari* ('noble')+*Maspii*, a Persian tribe (Hdt. i. 125)?). Hdt. iii. 116 is pertinent here. According to this passage the north produces most gold (which Herodotus connects with the griffins and Arimaspi); we are not entitled to associate this northern gold (the gold of the Urals) with that of Baltistan and Tibet. Indeed, if we compare the fragment of Damastes [39 f.] where the Rhipaean mountains are mentioned, but not the griffins, with Hdt. iv. 13 [T. 1] where the griffins are mentioned, but not the Rhipaean mountains, we may doubt if Aristeas had anything to say about the gold-guarding griffins at all; for the fragment of Damastes seems likely to be closer to the text of Aristeas than is Herodotus, as being more consistent and detailed. The griffins belong to India (Herodotus and Ctesias), and it would be natural [for Herodotus, presumably, for the Scythians could hardly know so much] to say that the northern gold was got in the same way as the eastern gold.

The shifting of peoples in eastern Europe took place in or before the time of Aristeas; there were no more changes between him and Herodotus. Therefore, as Aristeas says that the Issedonians were the next-door neighbours of the Scyths and had caused them to migrate, his Issedonians are to be identified with the Sauromatae, whose womenfolk were equal with the men (cf. what is said about the Issedonians in c. 26); and it is tempting to see the Arimaspi in the Massagetae.

There is a marked discrepancy between the scrupulous way in which Westberg treats the evidence of Herodotus concerning the trade-route to the Argippaei (except perhaps for the glossing over of the 'separate' Scyths) and that in which he treats the same author's testimony concerning the content of the *Arimaspea*. We cannot thus over-ride Herodotus when he says plainly that Aristeas put the gold-guarding griffins beyond the Arimaspi; and that he did not insert this himself on the analogy of the ant/Indian story [66] is proved by Aeschylus' association of Arimaspi with gold and griffins in the *Prometheus Vinctus*. Also, the identification of the Issedonians with the Sauromatae is precluded if it is true that the latter were aboriginals, already occupying the country when the Scyths arrived [51 f.].

4. Hermann: The placing of the Issedonians in the far east, under the influence of Ptolemy, is wrong. Only the evidence of Herodotus and Aristeas is of any value, and this shows that they were Indogermanic nomads living east of the Urals about the lower Tobol and the Iset, which is obviously named after them (they appear too in Ptolemy in this neighbourhood as *Iastae* [?]). The evidence of later writers has been distorted by false associations.

Aristeas called them *Issedi*, but, as Alcman shows, the longer form was soon in use. Hecataeus is the first to our knowledge to use *Issedones*; the form *Essedones*, it may be conjectured [why?], was given currency by a younger Ionian geographer, Dionysius of Miletus. The Greeks first heard of them from Aristeas (second half of seventh century), who appears really to have visited them. He placed them north of the Scyths and south of the Arimaspi and griffins. His placing of the Rhipaean mountains north of these last merely reflected older mythological ideas: they are the northern range which was invented by the imagination of the old astronomers.[6] The same can be said of the Hyperboreans.

The *Arimaspea* influenced poets (e.g. Alcman) and geographers. Hecataeus undoubtedly [?] put the Arimaspi under the eastern part of the Rhipaeans, which extended right through Europe, and beneath them the Issedonians, as a subdivision of the Scythians. The view of Kiessling, that Hdt. i. 201 [where Herodotus says that the Issedonians 'face' the Massagetae] derives from Hecataeus, is wrong; it was a later modification of Hecataeus' work that made the Issedonians an Asiatic people; for though Stephanus puts the Issedonians of Hecataeus in Asia we know that for the Ionian cartographers the continental boundary was the Phasis [but cf. 190!].

It was probably Dionysius of Miletus who more accurately defined the country of the Issedonians, as a result of information about a caravan route beyond the Tanais. Not one fragment of Dionysius

remains [!], but we know Herodotus used him for his account of
Scythia [?], as did a later historian (Theophanes of Mytilene?), from
whom Pliny vi. 19 and Mela i. 116 f. derive. These passages enable us
to determine what Dionysius had to say about the situation of the
Issedonians. He, like Aristeas and Hecataeus, put them north of
the Pontus but west of the Tanais; it was beyond the Tanais that the
tribes about which he had new information dwelt. The peoples west
of the Tanais were, from north to south, the Arimaspi, Issedonians,
Scyths; and east of the river Arimphaei, Thyssagetae, Tyrcae, Budini,
Sauromatae (when Mela and Pliny put the Issedonians west of the
Tanais they merely repeat Dionysius).

Herodotus, doubtless using information about the same caravan
route as Dionysius, moved the Issedonians over the Tanais to the far
north-east of the earth. Dionysius knew as his farthest people the
Arimphaei, with high mountains cutting off further knowledge;
Herodotus must have heard that east of them were the Issedonians,
so their neighbours the Arimaspi were shifted by him far away to the
east. The 'high mountains', in Herodotus north of the Argippaei
[= Arimphaei?], were probably originally a range running north to
south between the Argippaei and the Issedonians [why?]. As a result
of his new information about the way to these people, Herodotus was
forced to separate the Caspian Sea from the encompassing Ocean [in
which he did not believe [60]!]. This positioning of the Issedonians
accounts for their being 'opposite' (i.e. north of [?]) the Massagetae.

Later authors who misplaced the Issedonians in the region of the
Caucasus were misled by a confusion over Herodotus' Araxes (i. 202—
itself a confusion) with the Armenian Araxes. From Herodotus'
conjunction of the Issedonians and the Massagetae, and taking the
Araxes here as the Jaxartes, Marinus of Tyre supposed there to be an
Issedon Scythica (Ptol. *Geog.* vi. 16. 7; cf. Amm. Marc. xxiii. 6. 66); his
Issedon Serica farther east is based on a misunderstanding of the
Itinerary of Maës (end of first century A.D.), whose knowledge of the
east Turkestan silk-route came not from travellers themselves but an
Iranian guide-book. It is possible with the help of c. 96 of the *Han
Annals*, which uses this same source, to reconstruct it exactly and see
where Marinus and Ptolemy followed, expanded, or altered it. From
this it seems that Marinus thought the Massagetae were west of
Kashgar, and the inhabitants of the Tarim basin (who are not named
by the *Han Annals* or later Chinese authorities, and not being of
uniform stock probably never had a common name) to be Issedonians
also. It was Marinus, then, who put the Issedonians in east Turkestan;

as this was a palpable misunderstanding, his authority is worth-less.

Earlier discussion of the position of the Issedonians has been bedevilled by an uncritical acceptance of the various ancient traditions. Toma-schek's identification of them with Tibetans, unlikely enough in itself, does not in the least fit the time to which Ptolemy's authority belonged; and his whole inquiry suffers because he continually interprets Herodotus' evidence in favour of Ptolemy. (Kiessling accounted for the varying traditions about their position by postulating that the Issedonians themselves moved about.)

The only authorities of value we have are in fact Aristeas and Herodotus; and to them we must limit ourselves. Now as Aristeas' route was from south to north, we might think we were concerned with the prehistoric amber-route from the Baltic to the Black Sea [the existence of which is unproved: *P.–W.* iii. 298 f.]; but as there are no remarkable mountains on this route we must give Aristeas another direction (no doubt the notion of a great northern range and Hyper-boreans caused him to give his route a more northerly orientation theoretically than in fact it had). In his time we must remember that the Scyths stretched as far as the Volga; so our thoughts are turned to that old trade-route mentioned by Herodotus and Dionysius. This would follow the Volga north, until it turned north-east and east at the junction with the Kama. Up to this point there would be, in Aristeas' time, Scythians and the related Geloni. Dionysius did not know of Issedonians on this trade-route; his knowledge stopped at the Urals, in which he saw a branch of the Rhipaean mountains (and therefore gave them a west–east direction). Herodotus is better in-formed, and does not say that these are the Rhipaeans; he speaks only of them as high and impassable, and puts the Argippaei at their foot, the Issedonians to the east. We have now reached the eastern side of the Urals, in the neighbourhood of west Siberian steppe; here were the Issedonians of both Aristeas and Herodotus, a placing which is confirmed by the name of the river Iset (the river mentioned by Zenothemis?), where in the seventeenth century there was a district called Issetia. Westberg's identification of the Issedonians of Aristeas with the Sauromatae of Herodotus fails because the latter were east of the Scyths, not in the path of Aristeas' northerly journey. We have seen that there is no need to give any weight to Herodotus' conjunc-tion of the Issedonians with the Massagetae in the neighbourhood of the Aral Sea.

The Arimaspi would be on the old trade-route from the Tobol to

Omsk and then up the Irtysh to the Altai, which with its rich gold deposits provides the best scene for the griffins and the Rhipaean mountains.

I concur with Hermann's dismissal of the evidence of Ptolemy, if only because it is half a millennium later than that of Herodotus, during which period there had been much movement of the Eurasian tribes. But his cock-sure reasoning about the true situation of the Issedonians, apart from being at times hard to follow, I find quite unacceptable in its premisses. Useful though it is to examine closely Herodotus' account of the peoples along the Scythian trade-route, in order to try to discover where he put the Issedonians, there is no ground for the assumption that this was the route which Aristeas himself followed (Hermann seems to imagine that the Scyths came from north Europe, when he says that in Aristeas' day they would have extended as far as the junction of the Volga and the Kama—in heavy forest!). And even granting that the river called Iset preserves the name of the Issedonians, nothing more can be inferred from it than that this people lived *at some time* near it; just as the migrant tribes of Rus (Ros) and As left their names in passing to rivers in south Russia (Vernadsky 97; 148).

All these modern theories about the Scythian trade-route are helpful, yet none is in my opinion entirely satisfactory. Though Herodotus gives us little in the way of distances, he does tell us enough about the characteristics of the terrain and the various tribes along the way to show the sort of country through which it passed. After the Sauromatae in the steppe, it traversed woodland mixed with pasture (Budini and Geloni), a wilderness (which may have been uninhabited forest), then eastwards through forested uplands—forested, because the inhabitants, the Thyssagetae, were hunters; uplands, because a number of rivers had their source there. The forest must have been thinning out in the country of their neighbours, the Iyrcae. Another easterly inclination now brings us to a branch of the Scyths; that is, we are out on the steppe again. A stony tract next leads us to the Argippaei (Turco-Tatars?) in a region where the trees are not too dense to prohibit the rearing of flocks, at the foot of high mountains.

I would accept Westberg's exposition of the route as far as the
territory of the Thyssagetae, but this people I would spread over
both sides of the southern Ural in the area Belaya–Kama–Iset–
Tobol (cf. Tomaschek). The Iyrcae would then be in the semi-
steppe about the middle Ishim, and the 'separate' Scyths in the
steppe to the south-east. The road would now follow the northern
edge of the Kazak uplands, a region of low broken hills and
granite outcrops (Humboldt ii. 122–37)—the 'rough, stony tract'
of Herodotus—to the vicinity of Semipalatinsk, across the middle
Irtysh to the semi-steppe between that and the Ob, on the
western skirts of the Altai (the Argippaei). I would place the
Issedonians not east but south and south-west of these, in
the steppe extending from the Irtysh to the head-waters of the
Ishim, and perhaps farther towards the Syr, to 'face' the Massagetae beyond it[7] (the Issedonians were a large tribe, according
to Zenothemis [68]). This violence I would excuse by supposing
that the Rhipaean range was not simply the Altai but the whole
western fringe of the central Asiatic massif; if these Rhipaeans
were imagined (as they were later) as being in the 'proper' place
for the home of Boreas, the north, and so slewed round to run
from west to east, carrying the peoples at their foot with them,
the Issedonians would be thought of as east of the Argippaei!

But how could Aristeas ever have supposed that his Issedonians
were in the north, if they were in fact in the same latitude as the
Palus Maeotis? The answer to this crucial question I believe to
be, quite simply, that he did not. Speculation on his geography
has been dogged, both in ancient and in modern times, by the
assumption that his Boreas, the only apparent clue we have to
the orientation of his journey, represents a cardinal point. But the
concept of fixed cardinal points is an advanced one, formed as
astronomical science and mathematical geography progressed.
Though the names of the winds were to be used for these points
by a more scientific age, it is anachronistic to suppose that this
could have taken place already in the seventh century B.C. The
germ of the idea is no doubt to be seen in the two pairs of oppos-
ing winds in *Od.* v. 331 f., but even supposing that the east
and west winds were then defined by reference to heavenly

phenomena—the rising and setting sun—(and Homer nowhere implies this), it is still a long step to *fixing* east and west (for the points at which the sun rises and sets vary through the year), and an even longer step to fixing north and south. Homer's conception, mythical though it is, that all the winds had a common starting-point (the Aeolian isle) indicates that the association of winds and 'points of the compass' had not yet got very far.[8]

In the first place the various winds would be identified, not with the help of astronomy, but by the locality from which they blew at any particular place, or by their effects.[9] Thus Boreas is a cold and powerful wind; and, for the Greeks on the western seaboard of Asia Minor, blows from Thrace. But when Aristeas had left Thrace far behind how could he identify Boreas? Only by its characteristics of coldness and force; characteristics which may be found also in the prevailing *easterly* winds of south-east Russia (*E.B.* xxiii 881b). It might be thus that Aristeas gave his route an easterly direction, thinking that he was marching towards the Hyperboreans beyond the source of Boreas; and that source he might well have imagined he had found if he heard of the bitter hurricanes which sweep through the Dzungarian Gate, and of the Cave of the Winds there.

Here I must forestall a possible objection, that in fr. 4 Aristeas himself says that the Arimaspi dwell beyond the Issedonians καθύπερθε πρὸς βορέω, and that καθύπερθε in itself means 'to the north [of]'. That this is a misunderstanding of the word is sufficiently demonstrated by Hdt. iv. 174, τούτων δὲ κατύπερθε πρὸς νότον ἄνεμον . . . οἰκέουσι Γαράμαντες. It seems to be based on an interpretation of *Od.* iii. 169–72 which is not obligatory. Here Menelaus comes upon Nestor's fleet at Lesbos, wondering whether to round Chios by the north and west or by the east and south:

> ἐν Λέσβῳ δ' ἔκιχεν δολιχὸν πλόον ὁρμαίνοντας,
> ἢ καθύπερθε Χίοιο νεοίμεθα παιπαλοέσσης,
> νήσου ἔπι Ψυρίης, αὐτὴν ἐπ' ἀριστέρ' ἔχοντες,
> ἢ ὑπένερθε Χίοιο, παρ' ἠνεμόεντα Μίμαντα.

Psyra is west of Chios, Mimas east; they might represent different stages on each course, but they might (and I think do) rather give exactitude to the prepositions: 'above' means not 'to the north of' but 'on the far side of'; 'below', not 'to the south of' but 'on the near side of'—from the point of view of the poet and his audience in *Ionia*. So too καθύπερθε in *Il.* xxiv. 544 f. can have no reference to the north (Achilles is describing the extent of the kingdom of Priam):

> ὅσσον Λέσβος ἄνω, Μάκαρος ἕδος, ἔντος ἐέργει
> καὶ Φρυγίη καθύπερθε καὶ Ἑλλήσποντος ἀπείρων.

Here καθύπερθε means 'inland' (and ἄνω 'out to sea'?); the baseline of reckoning, which gives the word its sense, may be either the poet himself (as in the former example[10]) or one of his characters who is speaking (as perhaps in the latter). The Greeks seem to have thought of a coastline as a sort of trough: you ascended from it whether you went out to sea (ἀναπλεῖν) or inland (ἀναβαίνειν). So καθύπερθε is used in topographical descriptions with reference to an imaginary observer on the coast, and means simply 'up-country' (cf. the use of ὑπέρ with the genitive, e.g. in Hdt. iv. 170 f.[11]).

There is evidence enough that the ancients came to think of the north of the earth as being higher than the south, but this must have been the result of considerable scientific advance. First had to come the discovery of the celestial north pole; then would be asked, why is this pole not in the zenith (for the questioner would naturally assume that he was at the centre of things)? The earliest answer to this question was, that the flat disk of the earth was tilted towards the south; but this was long after Aristeas' day,[12] and should not be connected with the use of καθύπερθε which I have been discussing.

Though such I believe to have been the state of affairs in Aristeas' time, in the following two centuries, as a result of the flowering of Ionian science, the quarters of the winds came to be defined more and more exactly with the aid of astronomy.[13] As a result Boreas begins really to stand for the cardinal north;[14] and so the Rhipaean mountains of Aristeas are shifted by the carto-graphers from their true position in the east to the north.

There is, then, no objection on the score of direction to my placing of the Issedonians; and that they were in that position in Aristeas' time as well as in the time of Herodotus would be probable, because there had been no major migration in between, and is confirmed by the central Asiatic folk-lore which they retailed to Aristeas. The region of the griffins, rich in gold, *might* be the Altai and Kuznetsk mountains; but it might also be located in the Tarbagatai mountains, between Ala Kul and Lake Zaysan in the river Irtysh, on whose northern slopes are auriferous streams whence in olden times gold was extracted (Humboldt ii. 83; cf. iii. 501). Here, therefore, about the upper Irtysh (Aeschylus' *Pluton*?), I would put the one-eyed Arimaspi, a branch of the one-eyed Kuei (Mongols[15]), who had pushed the Issedonians farther away from Mongolia and Dzungaria. I would see the home of Boreas in a legendary cave in the neighbourhood of the Dzungarian Gate; and the Rhipaean range in the succession of heights, forested on their lower slopes but often rising to regions of perpetual snow, which form the western and northwestern extremity of the highlands of central Asia—perhaps called *Caucasus* by Aristeas: it will not escape remark that later the native informants of Alexander's expedition called the southerly mountains of this group by a name which was interpreted as Caucasus.[16] (This may be the reason why Herodotus does not name the 'Rhipaean' mountains [42] : because they were called *Caucasus* by Aristeas, but he knew the Caucasus as the historic Caucasus.)

Here, then, was the limit of Aristeas' journey. The way by which he travelled there, however, can only be guessed. It was probably through the 'corridor of the steppes', by which his Scythian hosts must have come, and over which at that time they may still have been strung out, rather than by the trade-route described by Herodotus, except in its initial stages: he may have followed the Tanais and the Volga (which he conflated into the Phasis?) to the vicinity of Saratov, and seen the Sauromatae or Maeotians, whom he took for Amazons (the Sauromatae are called Scythian by Hippocrates (*Airs*, &c. 17)). Had he followed the trade-route throughout, through many peoples clearly non-Scythian, he would hardly have said that the Issedonians were the Scythians' neighbours. More we cannot say.

VI

THE POET

ABOUT Aristeas himself fabulous tales were told from our earliest
testimony onwards. So far I have used his name as a convenience
for 'the author of the *Arimaspea*' : it is now time to examine the
evidence about him in detail, to review the theories of some
modern scholars, and to see if there is any good reason to discount
the ancient ascription of the *Arimaspea* to him. I start by repeating
the story in Herodotus [T. 12].

According to a tale that Herodotus had heard at Proconnesus
and Cyzicus, Aristeas,

who belonged to one of the noblest families in the island, had entered
one day a fuller's shop, when he suddenly dropped down dead. Hereupon the fuller shut up his shop, and went to tell Aristeas' kindred
what had happened. The report of the death had just spread through
the town, when a certain Cyzicenian, lately arrived from Artace, contradicted the rumour, affirming that he had met Aristeas on the road
to Cyzicus, and had spoken with him. This man, therefore, strenuously
denied the rumour; the relations however proceeded to the fuller's shop
with all things necessary for the funeral, intending to carry the body
away. But on the shop being opened, no Aristeas was found, either
dead or alive (οὔτε τεθνεῶτα οὔτε ζῶντα φαίνεσθαι Ἀριστέην). Six
years afterwards he reappeared, they told me, in Proconnesus (μετὰ
δὲ ἑβδόμῳ ἔτεϊ φανέντα αὐτὸν ἐς Προκόννησον), and composed the poem
which the Greeks now know as the *Arimaspea*, after which he disappeared a second time (ἀφανισθῆναι τὸ δεύτερον). This is the tale
current in the two cities above mentioned.

What follows I know to have happened to the Metapontines in Italy
two [*v.l.* three] hundred and forty years after the second disappearance
of Aristeas, as I discovered by calculations I made at Proconnesus
and Metapontum (τάδε δὲ οἶδα Μεταποντίνοισι τοῖσι ἐν Ἰταλίῃ συγκυρήσαντα μετὰ τὴν ἀφάνισιν τὴν δευτέρην Ἀριστέω ἔτεσι τεσσεράκοντα καὶ
διηκοσίοισι [*v.l.* τριηκοσίοισι], ὡς ἐγὼ συμβαλλόμενος ἐν Προκοννήσῳ
τε καὶ Μεταποντίῳ εὕρισκον). Aristeas then, as the Metapontines affirm,
appeared to them in their own country in person (αὐτὸν Ἀριστέην

φανέντα σφι ἐς τὴν χώρην), and ordered them to set up an altar in honour of Apollo, and to place near it a statue to be called that of Aristeas the Proconnesian. Apollo, he told them, had honoured them alone of the Italiotes with his presence (φάναι γάρ σφι τὸν Ἀπόλλωνα Ἰταλιωτέων μούνοισι δὴ ἀπικέσθαι ἐς τὴν χώρην); and he himself accompanied the god at the time, not however in his present form, but in the shape of a raven. Having said so much he vanished (εἰπόντα ταῦτα ἀφανισθῆναι). Then the Metapontines sent to Delphi, and inquired of the god what they were to make of this apparition. The priestess in reply bade them attend to what the spectre said, 'for so it would go best with them'. Thus advised, they did as they had been directed; and there is now a statue bearing the name of Aristeas, close by the image of Apollo in the market-place of Metapontum, with bay trees standing round it.

In this, the earliest story we have about Aristeas, there are, first, a miraculous disappearance—the dead body is animated and rapt away by some supernatural agency (Apollo, one supposes)—and, secondly, *two* supernatural reappearances. For though, disregarding Aristeas' death in the fuller's shop, his first disappearance from Proconnesus, followed six years later by his reappearance there, would be perfectly compatible with ordinary absence on travel, the words Herodotus uses about this reappearance are the same as those he uses to describe the second, undoubtedly spectral, appearance to the Metapontines. The *Arimaspea*, then, was composed by a ghost (or rather, a zombie!), and the second disappearance too from Proconnesus we may conclude was as mysterious as the first.

A century after Herodotus we meet a different story. In the second chapter of the *Historiae Mirabiles* of Apollonius—a passage probably derived from Theopompus[1]—we read [T. 14]:

It is reported of Aristeas the Proconnesian that at the very time of his death in a fuller's shop in Proconnesus many saw him in Sicily teaching (γράμματα διδάσκοντα). This kind of thing happened to him often and over a long period of time his appearances in Sicily became quite frequent (πυκνότερον φανταζομένου) and generally known, so that the Sicilians accorded a shrine and sacrifices to him as a hero (ἱερόν τε καθιδρύσαντο αὐτῷ καὶ ἔθυσαν ὡς ἥρωϊ).

On the face of it, all these Sicilian appearances are *post mortem* there is no indication that the death in Proconnesus was not a true death, and the phrase πολλάκις αὐτῷ τοῦ τοιούτου συμβαίνοντος need only refer to the phantasmal manifestations, and not imply a new 'death' on each occasion. It would, however, also be compatible with the latter interpretation; and there was another version of the Aristeas-legend in which his 'death' was but a death-like trance, occasioned by the temporary absence of his soul on disembodied peregrinations. 'Suidas' gives a report that the soul of Aristeas could go forth from his body and return at will [T. 11]; and it is this that Pliny means in a passage of proofs that even death may be deceptive:

The soul of Hermotimus of Clazomenae would leave his body, range abroad, and report distant happenings unknowable except to an eye-witness,[2] while his body itself would be betwixt life and death. Finally his enemies, the Cantharidae, burnt it, and so deprived the soul on its return of its sheath. The soul of Aristeas too, about which many a tall tale is told, was seen flying from his mouth in Proconnesus in the form of a raven.

(*N.H.* vii. 174: 'reperimus inter exempla Hermotimi Clazomenii animam relicto corpore errare solitam vagamque e longinquo multa adnuntiare, quae nisi a praesente nosci non possent, corpore interim semianimi, donec cremato eo inimici, qui Cantharidae vocabantur, remeanti animae veluti vaginam ademerint; Aristeae etiam visam evolantem ex ore in Proconneso corvi effigie, magna quae sequitur ha*n*c fabulositate' [T. 15]). It looks as if Pliny knew of stories about Aristeas similar to that which he here tells about the psychic excursions of Hermotimus.

This form of the story finds a detailed exposition in two passages of Maximus of Tyre, a sophist of the second century A.D. According to the first [T. 19]

there was a man of Proconnesus whose body would lie alive, yes, but with only the dimmest flicker of life and in a state very near to death (ἔμπνουν μέν, ἀλλ' ἀμυδρῶς καὶ ἐγγύτατα θανάτου); while his soul would issue from it and wander in the sky like a bird, surveying all beneath, land, sea, rivers, cities, nations of mankind, and occurrences and creatures of all sorts (καὶ παθήματα καὶ φύσεις παντοίας); then returning into and raising up its body, which it treated like an instrument (ὥσπερ ὀργάνῳ χρωμένη), it would relate the various things it had seen and heard in various places.

The second passage concerns untaught sages: stories of inspiration or knowledge obtained by mysterious means, as of Hesiod receiving the gift of poesy together with a laurel bough from the Muses, of Minos receiving instruction in politics from Zeus in the Idaean cave, and so on, allegorize innate genius. So too Aristeas' edifying journeys in the spirit [T. 20]:

There was in Proconnesus a man who loved wisdom; his name was Aristeas. Yet at first he was not credited with his wisdom, for he could boast of none that had taught him it. So he thought of a device to overcome men's disbelief. He would tell how his soul would leave his body and, flying up into the sky, would traverse the lands both Greek and foreign, all islands, rivers, and mountains; how the limit of his journey was the country of the Hyperboreans (γενέσθαι δὲ τῆς περιπολήσεως αὐτῇ τέρμα τὴν Ὑπερβορέων γῆν); how he thus obtained a successive view of all usages customary and political, of varying landscapes and climates, of inroads of the sea and outpourings of rivers (φύσεις χωρίων, καὶ ἀέρων μεταβολάς, καὶ ἀναχύσεις θαλάττης, καὶ ποταμῶν ἐκβολάς); and how his soul then had a much clearer view of heaven than from below on earth (γενέσθαι δὲ αὐτῇ καὶ τὴν τοῦ οὐρανοῦ θέαν πολὺ τῆς νέρθεν σαφεστέραν).

Aristeas' knowledge was not confined to geography and astronomy; it was not even confined to present time, but included the future also, for he was an adept in prognostication, according to Clement [T. 21]. Here may be another similarity with Hermotimus, whose migrant soul not only brought back with it information of distant events but during its wanderings appeared visibly in various places and prophesied. So much is told by Apollonius (*Hist. Mir.* 3), who supplements the account of Pliny already quoted, possibly from the same ultimate source:

They say the soul of Hermotimus would wander away from his body and absent itself for years on end, and, appearing now in one place, now in another (? κατὰ τόπους γινομένην [leg. φαινομένην?]), would foretell events such as floods and droughts, earthquakes, plagues, and the like (ὄμβρους μεγάλους καὶ ἀνομβρίας, ἔτι δὲ σεισμούς τε καὶ λοιμοὺς καὶ παραπλήσια). After a certain time it would re-enter its body, which had been lying inert, as into a sheath (ἔλυτρον: there can be

little doubt that this is the word translated by Pliny's *vagina*), and
arouse it.

(There follows the story of the burning of the body by Hermotimus' enemies, after suborning his wife: this explains why no
woman is allowed to enter the temple which the Clazomenians
erected in honour of Hermotimus (ἱερὸν αὐτοῦ καθίδρυται—cf.
the phrase which Apollonius used of the Sicilians and Aristeas
[120]).³

So many coincidences have now been noticed between the
stories about Hermotimus and those about Aristeas that I think
we are entitled to postulate one more to account for Clement's
statement: the discarnate soul of Aristeas too had prophetic insight. This mantic capacity of Aristeas throws light on a rather
odd tale in Athenaeus, apparently from Theopompus (though
Jacoby has his doubts about this (ii. 389)) [T. 18]:

> Philomelus gave the golden laurel wreath, which the Lampsacenes
> had dedicated [at Delphi], to a Thessalian dancing-girl called Phar-
> salia. As soon as this Pharsalia entered the market-place at Metapon-
> tum a voice issued from the bronze laurel which the Metapontines set
> up at the time of the visitation (ἐπιδημίαν) of Aristeas the Proconnesian,
> when he said he had come from the Hyperboreans, and the seers in
> the market-place went mad and tore her to pieces. When they later
> inquired the reason for this [from Delphi, presumably] they found that
> the cause of her destruction had been the wreath belonging to the god.

The suggestion may be that the prophet Aristeas had the power
to impart the mantic gift to a clientele of hangers-on around the
monument of his visit to Metapontum, and on occasion to possess
them with a more than mantic frenzy, as he himself had once
been possessed by Apollo. On the other hand, the voice that issued
from the laurel may have been the voice of the god himself, just
as the Homeric Hymn to Apollo says that he gave oracles from
a laurel at Delphi (iii. 396; cf. Parke i. 3).

This is perhaps the place to record one further mention of
Aristeas, though its relation to the traditions so far given is not
readily apparent. It is in Gregory of Nazianzus [T. 23]:

> Let us leave this childishness to such Greek worthies as Empedocles,
> Aristaeus, Empedotimus, Trophonius, and the wretched mob of like

kidney. The first won divinity for himself, or so he thought, by jumping down the Sicilian crater, but was given away by his own sandal, which the fire cast out . . . while the others, through this same disease of self-importance, hid themselves away in cells (ἀδύτοις τισίν) but were found out, and earned more contempt from their exposure than they had honour from their deceit.

The views of modern scholars about Aristeas may be divided into three groups. First, there are those who hold that he was a mythical personage (and therefore could not be the author of the *Arimaspea*) ; second, those who hold that he was historical, but not the author of the *Arimaspea*; third, those who hold that he was the author of the *Arimaspea* (and therefore historical). Of the first group, Crusius is perhaps the most outspoken (Roscher i. 2814) : the poetic fantasy called *Arimaspea* originated among the Ionian colonies of the Sea of Marmara and came to be ascribed to the miracle-monger (*Wundermann*) Aristeas of Proconnesus, who has been recognized as a mythical figure of the cult of Apollo, like Olen and Abaris. It would seem that Bethe thinks similarly (876) : Aristeas was a *Wundermann* like Abaris and Epimenides, given a local habitation in Proconnesus and Metapontum; the probable date of the *Arimaspea*, wherein Aristeas appears to have been named as author, is the sixth century, an era to which is well suited that combination of fantasy and religion which he, like Abaris, Salmoxis, and Hermotimus, exemplifies. To Diels Aristeas was a fabulous traveller so well known in antiquity that it was as natural to ascribe a fantastic travel-poem to him as it was to ascribe cosmogonies to Orpheus or cookery-books to Apicius (21). For Rhys Carpenter he is but another type of the 'bear-hero', identical with Aristaeus and Salmoxis (162 f.). I am not sure how much historicity Jacoby would grant to the *Wundermann* whose works he rejects as spurious (i. 519) ;[4] or whether Guthrie regards him as an entirely legendary figure (he is one of the 'strange servants' of Apollo, 'figures of legend'; but elsewhere 'other figures also' besides Aristeas (Abaris, Hermotimus, Epimenides) 'emerge from the twilight between myth and history' (193; 195)). I hope I do them no great injustice by including them in my first group.

Representatives of the second group are Rohde, who, though seeing no reason to doubt the historicity of Aristeas, yet is non-committal about his authorship of the *Arimaspea* ([i] 329 f.; [ii] 186); and Hennig (71), who sees a gap of at least two centuries between Aristeas and the author of the *Arimaspea*—if indeed the former lived at all, for Hennig circumspectly will not go beyond admitting the possibility of this (he follows Bethe in dating the poem in the sixth century, and the 'better tradition' in reading τριηκοσί-οισι in Hdt. iv. 15. 1).

The third group follows ancient tradition in allowing not only that Aristeas existed but even that he composed the poem with which he was credited. This view was expressed a century ago by Tournier (4 ff.), but went out of fashion with a later and more sophisticated generation of scholars. Today Tournier does not lack supporters; but whereas he also thought that Aristeas was a genuine explorer, there is a disposition among these modern scholars to doubt whether he actually made the journey which he professed to have made in his poem.

Years ago Rohde, contrasting the account in Herodotus of Aristeas' death and disappearance from Proconnesus with the other traditions given above, concluded that Herodotus had conflated two incompatible versions: according to one, Aristeas did not die but was translated, body and soul: according to the other, Aristeas 'died' not once but often, when his soul left his body temporarily to wander abroad. This latter, preserved in the non-Herodotean sources, is yet really the more primitive and original version ([i] 328 f.). In 1935 this argument was carried a stage farther by K. Meuli: drawing attention to the many similarities between the stories about Aristeas and modern knowledge of Siberian shamanism—which, he infers from Hdt. iv. 73 ff., was not unknown to the ancient Scythians, whose regions were the scene of Aristeas' travels—he suggested that Aristeas was a sort of Greek shaman, and the *Arimaspea* a 'shamanistic' poem.

Meuli's theory, cogently argued and supported with a wealth of learning, has been enthusiastically received and may be considered orthodox today. Among English scholars it has been accepted by, for instance, Cornford (ch. 6), Dodds (ch. 5), Phillips

(176), and Bowra (2). The similarities between Aristeas and the shamans are certainly impressive. The soul of the shaman leaves its body behind and makes long ecstatic journeys to places both real and imaginary (cf. Phillips 176) : so did the soul of Aristeas. During these journeys it meets with fantastic adventures : so did Aristeas, and related them in the *Arimaspea* as the shaman recounts his adventures to his audience. The shaman can appear in two places at once, as did Aristeas; or his soul issues from him as a bird, as Pliny tells us the soul of Aristeas issued from his mouth in the shape of a raven (old Siberian myth even called the prototype of shamans 'the Great Raven'—Meuli 158). The shaman is an adept in divination : so was Aristeas. When we consider further that the scene of Aristeas' travels was the very country of these medicine-men, and that he himself stated that he made his journeys 'possessed by Apollo', that is, in some unusual state, the case seems pretty conclusively proved. There are, however, some awkward difficulties, shortly to be discussed.

I agree with Rohde that there are inadequate grounds for doubting that Aristeas was an historical character. Though there is some evidence of confusion between him and Aristaeus the son of Apollo and Cyrene, he does not show signs of being a 'faded god' or hero. Antiquity provided him with a birth-place that was only founded in comparatively recent times, with a father not otherwise known but with a convincingly human name [131], and even with a date—or rather, dates, for our two authorities on this subject disagree.

According to 'Suidas' [T. 11], Aristeas was a contemporary of Croesus and Cyrus, flourishing in the fiftieth Olympiad (580/77) : γέγονε κατὰ Κροῖσον καὶ Κῦρον, 'Ολυμπιάδι ν' [η' F; ὀγδόη V (i.e. 748/5, surely from a confusion of *N* and *H*); νη' Rohde (548/5), accepted by Meuli]. I take it that the combination of the more precise dating of the Olympiad with the vaguer 'in the time of Croesus and Cyrus' means that the former was Aristeas' *floruit.*[5] If this dating is right, Aristeas could not have been the author of the seventh-century *Arimaspea*; but reasons will be adduced to show that it may be part of an unreliable tradition [172].

Herodotus, as we have seen, says that Aristeas' appearance at Metapontum occurred two hundred and forty, or according to another reading three hundred and forty, years after his second disappearance from Proconnesus. The higher number, in spite of its respectable manuscript support, cannot be fitted into any scheme; it will not fit inside even the most extreme termini conceivably possible, the foundation-date of Proconnesus (at earliest *c.* 685, cf. Burn 132) and the year of Herodotus' death (at latest 425, cf. *P.-W.* suppl. 2, 232). The lesser figure, which is supported by Origen (*Cels.* iii. 26) and Tzetzes [T. 13]—to which must be added the interval between Aristeas' second and his first disappearance from Proconnesus: not less than seven years—can just be squeezed between these termini, but with uncomfortably little elbow-room; and it would make the appearance of the ghost of Aristeas to the Metapontines coincident with the last part of Herodotus' own life—indeed, when he was living next door, at Thurii, in which case it is almost incredible that he should not have remarked how recent it was. Anyway the whole story smacks of an earlier age. Rohde concludes that Herodotus has made an error of calculation.[6]

Some account of a mysterious appearance, or appearances, of Aristeas may have been known to Pindar. This is an inference from a remark of Origen; and even if it is justified we still cannot decide (as yet—papyri may give us the answer) whether this was, or included, the Metapontine appearance; if it did, of course even Herodotus' lower figure would be quite impossible. Origen quotes Celsus [T. 17]: 'Then take Aristeas of Proconnesus, who disappeared so strangely and again reappeared to the sight of men, and long afterwards was a visitant in many places bringing marvellous reports: Apollo ordered the Metapontines to regard him as divine, but no one now worships Aristeas.' He then adds that Celsus 'probably got the story from Pindar and Herodotus'.

It must be borne in mind that, though Origen thought that Celsus was using Herodotus and Pindar here, this does not mean that he was necessarily right; but it must mean that something in Pindar, as well as in Herodotus, afforded reasonable ground for his deduction. Knowledge of Herodotus' story alone could account for Celsus' first words, 'who disappeared so strangely and again reappeared', ἀφανισθέντα τε οὕτως δαιμονίως ἐξ ἀνθρώπων [the death and disappearance in the fuller's shop] καὶ αὖθις ἐναργῶς φανέντα [the reappearance in Proconnesus six years later]; πολλοῖς ὕστερον χρόνοις, 'long afterwards', too fits with Herodotus' long period between the second disappearance and the Metapontine reappearance. But with πολλαχοῦ τῆς οἰκουμένης, 'in many places',[7] we meet something non-Herodotean. We have indeed heard of a number of other appearances of Aristeas in Sicily [120]; and Plutarch tells how at the moment of his death in the fuller's shop he was met upon the road to Croton in south Italy [T. 16]. But the latter certainly, and the former possibly, are contemporaneous with a real or putative death of the man, not 'long afterwards'. Also, the evidence of Plutarch here must be treated with great reserve, for it looks too like a distortion of Herodotus' account [cf. 201]. Reasons will be given too to suspect that the Sicilian appearances are a late invention [169].

The next words, θαυμαστὰ ἀγγείλαντα, 'bringing marvellous reports', could be Herodotean, and refer to Aristeas' statement that Apollo had visited the Metapontines and that he himself had accompanied the god in the shape of a raven; but, when one recalls that Pliny uses adnuntiare (i.e. ἀγγέλλειν) of the marvellous clairvoyant reports that Hermotimus gave [121], one wonders whether Celsus did not know, and here refer to, similar reports given by Aristeas.

The clause τοῦ Ἀπόλλωνος ἐπισκήψαντος τοῖς Μεταποντίνοις ἐν θεῶν μοίρᾳ νέμειν τὸν Ἀριστέαν, 'Apollo ordered the Metapontines to regard Aristeas as divine', may be non-Herodotean, or it may be an inference from Herodotus' words. According to these Aristeas told the Metapontines to set up an altar to Apollo and a statue to himself; and the Delphic oracle confirmed this behest. There is no explicit statement here that a cult of Aristeas was thus to be established, though the passage might so be taken. He is indeed said to have been given heroic honours by the Sicilians [120], and divine or semi-divine rank is indicated by Theopompus' calling his appearance at Metapontum an ἐπιδημία [123; cf. Celsus' ἐπιδημήσαντα here], a word particularly used of divine visitations;

but in both these cases the evidence is suspect, showing signs of fourth-century working-over and touching-up (if not making-up).

If Aristeas was an historical personage such heroization, especially as early as the fifth century, would present peculiarities. He might have qualified as the minister of Apollo or the apostle of his cult (cf. Farnell ii 53 ff.) ; but canonization usually centred on, and depended upon the existence of, the supposed grave or relics of the hero. In a parallel case to that of Aristeas, that of the athlete Cleomedes, who vanished mysteriously in 492 B.C., his cult was established at his home, Astypalaea (Plut. *Rom.* 28; Paus. vi. 9. 6 ff.), so that Proconnesus rather than Metapontum would have been the natural place for a cult of Aristeas.[8] However, I suspect that divine honours were never paid to Aristeas *in fact*, but were a fiction of some fourth-century author with Pythagorean leanings. Pindar (fr. 127) and Empedocles (fr. 146) are evidence that for early Pythagoreanism the highest incarnation was to be a man of outstanding strength or wisdom, a king, or a seer. The next stage was escape from the flesh and graduation to divinity, as ἥρως (Pindar) or θεός (Empedocles) (cf. the 'Orphic' tablet of fourth/third century B.C. from Petelia, Diels–Kranz i. 15. 31). Such cults of hero-philosophers are indicated in the fourth century for Pythagoras and Anaxagoras (Arist. *Rhet.* ii. 23) ;[9] the idea is persistently expressed by Plato (e.g. *Phaedr.* 248 f.; cf. Boyancé 268 ff.), and it was, I suggest, some pupil of Plato (aided no doubt by the Herodotean account) who *invented* the story of the bestowal of divine honours upon Aristeas by the Metapontines at the bidding of Apollo (that is, of course, Delphi, the normal dispenser of heroic status) ; honours which Aristeas now merited as the philosopher [T. 20] and seer [T. 21] he had become. This argument would carry with it the story of the heroization by the Siceliotes too: there I think the important point is not so much that Aristeas appeared supernaturally but that he appeared as a teacher—though it is certainly strange that he should be described as teaching *letters* (γράμματα διδάσκοντα, usually of a schoolmaster![10]). The use of the words θεός by Celsus and θύειν (for ἐναγίζειν, cf. Hdt. ii. 44. 5) by Theopompus

[120] with reference to the *man* Aristeas also seems to me to indicate a later rather than an earlier date: at least post-Empedoclean, and so post-Pindaric (quite possibly fourth-century: after Empedocles' translation in the story by Heraclides Ponticus, Pausanias tells his friends that they must sacrifice to the vanished man as to one who has become a god, θύειν αὐτῷ δεῖν καθαπερεὶ γεγονότι θεῷ (D.L. viii. 68)).

If this is so there could have been nothing in Pindar about Aristeas' divinity, nor could Celsus in fact have had Pindar and Herodotus as his sources here. The only logical basis for Origen's inference that Pindar as well as Herodotus underlay Celsus' words must have been the phrase πολλαχοῦ τῆς οἰκουμένης ἐπιδημήσαντα, for which alone Herodotus provides no warrant: Origen may have known that Pindar told of a number of ghostly appearances of Aristeas similar to, and perhaps including, that at Metapontum. This is the most that can be said, and even so it may be pressing logic too far. It is noteworthy that Origen, in support of his statement that Celsus probably got the story from Pindar and Herodotus, proceeds to quote Hdt. iv. 14 f. *verbatim*, but of Pindar not one word. It is not impossible that Origen was really thinking of (or Celsus himself appealing to?) *Pythian* ix. 63 ff., about the bestowal of divinity on the child of Apollo and Cyrene, 'who will be called Zeus and holy Apollo, . . and by others Aristaeus', and that there was in fact nowhere in Pindar any mention of Aristeas of Proconnesus. (This would not be the only case of confusion between these two.)

An attempt has been made to save Herodotus' arithmetic at the expense of his text. E. Schwyzer proposed to read in iv. 15. 1: τάδε δὲ οἶδα Μεταποντίνοισι τοῖσι ἐν Ἰταλίῃ συγκυρήσας [for συγκυρήσαντα] μετὰ τὴν ἀφάνισιν τὴν δευτέρην Ἀριστέω ἔτεσι τεσσεράκοντα καὶ διηκοσίοισι, ὡς ἐγὼ συμβαλλόμενος ἐν Προκοννήσῳ τε καὶ Μεταποντίῳ εὕρισκον, 'what follows I know because I fell in with the Metapontines two hundred and forty years after the second disappearance of Aristeas . . .'. The effect of this then is to date the Metapontine visit of Herodotus himself, not of Aristeas, two hundred and forty years after the second disappearance of the latter; no date is then given for the ghost's

appearance at Metapontum, which can now be moved back into
the decently distant past; while, assuming what is probably true,
that Herodotus was in Metapontum some time in the thirties,
Aristeas can be one of the first colonists of Proconnesus two
hundred and forty-seven years before. Also, one can see how
Herodotus might have calculated the time of his own presence
in Metapontum relative to Aristeas' disappearance: by generations, which he might have heard recounted in Proconnesus,
plus the time between his own visits to Proconnesus and to Metapontum (this would work out at seven generations, or two hundred
and thirty-three years on his reckoning (ii. 142), plus seven years).

But the emendation fails to convince me on two grounds, linguistic and artistic. First, Μεταποντίνοισι συγκυρήσας should mean
'having come upon the Metapontines accidentally', whereas we
may be certain that Herodotus did not find himself in Metapontum quite by chance. Secondly, there is a point in giving the
time between Aristeas' disappearance and reappearance, but
none whatever in giving that between Aristeas' disappearance
from Proconnesus and Herodotus' own visit to Metapontum; it
would be a most curious era to choose for his dating.[11]

It seems, then, that attempts to defend even the lower figure
in the Herodotean manuscripts as historically accurate must be
abandoned. The most that we can deduce is that for Herodotus
Aristeas was a very remote figure, who would suit well enough
as one of the earliest colonists of Proconnesus.

The name of Aristeas' father, Caystrobius, appears to be of the
same class as Cephisodotus, Cephisodorus, &c. (cf. Nilsson [ii] 10):
the parents of Caystrobius in their desire for a child had prayed
for fertility to the river-god Cayster, and in gratitude for his
answer to their prayer had called their son 'he who owes his life
to the Cayster' (the form of the name is exactly paralleled by
Hermobius, who came from Temnus on the Hermus (Cic. *Fl.* 43)).
A river-god is naturally a local god, and so this Caystrobius must
have been born, or at least conceived, in Ionia. If the father of
Aristeas was the first of his family to bear this name, it is possible
to reason thus: when Herodotus says that Aristeas 'belonged
to one of the noblest families in the island' (he was τῶν ἀστῶν

οὐδενὸς γένος ὑποδεέστερος) he must mean that his family was one
of the original founder-families of the colony: that either Caystrobius or his father, or (less likely perhaps in view of Herodotus'
γένος) Aristeas himself had shared in the original foundation.
Even if this is right, all the suggested dates for Aristeas could still
be accommodated—even Rohde's emendation of the Olympiad
in 'Suidas'; but this last would now be rendered extremely unlikely, for it would necessitate a series of last-minute occurrences:
the latest possible foundation-date for Proconnesus (*c.* 650:
Strabo 590 and 587); Caystrobius born the same year or a year
or so before; Aristeas born when his father was verging on
senility.[12] The probabilities would point to a birth-date for
Aristeas between 680 and 620; in other words, we should arrive
at a likely date for Aristeas which matches remarkably the date
we found, by quite independent arguments, to be the likely one
for the poem which was ascribed to him. I have no qualms about
accepting this ascription.

A seventh-century date for the *Arimaspea* and its author poses
a problem for the 'shamanistic' theory. We have seen that the
poem contained matter the accuracy of which could only be
owed to real knowledge of central Asia. How did Aristeas come
to be so well informed? From some genuine Greek traveller or
Scythian trader? But the foundation of the earliest Greek entrepots
on the north side of the Black Sea does not appear to be much
before 600 B.C. (Olbia founded *c.* 610: Cook 71 f.; 76 ff.; 82);
and though there is some support for the view of Burn (135)
that there had been two or three generations of exploration and
commerce before this (Roebuck 118 f.), Greek trade with the
deep Scythian hinterland could not yet have been established.
And it is uneconomical to postulate an 'Ur-Aristeas'—an unknown Greek traveller to do in fact what Aristeas himself claimed
to have done—without sufficient cause. But if Aristeas made the
journey in the flesh and himself collected the information an
extraordinary state of affairs follows: we have to believe that he
returned to his home-town, where his absence of years would be
well known, went into a shamanistic trance, and then pretended
that during this he had been journeying in the spirit: surely an

unnecessarily elaborate as well as patently obviously deceit. No
wonder that Meuli was ready to accept Rohde's emendation of
'Suidas'' Olympiad as near the truth, and so bring Aristeas down
to a time when the flow of Scythian trade to the Black Sea
colonies could be supposed to have carried with it knowledge of
the far hinterland of Asia!

I hope to have shown that objections to a sixth-century date are
manifold and grave. Even if I have not succeeded, obstacles
remain to an easy acquiescence in the 'shamanistic' theory. Herodotus states that he heard the story of Aristeas' first disappearance
and reappearance from the Proconnesians *and Cyzicenes*. It is
a reasonable conjecture that the Cyzicene contribution was the
man of Cyzicus who met the 'dead' Aristeas on the mainland,
and that Herodotus himself has combined this with a Proconnesian account—of the corpse which vanished from the fuller's
shop—in a manner dramatically effective though chronologically absurd, for logic demands that the Cyzicene had left
the mainland before the death, if he was to arrive in Proconnesus,
a good four hours' voyage from Artace, just after it had been
announced. This is all we need suppose, and there is no cause to
follow Meuli in seeing in this episode proof of a much more
deep-seated tampering with, and rationalizing of, an original
trance-journey of Aristeas the shaman.[13] Also, if Aristeas was
lying all the time in Proconnesus 'shamanizing', his soul would
be flying through the *air*, perhaps even in the form of a bird, and
it is difficult to see how the *Cyzicenes* would come to have an
interest in the story at all.

An even more awkward absurdity is involved in regarding the
Arimaspea as a shamanistic poem. We are told emphatically and
unambiguously by Herodotus that in it Aristeas claimed only to
have got as far as the Issedonians, and admitted that what he had
to tell of the regions beyond was hearsay. But whoever heard of a
shaman's soul 'breaking down' in mid-flight and confessing that
henceforth it had to depend on the reports of the people among
whom it had made its forced landing? I find this so ridiculous
(the more so as it would be quite unnecessary) as to be incredible.

Once again we are confronted with that old dichotomy in the

tradition: according to one form of it Aristeas reached the Hyperboreans, according to the other he reached only the Issedonians.
In the former he travels in the soul (Maximus [122]); but the
latter derives from the *Arimaspea* itself. Attempts to paper over
this dichotomy have so far not been satisfactory. Dodds (141)
says 'whether Aristeas' journey was made in the flesh or in the
spirit is not altogether clear'; Phillips (176) suggests that he went
part of the way in the flesh and the rest in the spirit; Bowra
(2), that he claimed to have travelled both in the flesh and in
the spirit, and that Herodotus chose to emphasize one claim
and Maximus the other.

Yet it will be remembered that Aristeas in his poem said that
he had made his journey 'possessed by Apollo', rendered by
Herodotus as φοιβόλαμπτος γενόμενος. What are we to make of
this? Does it offer support to the view that Aristeas was a shaman?
It offers, I think, support to this extent, that it could mean 'filled
with prophetic insight'; and the mantic knowledge which Apollo
bestows upon his priest may be of contemporaneous events, and
is not necessarily confined to the future (cf. Hdt. i. 47). But such
a meaning seems barely possible in this context: the seer shares
the god's knowledge in the moment of possession, or the god
imparts it through the mouth of the seer, but there is no question
of the seer's soul going forth and as it were fetching the knowledge
back with it. Herodotus' language then, 'Aristeas said that,
possessed by Apollo, he reached the Issedonians', is either very
inexact or puts this interpretation out of court.

Moreover, I have yet to find characterized as φοιβόληπτος one
whose soul wanders while his body lies in a trance. The word is
never applied to the doyen of such, Hermotimus (for whose status
as an Apolline figure anyway the evidence is tenuous in the extreme[14]); and the fairly numerous others of whom similar stories
came to be told [148 ff.] are never described as 'possessed' by
any god when they undergo this separation of soul and body. In
fact, such uses as I have been able to find of this adjective,
and of related adjectives and verbs, have with one exception
implied inspiration or frenzy, and the *activity* of speech at least.

In Lycophron's *Alexandra* Cassandra calls herself ἡ φοιβόληπτος χελιδών (1460); and the slave, reporting her prophecies at the beginning of the poem, says (3)

> οὐ γὰρ ἥσυχος κόρη
> ἔλυσε χρησμῶν, ὡς πρίν, αἰόλον στόμα,
> ἀλλ' ἄσπετον χέασα παμμιγῆ βοὴν
> δαφνηφάγων φοίβαζεν ἐκ λαιμῶν ὄπα

'for not quietly as of old did the maiden loose the varied voice of her oracles, but poured forth a weird confused cry, and uttered wild words from her bay-chewing mouth' (trans. A. W. Mair). Cassandra's psychic disturbance, and the use of the verb φοιβά-ζειν, may here have been suggested by the literary tradition of the frenzied inspiration of the Pythia; but that such manifestations were expected of a prophet by the man-in-the-street too is in-dicated by the counterfeit seer in Diodorus Siculus (xxxiv and xxxv. 2. 6), who, to give authority to his utterances, even went so far as to breathe fire in accompaniment with them, and, raving so, would foretell the future (διά τινος μηχανῆς πῦρ μετά τινος ἐνθουσιασμοῦ καὶ φλόγα διὰ τοῦ στόματος ἠφίει, καὶ οὕτω τὰ μέλλοντα ἀπεφοίβαζεν[15]).

In these places derivatives of *Phoebus* have been used to denote the physical accompaniments of divine inspiration; but they are also used to suggest divine inspiration for the form or content of a man's utterances. So, after the high-handedness of Pompey and Caesar and the passage of the latter's agrarian law in 59 B.C., Cato, according to Plutarch, foretold in the Senate the mis-fortunes of Rome ὥσπερ ἐπίπνους καὶ φοιβόληπτος (*Pomp.* 48). Here no doubt it was primarily the *content* of Cato's speech which earned the epithets—his prophecies seemed god-given because they turned out true. But implied too may be the loftiness of the *form* in which they were expressed, as in three passages of the *de sublimitate*: Demosthenes enunciated his famous 'Marathon oath' as if suddenly inspired, καθάπερ ἐμπνευσθεὶς ἐξαίφνης ὑπὸ θεοῦ καὶ οἱονεὶ φοιβόληπτος γενόμενος (16, 2)—surely a case in point that there is nothing so conducive to lofty style as heartfelt passion, 'which breathes forth our words as if in the frenzy of divine inspiration, and gives them a sort of sanctity', ὥσπερ ὑπὸ μανίας τινὸς καὶ πνεύματος ἐνθουσιαστικῶς ἐκπνέον καὶ οἰονεὶ φοιβάζον τοὺς λόγους (8. 4); if they model themselves on such as this even those who are little prone to inspiration may draw upon and share something of the divine spirit of their great exemplars: οὕτως ἀπὸ τῆς τῶν ἀρχαίων μεγαλοφυΐας εἰς τὰς τῶν ζηλούντων ἐκείνους ψυχὰς ὡς ἀπὸ ἱερῶν στομίων ἀπόρροιαί τινες φέρονται, ὑφ' ὧν ἐπιπνεόμενοι καὶ οἱ μὴ λίαν φοιβαστικοὶ τῷ ἑτέρων συνενθουσιῶσι μεγέθει (13. 2).

On the other hand, yet another element of divine inspiration, fluency of composition, is emphasized by Strabo (675) when he relates how Diogenes of Tarsus, being set a subject, could throw off a poem on it 'as if inspired' (καὶ ποιήματα ὥσπερ ἀπεφοίβαζε τεθείσης ὑποθέσεως).

In all these examples of Apolline possession, literal or metaphorical, the simultaneous activity of speech at least is implied, as I have said. The subject has the god within him, who does the talking: he is ἔνθεος καὶ ἔκφρων, the god has displaced his own mind; meaning, not that his soul or mind is away from his body wandering ecstatically, but that it is for the moment of no account, thrust aside by another power which has taken control of the man. The one exception that I mentioned above, where not activity but serene contemplation is deemed to accompany the fact of possession, indeed brings out the meaning of φοιβόληπτος as ἔνθεος—he whom Apollo has seized has the god within him: Plotinus tells us that we must view Beauty not as something external but as something within ourselves, 'as if one possessed by Apollo or some Muse were to contemplate the deity within himself, were he capable of such a thing' (*Enn.* v. 8. 10: ὥσπερ εἴ τις ὑπὸ θεοῦ κατασχεθεὶς φοιβόληπτος ἢ ὑπό τινος Μούσης ἐν αὐτῷ ἂν ποιοῖτο τοῦ θεοῦ τὴν θέαν, εἰ δύναμιν ἔχοι ἐν αὐτῷ θεὸν βλέπειν).

Seizure by other deities too brings an unaccustomed activity of some sort to the possessed. 'Does it strike you as it strikes me, my friend,' asks Socrates of Phaedrus in that sequestered beauty-spot by the Ilissus, 'that a god has done something to me?' 'You certainly have an unwonted fluency, Socrates.' 'Then hear me in silence. We really are on holy ground, so don't be surprised if during my discourse I am perhaps seized by the nymphs (νυμφόληπτος); for already I am almost talking in dithyrambs' (*Phaedr.* 238c). Socrates expects seizure by the nymphs because they are appropriate to the setting; though the consequences he foresees are more appropriate to seizure by Apollo. Many Greeks, ancient or modern, would not share Socrates' serene humour in such a situation, for seizure by the nymphs is no laughing matter (cf. Lawson 142 ff.).

Hermias, in commenting on this passage of the *Phaedrus*, says εἰσὶ δὲ καὶ πανόληπτοι καὶ μητρόληπτοι καὶ κορυβαντισμοί (105). Now we have an account in Plutarch, derived from Posidonius, of a spurious μητρόληπτος, who pretended to be seized by the Sicilian goddesses called 'the Mothers', which is worth quoting because it shows us what symptoms were expected to accompany such a seizure (*Marc.* 20; the translation is Langhorne's in the main):

There is in Sicily a town called Enguium, not large, indeed, but very ancient, and celebrated for the appearance of the goddesses called the *Mothers*. . . . This town was strongly inclined to favour the Carthaginians; but Nicias, one of its principal inhabitants, endeavoured to persuade them to go over to the Romans, declaring his sentiments freely in their public assemblies, and proving that his opposers consulted not their true interests. These men, fearing his authority and the influence of his character, resolved to carry him off and put him in the hands of the Carthaginians. Nicias, apprised of it, took measures for his security, without seeming to do so. He publicly gave out unbecoming speeches against the *Mothers*, as if he disbelieved and made light of the received opinion concerning the presence of these goddesses there. Meantime, his enemies rejoiced that he himself furnished them with sufficient reasons for the worst they could do to him. On the day which they had fixed for seizing him, there happened to be an assembly of the people, and Nicias was in the midst of them, treating about some public business. But on a sudden he threw himself upon the ground, in the midst of his discourses, and after having lain there some time without speaking, as if he had been in a trance (ἀφῆκεν εἰς τὴν γῆν τὸ σῶμα, καὶ μικρὸν διαλιπών, οἷον εἰκός, ἡσυχίας σὺν ἐκπλήξει γενομένης κτλ.), he lifted up his head, and turning it round, began to speak with a feeble trembling voice, which he raised by degrees: and when he saw the whole assembly struck dumb with horror, he threw off his mantle, tore his vest in pieces, and ran half-naked to one of the doors of the theatre, crying out that he was driven by the *Mothers*. From a scruple of religion no one durst touch or stop him; all, therefore, making way, he ran towards the city gates, omitting neither sound nor gesture befitting one that was heaven-struck and distracted (δαιμονῶντι καὶ παραφρονοῦντι). His wife, who was in the secret, and assisted in the stratagem, took her children, and went and prostrated herself as a supplicant before the altar of the goddesses. Then pretending that she was going to seek her husband, who was wandering about in the fields, she met with no opposition, but got safe out of the town; and so both of them escaped to Marcellus at Syracuse.

Here we notice the sequence of events: the victim is behaving normally when he suddenly falls to the ground, where he lies for a short time bereft of his faculties; then springs into wild activity and is compelled to roam about. Nicias' fraud was clearly well conceived and executed (cf. Plutarch's οἷον εἰκός). A possible parallel can be discerned here with Herodotus' account of how Aristeas walked, apparently normal, into the fuller's shop, fell, apparently suddenly, into a state that simulated death, and later was gone from the shop; there is no parallel at all with the version of Maximus and others of the cataleptic Aristeas whose *soul* wandered. Such a state, as I have said, is not described by the ancients as seizure or possession.

This brings me to an illustration given by Rohde (¹ 328, on the *ekstasis* of Aristeas). Rohde believed that the version of Maximus was in origin earlier and truer than that of Herodotus; and that, when in the *Arimaspea* Aristeas said that he reached the Issedonians φοιβόλαμπτος γενόμενος, this at least meant 'in some strange way impossible for other men, i.e. in Apolline ecstasy (cf. . . . ἐν ἐκστάσει ἀποφοιβώμενος, *P. Mag. Par.*, p. 63 Wess.)'. Now the words in question may not refer to the *way* but to the *state* in which the poet travelled; and for the assertion that it was impossible for other men there is not a shred of justification. The parallel for 'Apolline ecstasy' (in Rohde's sense of cataleptic trance) from the magical papyrus looks at first impressive in spite of its lateness; but it looks less so when quoted in full: ἐὰν δὲ καὶ μόνος ᾖς καὶ ἐγχειρῇς τὰ ὑπὸ τοῦ θεοῦ εἰρημένα, λέγεις ὡς ἐν ἐκστάσει ἀποφοιβώμενος (= iv. 736 of *P. Graec. Mag.* ed. Preisendanz). This ecstasy too supposes the accompanying activity of speech, and ἀποφοιβώμενος has no sense that we have not already considered in its related derivatives: it refers here to the 'fine frenzy' displayed by those whom Phoebus inspires.

Rohde's assumption that *ekstasis* originally involved the idea of the soul's departure from the body has been challenged (cf. Dodds 94 f.): the word is used of mental disturbance of varying degrees, but not in passages where one would expect it if Rohde were right. In the question under discussion we must be more exact: we must distinguish between *three* conditions: that of possession, in which the subject is unwontedly active in some respect or respects; that of hypnotic or mediumistic trance, in which the subject is quiescent but palpably alive; and that of catalepsy, where the subject is so bereft of all faculties, even to the cessation of breathing and pulse, that he appears to be dead— though after revival he tells of perceptions made, and knowledge gained, 'in the spirit'.

All three of these are authenticated psychic phenomena; the last-named perhaps rarer than the others. Tyrrell gives some interesting modern examples of it (149 ff.), of which I quote one:

Dr. Wiltse, of Skiddy, Kansas . . . , lay ill with typhoid and sub-normal temperature and pulse, felt himself to be dying, and said goodbye to his family and friends. He managed to straighten his legs and arrange his arms over his breast, and sank into utter unconsciousness. Dr. S. H. Raynes, the only physician present, said that he passed four hours without pulse or perceptible heart-beat. He was thought to be dead and the church bell was tolled. The doctor, however, thought he could perceive occasionally a very slight gasp; he thrust a needle into the flesh but got no response. The percipient, however, says that at last he again came into a state of conscious existence and found he was still in the body, 'but the body and I no longer had any interests in common'. He seemed to be getting out of his body, rocking to and fro and breaking connection with the body's tissues. He seemed to feel and hear the snapping of innumerable small cords and then, he says, 'I began slowly to retreat from the feet toward the head, as a rubber cord shortens.' Presently he felt he was in the head and then emerging through the sutures of the skull. 'I recollect distinctly', he continues, 'how I appeared to myself something like a jellyfish as regards colour and form. As I emerged I saw two ladies sitting at my head. I measured the distance between the head

of my cot and the knees of the lady opposite the head and concluded
there was room for me to stand, but felt considerable embarrassment
as I reflected that I was about to emerge naked before her. . . . As I
emerged from the head I floated up and down and laterally like a soap-
bubble attached to the bowl of a pipe until I at last broke loose from
the body and fell lightly to the floor, where I slowly rose and expanded
into the full stature of a man. I seemed to be translucent, of a bluish
cast and perfectly naked.' The percipient fled towards the door, but
when he got there, found himself suddenly clothed, and his elbow came
in contact with one of two men standing in the doorway (they were
actually there) and to his surprise went through him without en-
countering any resistance. He tried to attract the attention of his
friends but without success, so he walked out of the door and into the
street. He says, 'I never saw that street more distinctly than I saw it
then. I took note of the redness of the soil and of the washes the rain
had made.' (There had been heavy rain and the roads were marked
by rain-washes.) He then noticed that he was attached by means of
a small cord, like a spider's web, to his body in the house, the cord
coming from his shoulders. He then seemed to be propelled, as if by a
pair of hands, and found himself on a roadway, while below him was a
scene of mountain and forest which looked very like the local scenery.
After various experiences he came to rocks blocking the road which
he tried to climb round. But at that moment a black cloud descended
on him; and he opened his eyes to find himself back on his sick-
bed.

Clearly the Aristeas of Maximus' tradition is a cataleptic,
accurately portrayed; there is no confusion with the symptoms of
possession. Ancient authors are not always so careful to keep the
two things apart; a notable example of such 'contamination' is to
be found at the end of the first book of Lucan, where a frenzied
Roman matron, possessed by Apollo, speaks as if her soul has left
her body and is flying over the face of the earth, viewing the
lands beneath; yet at the same time her body is tearing through
the streets of Rome (674 ff.).

I do not doubt that the events in the fuller's shop, as recounted
by Herodotus, preceding as they do Aristeas' departure on his
journey, constitute that 'seizure by Apollo' which the poet himself said he had undergone when he made his travels. This seizure
was possession, not catalepsy, and it perhaps ushered in a sense of

superhuman strength and confidence, like that imparted by Apollo to his devotees at Hylae:

In the territory of Magnesia, on the river Lethaeus, there is a place called Hylae, where is a grotto consecrated to Apollo. There is nothing very wonderful in the size of the grotto, but the image of Apollo is very old, and it imparts strength equal to any labour. Men sacred to the god leap down precipices and high rocks, tear exceedingly lofty trees from their roots, and walk with their burdens along the narrowest paths [mountain-paths, I take it] (Paus. x. 32. 6, trans. Frazer).[16]

There is some evidence that Apollo was a popular god in the environs of Proconnesus. He was said to be much worshipped by the natives in the neighbourhood of Cyzicus (Strabo 551). Cyzicus itself was named after a son of Apollo, and the god was somehow particularly closely connected with that city (Aelius Aristides xxvii. 5: τὰς μὲν γὰρ ἄλλας πόλεις διὰ τῶν οἰκιστῶν ᾤκισεν οὓς ἀπέστειλεν ἑκασταχόσε, ταύτης δὲ ἐκ τοῦ εὐθέος αὐτὸς γέγονεν οἰκιστής). It seems to me not impossible that Aristeas himself may have been a devotee or priest of Apollo, who, hearing perhaps of some exploratory venture to the northern shores of the Black Sea (and there may well have been such even as early as the mid-seventh century [132]), felt possessed by his god and impelled to visit Apollo's paradise among the Hyperboreans, who could not be far away if Boreas blew from Thrace. The act of divine possession,[17] followed by an abrupt departure from Proconnesus, would not need to be relayed through many mouths before it became a death and strange disappearance. Given this, the story of the acquaintance who met Aristeas near Cyzicus presents no difficulty, once we eliminate the preternatural element of speed; and this I have done [133]: the acquaintance met Aristeas *en route* on the mainland (Cyzicus may have been the starting place for the expedition), and some time later heard the rumour that he was dead by that time. This made a good story, and was preserved in Cyzicus even to Herodotus' day.

I have given my reasons for believing that the tradition about Aristeas represented by Maximus is not, after all, the truer and more primitive, as has been held by Rohde and others. It now remains to examine this tradition more closely, to see if we can establish when and how it arose.

VII

ARISTEAS PYTHAGORICUS

IN that unreliable catalogue of early Pythagoreans which Iamblichus gives at the end of his *Vita Pythagorica* (267) there occurs the name of 'Aristeas the Metapontine'. Tournier suggests (45) that this personage may be the Aristaeus, son of Damophon, who is said to have married Pythagoras' widow Theano and succeeded him as head of the school (Iambl. *V.P.* 265, where admittedly he is called a Crotoniate). But the untrustworthiness of this evidence is plain from its anachronistic talk of an early Pythagorean 'school' with a headship, which dates it at earliest to the fourth century B.C.—probably indeed later, to the Hellenistic 'Peripatetics' with their interest in φιλοσόφων διαδοχαί; the mention of Theano the wife of Pythagoras also betrays the influence of the 'Pythagorean romance' of later times.[1] We do not hear of this Aristaeus until nearly a millennium has passed since his supposed lifetime, and though a work περὶ ἁρμονίας was current under his name (an extract, duly written in pseudo-Doric, is given by Stobaeus (i. 176), and Iamblichus appears to refer to the book (*Theol. Arithm.* 41)), it is merely another example of a neo-Pythagorean forgery ascribed to a putative early Pythagorean.[2] I myself do not believe that Aristaeus, the Crotoniate successor of Pythagoras, ever existed, but that he is the ghost of a ghost: a phantom reflection of Aristeas of Proconnesus, who appeared at Metapontum and so is called a Metapontine in Iamblichus' list.[3]

If Aristeas was supposed to have been a Pythagorean it would account for the interest he held for later Pythagoreans, who, according to Iamblichus [T. 22], not only believed the tales told about Aristeas, Abaris, and the like, but in many ways tried to emulate them. Iamblichus has just been speaking of the divine nature of the arts of divination, μαντική, and ritual, τελεστική—almost 'magic'—and implies that in Aristeas and Abaris we have two experts in these arts: he emphasizes them as religious teachers, θεολόγοι. It was their skill in divination (carried out in a certain way, i.e. through the trance?), and perhaps apotropaic magic, which these later Pythagoreans cultivated, as they were said to have been cultivated in the circle of the Master himself:

It is still remembered how infallibly Pythagoras prophesied earthquakes, how swiftly he averted plagues, how he quieted tempests and hailstorms, and how he smoothed the waves of river and sea to ease his friends' crossing. Such powers, we hear, were shared too and often exercised by Empedocles, Epimenides, and Abaris. Their own poems are clear enough evidence of this; besides their nicknames—Empedocles the Galestayer (ἀλεξάνεμος), Epimenides the Purifier (καθαρτής), and Abaris the Sky-traveller (αἰθροβάτης), so-called because, the story went (ἄρα), riding on the arrow of the Hyperborean Apollo which had been given him he traversed rivers, seas, and steeps, in a manner 'walking the air' (ἀεροβατῶν τρόπον τινά). Pythagoras, some have thought, had a similar experience (ὅπερ . . . . πεπονθέναι) when he conversed with the societies at Metapontum and Tauromenium on the same day (Porph. *Vita Pythagorae* 29; cf. Iambl. *V.P.* 135 f.; Lévy ¹ 90 ff.).

I have quoted Porphyry's words at length here, not only to illustrate the magical feats which Pythagoras and his strange friends were supposed to perform, but to draw attention to two more cases of bilocation like those of Hermotimus and Aristeas. It is clear from Porphyry's language that someone had suggested that the tale of the Hyperborean Abaris flying about the world on his arrow allegorized the ability of his soul to leave his body and travel about; and had likened this to an appearance of Pythagoras in places 200 miles apart, and separated by sea, on the same day—this was another 'journey in the soul'. Such a suggestion about Abaris could not have been made before the fourth century B.C., for the tale of his *riding* his arrow is no earlier than that (it is from Heraclides Ponticus [158]). Tauromenium too was not founded until the beginning of that century, at least 100 years after the death of Pythagoras; but this seems to be merely a distortion, deliberate or otherwise, of another story, that Pythagoras appeared simultaneously at Metapontum and *Croton* (Aristotle *ap.* Apoll. *Mir.* 6; cf. Lévy ¹ 99). There may be a reference to a trance journey in a remark ascribed to Pythagoras, 'when out of the body I have heard a musical scale being sounded'; the Music of the Spheres must here be meant, but the bodiless state in which Pythagoras had this experience may have been between bodily incarnations rather than a trance (schol. Ambros. *ad* Hom. *Od.* i. 371 : ἔξω γενόμενος τοῦ σώματος ἀκήκοα ἐμμελοῦς ἁρμονίας; cf. Lévy [ii] 148. Voss (57) assigns this saying to a work of Heraclides Ponticus, but this is no more than a likely guess).

A further connexion of Aristeas with Pythagoras and early Pythagoreans, imaginary or real, is implied in that curious passage of Gregory of Nazianzus [123 f.], where his name is associated with that of Empedocles, who tried to gain credence for his own apotheosis by destroying all relics of his body and so disappearing from human ken, but was betrayed by the preservation of his sandal; and of Trophonius and others not mentioned, who tried to win some supernatural reputation by hiding away in cells (ἀδύτοις). This latter ruse is illuminated by a story in Herodotus of the Thracian Salmoxis, 'a servant of Pythagoras', according to some, who, after his emancipation and return home,

had a chamber built, in which from time to time he received and feasted all the principal Thracians, using the occasion to teach them that neither he, nor they, his boon companions, nor any of their posterity would ever perish, but that they would all go to a place where they would live for aye in the enjoyment of every conceivable good. While he was acting in this way, and holding this kind of discourse, he was constructing an apartment underground, into which, when it was completed, he withdrew, vanishing suddenly from the eyes of the Thracians, who greatly regretted his loss, and mourned over him as one dead. He meanwhile abode in his secret chamber three full years, after which he came forth from his concealment, and showed himself once more to his countrymen, who were thus brought to believe in the truth of what he had taught them (iv. 95).

We hear of a similar trick played by Pythagoras himself on the Italiotes—but on no earlier or better authority than that of Hermippus (*ap.* D.L. viii. 41).[4] That the two stories are related is obvious, but which gave rise to the other is not so clear; probably the Salmoxis story is indeed the earlier, based on certain similarities between the teaching and methods of Pythagoras and the Thracian cult of Salmoxis (as is well argued by Morrison (139 ff.)), and then adapted by ill-wishers to Pythagoras himself. Some such tale about more than one personage appears to have been known to Sophocles, for he makes Orestes say (*El.* 62 ff.)

ἤδη γὰρ εἶδον πολλάκις καὶ τοὺς σοφοὺς
λόγῳ μάτην θνῄσκοντας· εἶθ᾽, ὅταν δόμους
ἔλθωσιν αὖθις, ἐκτετίμηνται πλέον.

'Before this I have marked more than one occasion when clever men have died by false report; then, when they come home again, they are henceforth respected more than ever.' Orestes plans to put about a report that he has been killed, to lull his enemies' suspicions; he has disappeared, and the presumption of his death must be encouraged. The stories about Salmoxis and Pythagoras just mentioned would provide a good parallel to his present case; so would the Herodotean ('anti-shamanistic') story of Aristeas; the 'shamanistic' tradition of Maximus and others, none at all.[5]

Gregory's words are the only inkling that the disappearance and reappearance of Aristeas may have been explained by someone as a withdrawal into a cellar, after the manner of Salmoxis and Pythagoras. This would have been a handy bit of support for Rhys Carpenter's theory that Salmoxis, Trophonius, and Aristeas–Aristaeus, to name only a few, were originally hibernating bears (112 ff.); but unfortunately Empedotimus, who is charged by Gregory with the self-same fraud as Trophonius and Aristaeus, was almost certainly a character invented by Heraclides Ponticus, so could hardly have been a bear (cf. Rohde [i] 330; Bidez, ch. vii. I may add that the earliest authority we know to have given the famous story of Empedocles' leap into Etna and his betrayal by his bronze sandal is this same Heraclides (D.L. viii. 67 ff.)). I rather think that Gregory is somewhat indiscriminately lumping together here a number of 'supernatural' men with certain features in common, the lowest common denominator being a connexion of some sort with Pythagoras or Pythagoreanism

(Trophonius might qualify for inclusion by having his oracle underground, but also his consultants were said to have visions of a Pythagorean type, cf. Plut. *gen. Socr.* 21 f.).

In the last chapter I suggested that the bestowal of divine honours upon Aristeas may have originated in the fancy of some fourth-century author with Pythagorean leanings [129], and already in this chapter we have met pointers to the same period, in the indications that Heraclides may in some way underlie the Gregorian passage, and in the 'journeys in the soul' of Abaris and Pythagoras (where again there was cause to mention the name of Heraclides). Such journeys in the soul are, of course, the central theme of the non-Herodotean or 'shamanistic' tradition about Aristeas: I therefore propose now to examine more closely the history of this notion among the Greeks.

The edifying flight of the soul and its keener perception when separated from the body was a topic dear to the Hellenistic age (cf. especially Festugière ii. 441 ff.). Pindar perhaps had already spoken of the far-reaching flight of mind: '[His] intellect flies everywhere, in Pindar's words "beneath the earth" and measuring the earth's surface, "and above the heaven" observing the stars, and nosing out the nature of all things everywhere' (Plat. *Theaet.* 173e: ἡ δὲ διάνοια . . . πανταχῇ πέτεται κατὰ Πίνδαρον "τᾶς τε γᾶς ὑπένερθε" καὶ ἐπίπεδα γεωμετροῦσα, "οὐρανοῦ θ' ὕπερ" ἀστρονομοῦσα, καὶ πᾶσαν πάντῃ φύσιν ἐρευνωμένη);[6] like Empedocles' God, who is 'holy mind alone . . . traversing the entire universe with swift thoughts' (fr. 134. 4: φρὴν ἱερὴ . . . φροντίσι κόσμον ἅπαντα καταΐσσουσα θοῇσιν). This faculty is enhanced in proportion as the soul is freed from the encumbrance of an importunate body, hence the philosopher will welcome death eagerly, as offering to his liberated soul a clear sight of universal truth. This note was struck for later ages by Plato (*Phaedo* 62–68, especially 66e): 'For if we cannot have pure knowledge of anything in company with the body there are only two possibilities: knowledge is obtainable by the dead or not at all; for then and not till then will the soul be on its own, untrammelled by the body.'

Pindar's theme is taken up in the proem of the pseudo-Aristotelian *de mundo*, in praise of philosophy: 'Since it was not possible

to reach the heavens in the body, the soul at least, by means of
Philosophy and under the leadership of Intellect, has made the
crossing and sojourned there, and in the understanding has
annihilated the greatest distances in space; easily recognizing its
kin, apprehending the divine—for the soul sees with divine eyes—
and proclaiming it to men' (391a: ἐπειδὴ γὰρ οὐχ οἷόν τ᾽ ἦν τῷ
σώματι εἰς τὸν οὐράνιον ἀφικέσθαι τόπον . . . ἡ γοῦν ψυχὴ διὰ
φιλοσοφίας, λαβοῦσα ἡγεμόνα τὸν νοῦν, ἐπεραιώθη καὶ ἐξεδήμησεν . . .
καὶ τὰ πλεῖστον ἀλλήλων ἀφεστῶτα τοῖς τόποις τῇ διανοίᾳ συν-
εφόρησε, ῥᾳδίως, οἶμαι, τὰ συγγενῆ γνωρίσασα, καὶ θείῳ ψυχῆς
ὄμματι τὰ θεῖα καταλαβομένη, τοῖς τε ἀνθρώποις προφητεύουσα)—
a theme to be often repeated by later writers.

The variation in the *Phaedo* too is used by Cicero (from Posidonius?) in *T.D.* i. 44 f.: that love of beauty, which compels us to
philosophize, will be really gratified after death. Those who have
travelled to the Propontis or the Pillars of Hercules think they
have seen something: 'Can we imagine what a sight it will be
when we can take in the whole earth at a glance, its position,
shape, and circumference, its habitable zones and its zones uninhabitable by reason of heat or cold?' So too Seneca pictures
Cremutius Cordus welcoming his grandson to heaven and teaching him the secrets of the universe he sees around and below
him, from the fund of true knowledge now, no longer from guesswork ('ille nepotem suum . . . adplicat sibi nova luce gaudentem
et vicinorum siderum meatus docet, nec ex coniectura sed
omnium ex vero peritus in arcana naturae libens ducit . . . et in
profunda terrarum permittere aciem ⟨iubet⟩; iuvat enim ex alto
relicta respicere' (*Dial.* vi. 25). Cf. Luc. ix. 1–14).

All this is not unlike what Maximus says of Aristeas, that his
soul in its flight through the air over lands Grecian and barbarian
saw all the features of earth and the customs of its inhabitants,
while having a clearer view of the celestial bodies than we have
here below [122]. There is, however, this difference to be noted
between Maximus' Aristeas and the other passages: in the latter,
from the *de mundo* onwards, the thought is never far away of the
pettiness of the things of earth, as contrasted with the view of the
cosmos (Festugière calls it a contrast of a moral order (ii. 446 ff.)).

This is absent from the former, a fact which may indicate a pre-Hellenistic source.[7]

There is of course another difference. In Pindar and the pseudo-Aristotle the metaphorical flight of the mind (διάνοια, νοῦς) is meant, and in Cicero and Seneca the actual flight of the understanding soul after death has released it from the anchor of the body. But Aristeas' soul bears his understanding mind between the face of earth and heaven before this final separation from the body: he anticipates death.

This notion too is popular in Hellenistic times. For an understanding of its history two texts are of major importance; both of them fragments of the work *On Sleep* of Aristotle's pupil Clearchus of Soli (frr. 7 and 8). One relates a kind of hypnotic experiment carried out on a boy by means of a ψυχουλκὸς ῥάβδος, or 'magic wand', which persuaded Aristotle, who witnessed it (according to Clearchus), 'that in truth the soul is a separate entity from the body, that it enters into the body and uses it as a sort of hostel' (ὡς ἄρα χωρίζεται τοῦ σώματος ⟨ἡ ψυχὴ⟩ καὶ ὡς χρῆται αὐτῷ οἷον καταγωγίῳ). Striking the child with his wand, the operator 'drew the soul forth, and seeming to lead it by means of the wand away from the body demonstrated that the latter, remaining motionless and uninjured [i.e. not reacting to the injuries?], was as insensible to pricks as a corpse' (τὴν ψυχὴν ἐξείλκυσεν καὶ οἷον ἄγων δι' αὐτῆς πόρρω τοῦ σώματος ἀκίνητον ἐνέδειξε τὸ σῶμα καὶ ἀβλαβὲς σῳζόμενον ἀναισθητεῖν πρὸς ⟨τὰς πληγὰς⟩ τῶν γναπτόντων ὅμοιον ἀψύχῳ). After the soul had been returned to its body it recounted all that had happened (ἀπήγγειλεν ἕκαστα). [Cf. 139 f.]

Such a temporary separation of soul from body might happen spontaneously. Speaking of men of old who died and lived again —Aristeas, Hermotimus, Epimenides, for example [T. 24]— Proclus (our intermediary for this as for the previous fragment) quotes Clearchus[8] again: Cleonymus the Athenian, on the death of a dear friend, pined away so that he seemed to die (ἀθυμήσας ἐλιποψύχησεν). Two days later, just as his funeral was about to take place, he revived and told all that he had seen and heard when absent from the body. He said that his soul, freed, as it were, from its corporeal chains, was raised heavenwards and saw upon the earth beneath 'places of different shapes and colours, and rivers that no man could look upon' (ἀρθεῖσαν ὑπὲρ γῆς ἰδεῖν τόπους ἐν αὐτῇ παντοδαποὺς καὶ τοῖς σχήμασι καὶ τοῖς χρώμασιν καὶ ῥεύματα ποταμῶν ἀπρόσοπτα ἀνθρώποις). Finally he reached a place sacred to Hestia, where were indescribable female demons; there he met another, a Syracusan, who was in the same condition as himself. A mysterious voice told them to stay quiet and watch what went on, and they saw 'souls being judged and punished and purified one after the other under the supervision of the Furies' (ψυχῶν ἐκεῖ κολάσεις τε καὶ κρίσεις καὶ τὰς ἀεὶ καθαιρομένας καὶ τὰς τούτων ἐπισκόπους Εὐμενίδας). They were then ordered to return to earth; they arranged to look each other up if possible, and later did meet and recognize each other in the flesh.

This story, or rather the father of it, pretty clearly underlies that in a work of Cornelius Labeo (?*de dis animalibus*) : 'Two men died on the same day and met at a sort of crossroads; then were ordered to return to their bodies. They made a pact that they would be friends for the future, and so they were until they actually did die' (Aug. *C.D.* xxii. 28 : 'Labeo enim dicit, duos uno die fuisse defunctos et occurrisse invicem in quodam compito, deinde ad corpora iussos fuisse remeare et constituisse inter se amicos esse victuros, atque ita esse factum donec postea morerentur'). I mention this for an interesting variation: the 'place sacred to Hestia' of Clearchus is here a crossroads (*compitum quoddam*, apparently a rendering of τρίοδος) ; the significance of this will appear shortly.

The experience of Cleonymus strongly reminds us also of those of Timarchus in the oracle of Trophonius and of Thespesius as a result of a concussion (Plut. *gen. Socr.* 21 f.; *ser. num. vind.* 22). The souls of both ascended temporarily from their bodies[9] and witnessed the fate of the dead in 'the Hades in the air'. The information they brought back was eschatological only; but in Cicero's *Somnium Scipionis*, in the sixth book of the *de republica*, Scipio Aemilianus seems to ascend in sleep to the region of the Milky Way, where the spirit of his grandfather, the great Africanus, drives home a religious and moral lesson by means of a cosmical discourse: the smallness of the earth, and hence the pettiness of earthly ambition, are thrown into relief by the majesty and harmony of the celestial spheres, and the beauty of the Galaxy, where dwell the souls of the virtuous—above all, of virtuous statesmen. 'The very earth now seemed so small to me', says Aemilianus (16), 'that I quite resented our empire, which covers no more than a speck of it.' For small as the earth is, it is only a small part of it which constitutes our world (οἰκουμένη): 'the world which you inhabit', explains Africanus, 'is nothing but an islet embraced by the sea which you call the Atlantic, or the Great Sea, or the Ocean; grand names, but you can see how mean it really is. Yet even within this world you know, has the fame of you or any other Roman ever overleaped the Caucasus you see there, or the Ganges here?'

Undoubtedly the first-parent of all these visions, in their eschatological aspect, is the myth of Er in the tenth book of Plato's *Republic*; in their physical and geographical aspect, perhaps the notion of the all-pervading understanding wedded to portions of the myth of Er (e.g. 615a τὰς δ᾽ αὖ ἐκ τοῦ οὐρανοῦ εὐπαθείας διηγεῖσθαι καὶ θέας ἀμηχάνους τὸ κάλλος; cf. *Phaedr.* 246e ff.) and of that in the *Phaedo*—especially where Socrates describes how the earth would appear 'if one were to view it from aloft' (110b: εἴ τις ἄνωθεν θεῷτο). One seems to hear in Clearchus' words concerning the 'places on the earth's surface of different shapes and colours', τόποι ἐν τῇ γῇ παντοδαποὶ καὶ τοῖς σχήμασι καὶ τοῖς χρώμασιν, an echo of *Phaedo* 109b, 'there are dotted about the earth's surface many hollows of different shapes and sizes', εἶναι γὰρ πανταχῇ περὶ τὴν γῆν πολλὰ κοῖλα παντοδαπὰ καὶ τὰς ἰδέας καὶ τὰ μεγέθη, and 110b—the earth is 'marked off in variegated colours', ποικίλη, χρώμασιν διειλημμένη; his 'rivers that no man could look upon' remind one of the mysterious rivers of legend for which Socrates finds a geographical location (112e ff.); while the 'place sacred to Hestia' attended by female demons (δαιμόνιαι δυνάμεις) is the 'demonic place' (τόπος δαιμόνιος) of *Rep.* 614c, where the judgement of the dead takes place.

The trail takes us no farther back than Plato. The fact that Plato calls Er a Pamphylian, the son of Armenius, suggests that the ultimate source of such trance visions is to be sought in Asia

Minor or the Middle East; but confirmation is lacking, and is not provided (Clemen, for example, (133) is mistaken here) by the fact that Zoroaster replaces the name of Er in some traditions [159].

But between Plato and Clearchus two developments have occurred: the geographical and eschatological features of the visions have been conflated (a process which would have been helped by the cosmological disquisition in *Rep*. 616b ff.), and the place of the souls' punishment has been raised from under the earth (as it is in *Rep*. 614d *al.*) to the air (in *Rep*. 614c the *righteous* souls only traverse the heaven). This is implied in Clearchus—Cleonymus could not have witnessed the punishment of souls from his station in the sky had it taken place beneath the earth—and is explicit in Plutarch.

Now Servius auct. *ad Geor*. i. 34 has this: 'Varro says he had read that a Syracusan called Empedotimus had his eyes opened with a more than human vision by some divine power, and saw among other things three gates and three roads: one by the sign of Scorpio, which was the way Hercules was reported to have ascended to heaven; another by the path between [*or* through the boundary between] Leo and Cancer; and the third between Aquarius and Pisces' ('Varro ait se legisse Empedotimo cuidam Syracusano a quadam potestate divina mortalem aspectum detersum, eumque inter cetera tres portas vidisse tresque vias: unam ad signum Scorpionis, qua Hercules ad deos isse diceretur; alteram per limitem qui est inter Leonem et Cancrum; tertiam esse inter Aquarium et Pisces'). Proclus adds to our information: once when out hunting Empedotimus found himself alone in a deserted spot and saw an appearance of Pluto and Persephone. He was dazzled by the light that encircled the gods, and through it saw all the truth about the fate of souls as if witnessing a drama (*in Plat. remp.* ii. 119: καταλαμφθῆναι μὲν ὑπὸ τοῦ φωτὸς τοῦ περιθέοντος κύκλῳ τοὺς θεούς, ἰδεῖν δὲ δι' αὐτοῦ πᾶσαν τὴν περὶ τῶν ψυχῶν ἀλήθειαν ὡς ἐν αὐτόπτοις θεάμασιν). The story is told by Heraclides Ponticus, says Proclus.[10]

Little of the truth about the dead which was revealed to Empedotimus in his vision has been preserved for us. Philoponus

reports that Empedotimus called the Milky Way 'the path of
the souls who traverse the Hades in the sky' (ad Arist. Meteor.
i. 8: φησὶ γὰρ ἐκεῖνος ὁδὸν εἶναι ψυχῶν τὸ γάλα τῶν τὸν Ἅιδην
τὸν ἐν οὐρανῷ διαπορευομένων); Olympiodorus, that Empedotimus said that the realm of Pluto [Hades] comprised all beneath the sphere of the sun (in Plat. Phaed. 238).[11]

Empedotimus was the author of a work on natural philosophy
(περὶ φυσικῆς ἀκροάσεως), according to 'Suidas', who quotes
Julian as saying that 'we believe Empedotimus and Pythagoras,
and what Heraclides Ponticus says on their authority' (s. Ἐμπε-
δότιμος: ἡμεῖς δὲ Ἐμπεδοτίμῳ καὶ Πυθαγόρᾳ πιστεύοντες, οἷς τε
ἐκεῖθεν λαβὼν Ἡρακλείδης ὁ Ποντικὸς ἔφη). But it is clear, as
Rohde says ([1] 330), that he is, in fact, no more than a fictitious
character in a dialogue of Heraclides. His very name is merely
a conflation of Empedocles and Hermotimus (cf. Bidez 55). The
belief that souls inhabit the Milky Way is elsewhere ascribed
to Heraclides himself, and to Pythagoras (Stob. i. 378; Nu-
menius ap. Procl. in Plat. remp. ii. 129). From this, and from
Julian's words, we may deduce that Pythagoras too featured in
some way in this same dialogue (cf. Voss 60). 'Suidas' statement
that Empedotimus himself wrote a book is probably a mistaken deduction from references to 'the discourse of Empedotimus [in the dialogue]', ὁ Ἐμπεδοτίμου λόγος, and the like (so
Rohde).[12]

The influence of this work of Heraclides was considerable. It
explains the transfer of the site of Hades from beneath the earth to
the air which recurs in authors from Clearchus onwards. The 'tres
portae tresque viae' which Empedotimus saw underlie the title
of Varro's satire Τριοδίτης Τριπύλιος, περὶ ἀρετῆς κτήσεως. The
τρίοδος is the compitum quoddam of Labeo, where Cleonymus met
the Syracusan Lysias in Clearchus' story; this infernal road junction appears first in the myth of the Gorgias (524a),[13] but that Heraclides is behind Clearchus here is indicated by his location of
Hades in the air.[14] Wehrli has gathered over 200 mentions
of him by many authors, Latin as well as Greek—Varro clearly
knew his work well, and the four fragments which Cicero has
transmitted are no measure of his considerable acquaintance

with Heraclides' writings (the *de republica*, for instance, is very probably a sample of a Heraclidean type of dialogue: Voss 23 f. Cf. fr. 27 a–f W.).

Even so, Empedotimus differs from his successors (better perhaps, his descendants), Cleonymus, Timarchus, and Thespesius, inasmuch as they witnessed the fate of the dead in the spirit—their souls visited the scene—whereas Empedotimus witnessed it in the body, not by any transportation but clairvoyantly; as Proclus says, 'Some have seen these things [the next world] in the body, as we are told Empedotimus did;[15] others in the spirit (ἄνευ σώματος), like the Athenian Cleonymus' (*in Plat. remp.* ii. 122). Nor do we know that his lesson in eschatology included any geography, as Scipio's did; indeed, it is hard to see how it could have done, for such a panorama of terrestrial features demands that the observer be suspended aloft, as Empedotimus was not.

Nevertheless Heraclides also treated at length that phenomenon of catalepsy of which Aristeas appears to have been so remarkable an example. Pliny, discussing men who have 'died and lived again' (*N.H.* vii. 173 ff., perhaps directly from some Roman authority—Varro or Messalla Rufus?), enumerates among others Hermotimus, Aristeas, and Epimenides; then adds that women are particularly liable to 'this affliction' (*huic morbo*): 'relevant here is that work of Heraclides, well-known among the Greeks, about the woman who was revived after being dead for seven days' (she might provide evidence of the possibility of resurrection to convince those sceptics who will not accept the story of Er, says Origen (*Cels.* ii. 16)).

We know a certain amount about the setting of this disquisition of Heraclides. It seems to have been in dialogue form, part of, if not identical with, the work *On Diseases* (Voss 69). Its preamble featured Pythagoras conversing with Leon, tyrant of Sicyon, on the subject of philosophers (D.L. i. 12; cf. Cic. *T.D.* v. 8 f.). After the manner of Heraclides (Voss 23), this preamble was only loosely connected with the main part of the book, in which Empedocles related to his friend Pausanias, at an *al fresco* banquet, the case of the Cataleptic Woman, whom he had cured after she had been for thirty days without pulse or breath (τριά-κοντα ἡμέρας ἄπνουν καὶ ἄσφυκτον τὸ σῶμα). Later on in the night when Empedocles had described this case, one guest saw a 'light from heaven, and heard a great voice calling Empedocles', who in the morning had disappeared—translated to the gods, apparently, wherefore Pausanias told his fellows that they must now pay divine honours to Empedocles (as happened, we recall, to Pythagoras, Hermotimus, and Aristeas [129; 123]). A more sceptical and naturalistic explanation of the disappearance was also expressed in the dialogue—by another character?—which Pausanias disputed: that Empedocles had jumped down the crater of Etna (D.L. viii. 60–71).

Because of this feat with the cataleptic, Heraclides called Empedocles both a healer and a seer (καὶ ἰητρὸν καὶ μάντιν), confirming these titles also from some lines of Empedocles' own, according to Diogenes (fr. 112. 1–11). In these lines Empedocles says that men come to him demanding oracles and remedies against disease, which certainly implies that he is both healer and seer; but the poetic form ἰητρός which Heraclides used indicates that he also quoted some other passage of Empedocles in which it actually occurred—probably fr. 146, where the final incarnation of the soul before deification is said to be as a *seer*, a poet, a *healer*, and a champion of men:

> εἰς δὲ τέλος μάντεις τε καὶ ὑμνοπόλοι καὶ ἰητροὶ
> καὶ πρόμοι ἀνθρώποισιν ἐπιχθονίοισι πέλονται,
> ἔνθεν ἀναβλαστοῦσι θεοὶ τιμῇσι φέριστοι.

This would fit excellently with the dramatic ending of Heraclides' book, where Empedocles is translated to heaven.

We can readily see how his success with the cataleptic woman would attest Empedocles' skill as a doctor; but how would it reveal him as a seer also? Did the woman on her recovery impart to him knowledge she had preternaturally acquired when in her deathlike state? At that time she would have been especially capable of clairvoyance and prophecy; for, just as on the point of its separation from the body at death the soul has prophetic insight,[16] so in the deathlike trance of catalepsy it has the same power. This is well illustrated by a fragment of Aristotle preserved in an Arabic source:

Aristotle tells of the Greek king whose soul was caught up in ecstasy, and who for many days remained neither alive nor dead. When he came to himself, he told the bystanders of various things in the invisible world, and related what he had seen—souls, forms, and angels; he gave the proofs of this by foretelling to all his acquaintances how long each of them would live. All he had said was put to the proof, and no one exceeded the span of life that he had assigned. He prophesied too that after a year a chasm would open in the country of Elis, and after two years a flood would occur in another place; and everything happened as he had said.[17] Aristotle asserts that the reason of this was that his soul had acquired this knowledge just because it had been near to leaving his body and had been in a certain way separated from it, and so had seen what it had seen (Ross, *Aristotle Translated* xii. 23).

Galen refers several times to this work of Heraclides. One passage is of particular interest to the present investigation (viii. 414 = fr. 79 W.): women afflicted with one kind of hysteria lie bereft of sense and movement, with only the faintest pulse or none at all; 'this kind, which is described in Heraclides' book, is very puzzling. There, a woman is said to have passed into a state where neither respiration nor pulse was manifest, only distinguishable from death inasmuch as there was a trace of warmth about the middle portion of the body. . . . The doctors present disputed whether she were not actually dead' (ἐγὼ δὲ θεασάμενος πολλὰς γυναῖκας ὑστερικάς, . . . τινὰς μὲν ἀναισθήτους τε ἅμα καὶ ἀκινήτους κειμένας, ἀμυδρότατόν τε καὶ μικρότατον ἐχούσας σφυγμὸν ἢ καὶ παντελῶς ἀσφύκτους φαινομένας. . . . ἡ μὲν οὖν πρώτη λελεγμένη διαφορὰ κατὰ τὸ τοῦ Ποντικοῦ Ἡρακλείδου γεγραμμένον βιβλίον ἀπορίαν ἔχει πολλὴν ὅπως γίγνεται. λέγεται γὰρ ἄπνους τε καὶ ἄσφυκτος ἐκείνη ἡ ἄνθρωπος γεγονέναι, τῶν νεκρῶν ἑνὶ μόνῳ διαλλάττουσα, τῷ βραχεῖαν ἔχειν θερμότητα κατὰ τὰ μέσα μέρη τοῦ σώματος. ἐπιγέγραπται γοῦν τὸ βιβλίον ἄπνους Ἡρακλείδου, καὶ ζήτησιν ἔφη γεγονέναι τοῖς παροῦσιν ἰατροῖς, εἰ μήπω τέθνηκεν). The words κειμένας ἀμυδρότατον . . . ἐχούσας σφυγμὸν . . . λέγεται ἄπνους γεγονέναι, τῶν νεκρῶν ἑνὶ μόνῳ διαλλάττουσα are curiously like those of Maximus on Aristeas [121], τὸ μὲν σῶμα ἔκειτο ἔμπνουν μέν, ἀλλ᾽ ἀμυδρῶς καὶ ἐγγύτατα θανάτου. There is also a similarity between Plutarch's explanation of the Cretan Epimenides' ability to maintain life by means of the plant called ἄλιμος—'because nature can nourish the vital spark and preserve the organism on a quite minute supply of heat' (*fac. in orb. lun.* 25. 940c)—and what Galen says of Heraclides' cataleptic: in those in whom an excess of heat agglomerates about heart or lungs the breathing is fast, but in those in whom the temperature has been lowered the opposite occurs, even to the extent of simulating death (fr. 80 W.: ἐν οἷς δὲ ἀπέψευκται τὸ θερμόν, ἡ ἐναντία, ὥστε καί τισιν ἤδη τελέως ἔδοξεν ἀπολωλέναι, καὶ ἦν ὁ Ποντικὸς Ἡρακλείδης ἄπνουν ἔγραψεν ἥδε ἐστίν). Epimenides might indeed be called the prince of cataleptics, having slept solidly for fifty-seven years without physical ill-effects, during which time he claimed to have been in the presence of the gods, to have heard divine discourse, and to have witnessed Truth and Righteousness (Max. Tyr. x. 1: ὄναρ ἔφη ἐντυχεῖν αὐτὸς θεοῖς καὶ θεῶν λόγοις καὶ ἀληθείᾳ καὶ δίκῃ). It should come as no surprise now to learn that Epimenides' soul also, like those of Hermotimus and Aristeas, could leave and return to his body at will (Suid. *s.* Ἐπιμενίδης).

I suggest that the dissertation of Heraclides περὶ τῆς ἄπνου discussed the physical causation of a phenomenon which also had an occult side to it: that of the deathlike catalepsy wherein the soul seems to acquire paranormal knowledge of events distant in time or place; that it centred round Empedocles' female patient, but that strange stories about other people were adduced as instances of the same phenomenon—Hermotimus, Epimenides who was said to have slept so long, Aristeas who travelled so far and appeared elsewhere after his 'death', perhaps Abaris the Hyperborean seer who was also like Epimenides in that he too journeyed in the soul and had some means of maintaining life without eating (Hdt. iv. 36), and Pythagoras himself, who could remember his soul's experiences out of the body. All these figures, including Empedocles, come to be connected with Pythagoras, and the ability to pass at will into a prophetic trance comes to be treated as a particularly Pythagorean aptitude; for which perhaps Heraclides may be responsible too.

It may be felt that my suggestion that Aristeas was mentioned in the περὶ τῆς ἄπνου is too speculative. However, he almost certainly found a place in another work of Heraclides, perhaps the book *On Oracular Utterances* (περὶ χρησμῶν) or that *On Oracles* (περὶ χρηστηρίων). I have long thought that a passage of Clement [T. 21] was Heraclidean, and am glad to see that Wehrli is also of this opinion, though he assigns it to one of the works *On the Soul* (fr. 90): 'Prognostication was practised by the great Pythagoras, by Abaris the Hyperborean, by Aristeas of Proconnesus, by Epimenides the Cretan, he who went to Sparta, by Zoroaster the Mede and Empedocles of Acragas and Phormio the Spartan; also to be sure by Polyaratus of Thasos and Empedotimus of Syracuse and especially by Socrates the Athenian' (here Wehrli ends the fragment; there follows a quotation from the *Theages*, and a reference to a method of divination used by a Phocian tyrant called Execestus on the authority of Aristotle in *The Phocian Constitution*[18]).

The appearance of Empedotimus immediately points to Heraclides as the ultimate source of this passage, and we have already seen that Pythagoras and Empedocles played a part in his writings. About Polyaratus I can discover nothing more, and the mention of Socrates is of no help; but an examination of the other names yields interesting results.

Heraclides believed, or spoke as if he believed, that the Hyperboreans really existed, and that in his own day. Plutarch records that Heraclides claimed to have heard a report from the west that a Hyperborean army had captured a Greek city called Rome, which was situated somewhere near the Great Sea. 'But it would not surprise me', continues Plutarch, 'that Heraclides, inventor of fairy tales as he is (μυθώδη καὶ πλασματίαν ὄντα), had grafted this nonsense about Hyperboreans and the Great Sea on to a true account of the capture of Rome [by the Gauls]' (*Cam.* 22).[19] In at least two of Heraclides' books a particular Hyperborean, Abaris, appeared or was mentioned: in that *On Righteousness* (περὶ δικαιοσύνης), and in that *Concerning the Sayings ascribed to Abaris* (περὶ τῶν εἰς Ἄβαριν ἀναφερομένων.[20] Frr. 51c; 74, 75 W.).

Pindar is the first author we know to have mentioned Abaris. He said that he came to Greece in the time of Croesus (fr. 283); Herodotus, that he traversed the whole earth carrying an arrow and eating nothing (iv. 36); Plato, that he was a purveyor of spells (ἐπῳδαί: *Charm.* 158b). A contemporary of Heraclides, the orator Lycurgus, provides more information in his speech *Against Menesaechmus*: as a result of a famine among the Hyperboreans Abaris came and served Apollo [at Delphi, presumably], and, obtaining mantic power from him, went round Greece prophesying, having as his badge the god's weapon [the arrow] (fr. 85: λιμοῦ γενομένου ἐν τοῖς Ὑπερβορέοις ἐλθὼν ὁ Ἄβαρις ἐμισθώτευσε τῷ Ἀπόλλωνι, καὶ μαθὼν χρησμοὺς παρ' αὐτοῦ, σύμβολον ἔχων τὸ βέλος τοῦ Ἀπόλλωνος περιήει ἐν τῇ Ἑλλάδι μαντευόμενος). The arrow here seems to have been meant as a guarantee of the genuinely Apolline quality of Abaris' divination; but Heraclides makes it do a real job of work. For him it is a huge weapon, the personal property of Apollo, on which Abaris comes riding, like a witch on a broomstick (fr. 51 W.), to discourse with Pythagoras in the presence of Phalaris on a most appropriate subject for a Hyperborean, Justice.[21] It has been suggested that Heraclides in fact preserves the original version in which the arrow was the carrier and not the carried, and that Herodotus has rationalized the story;[22] but the evidence of Lycurgus, which is independent of Herodotus, is against this.[23]

It seems, then, that Heraclides, just as he improved on the capture of Rome by the Gauls by adding romantic touches about Hyperboreans and so on, in the same manner has improved on earlier stories of Abaris and his arrow; perhaps (somewhere, if not in the περὶ δικαιοσύνης) suggesting that Abaris' transportation on the arrow symbolized his ability to make trance journeys in the soul [143]—at any rate this suggestion could not have been made before Heraclides, if he invented the tale that the arrow carried Abaris;[24] and associating him for the first time with Pythagoras, thus causing his inclusion in the catalogue of early Pythagoreans given by Iamblichus [142], and also the legend that he was a teacher of Pythagoras: for the latter was a disciple not only of Pherecydes and Hermodamas in Samos, but later of

Abaris and 'Zaratas the Magus', according to a scholiast on Plato (*in remp.* 600b : vi. 360 Hermann).

This Zaratas is the same as the Iranian religious teacher more commonly called Zoroaster, also mentioned in the passage of Clement under consideration. His name was apparently known to Greek learning as early as the fifth century B.C. (to Xanthus of Lydia); it was certainly known in the fourth, to the early Academy and the Lyceum; and, most pertinently for the present investigation, Heraclides Ponticus wrote a work entitled *Zoroaster* (Plut. *Col.* 14 = fr. 68 W.; cf. Voss 61).

We have no fragments specifically from this book, but it is fortunately possible to make important deductions about it with considerable assurance. In it Pythagoras visited Babylon and there sat at the feet of Zoroaster, by whom he was purified and taught not only to maintain this purity by abstention from beans but also truths about the soul and about natural philosophy.[25] Whether in this dialogue Zoroaster also claimed to have made journeys in the soul and to have had previous incarnations can only be surmised; but the former claim was certainly current by the early third century B.C., for Colotes, a pupil of Epicurus, found grounds for asserting that the original hero of the myth in the tenth book of the *Republic* was not Er but Zoroaster (Procl. *in Plat. remp.* ii. 109),[26] and later apocryphal works of Zoroaster appeared in which he personally professed to supernatural knowledge gained in the next world by the process of 'death and resurrection' (Bidez–Cumont ii. 158).

As to the claim to previous incarnations, there is no direct evidence that any such was made on behalf of Zoroaster,[27] but there are discrepancies in the later Greek tradition about him that could be explained on the assumption that somewhere it was made. It was asserted by some authority that he was a Greek and a Proconnesian. A scholiast on the Platonic *Alcibiades I* states that 'some people made Zoroaster a Greek, others the son of one of the invaders from the continent beyond the Great Sea; and they say that he was taught all wisdom by the good deity' (122a (Bidez–Cumont ii. 23) : οἱ μὲν Ἕλληνα, οἱ δὲ τῶν ἐκ τῆς ὑπὲρ τὴν μεγάλην θάλασσαν ἠπείρου ὡρμημένων παῖδά φασι, πᾶσάν τε σοφίαν ἐκ τοῦ ἀγαθοῦ δαίμονος ἐκμαθεῖν). Pliny preserves a tradition that there was a Zoroaster of Proconnesus living in the sixth century (*N.H.* xxx. 8: 'diligentiores paulo ante hunc [Ostanes, who accompanied Xerxes in his invasion of Greece] ponunt Zoroastren alium Proconnensium'). It has been suggested that this was Aristeas himself, a conjecture which does not commend itself to Bidez–Cumont (i. 23). I should explain it rather as a confused reminiscence of some assertion that Zoroaster (or rather Zaratas) was a *reincarnation* of Aristeas.

There is, of course, a glaring chronological inconsistency between the teacher of Pythagoras, who for Heraclides was a contemporary of Phalaris, and the Persian magus who lived 6,000 years before Plato (as stated by the scholiast on the *Alcibiades* just quoted; cf. Arist. *ap.* D.L. i *pr.* 1 f.; Plin. *N.H.* xxx. 3); but there is the further curiosity that, although the work of Heraclides was entitled *Zoroaster*, the sage therein who instructed Pythagoras at Babylon seems to have been called *Zaratas* or *Zaratus* (cf. the passages of Aristoxenus and Porphyry referred to in note 25). Now a Zaratas living in the sixth century B.C. is much closer in name and date to the founder of Mazdaism (Pehlevi *Zaratušt*, *c.* 600 B.C.: Bidez–Cumont i. 37; Henning 35 ff.) than a Zoroaster living in the sixty-fourth; perhaps Ζωροάστρης, 'Purely-astral', really was an etymological fiction based on Ζαράτας by someone trying to make a significant name for 'the first astronomer'. I advance this suggestion with great hesitation (cf. Bidez–Cumont i. 6); anyway, two forms of the name may have been known to Heraclides, who then in his dialogue made Zaratas, the teacher of Pythagoras, a later incarnation both of Aristeas of Proconnesus and of the Zoroaster who had lived 5,800 years before (Zaratus is distinguished from Zoroaster by Pliny, *N.H.* xxx. 5).[28]

We have already seen another name in Clement's list, that of Epimenides the Cretan, associated with Pythagoras [143]. He accompanied Pythagoras into the Idaean Cave when the latter was returning from his visit to the Magi (D.L. viii. 3), and is called a pupil of Pythagoras by Iamblichus (*V.P.* 222) in a story, appended to the résumé of the Heraclidean περὶ δικαιοσύνης, where

Epimenides is said to have caused his would-be assassins to go mad and slay each other (perhaps suggested by the tale of Cadmus and the Sparti). We have also seen that he was a cataleptic, who learned divine truth when in this state [156]. We only need to know that he was reincarnated for him to conform admirably to the pattern; and such a claim does seem to be made for him in a passage of Diogenes Laertius (i. 114): Epimenides said that he had first been Aeacus, had foretold to the Spartans their capture by the Arcadians, and had often 'lived again'.[29] This would explain a chronological problem in the legends about Epimenides. He is said to have visited Athens at the beginning of the fifth century by Plato (*Laws* i. 642d), a century earlier by Plutarch (*Sol.* 12; cf. Arist. *Ath. Pol.* 1; Suid. *s. 'Επιμενίδης*; D.L. i. 110). There is no difficulty about this for a man who lived to be more than 150 (so as early as Xenophanes: D.L. i. 111); but he would have to be much older than that to be able to prophesy to the Spartans their capture by the Arcadians, as Diogenes says he did. The only known incident to which this prophecy could refer is the capture of the Spartans by the Tegeans (Hdt. i. 66),[30] put by Pausanias in the reign of Charilaus in the ninth century (iii. 7. 3 *al.*), which could not have happened in Epimenides' lifetime even if we accept the Cretan version of his longevity, that he died aged 299! In fact, it *must* have happened in an earlier incarnation, if this was the distasteful prophecy for which the Spartans are said to have put Epimenides to death (Paus. ii. 21. 3: πρὸ δὲ τοῦ ναοῦ τῆς Ἀθηνᾶς Ἐπιμενίδου λέγουσιν εἶναι τάφον. Λακεδαιμονίους γὰρ πολεμήσαντας πρὸς Κνωσίους ἑλεῖν ζῶντα Ἐπιμενίδην, λαβόντας δὲ ἀποκτεῖναι, διότι σφίσιν οὐκ αἴσια ἐμαντεύετο). This view would account for the way in which Diogenes' mention of the prediction is sandwiched between Epimenides' claim to have been Aeacus and his claim to have often 'lived again' (cf. note 29).

About Phormio, the remaining name in Clement's list, Pausanias tells the following (iii. 16. 2 f.). He acquired a house in Sparta where once had dwelt the Dioscuri. These came to him in the likeness of foreigners; they said they had come from Cyrene, and asked him to put them up in the room that had been their

favourite when they were on earth. Phormio made them free of
the rest of the house, but would not grant their request for that
particular room, as it was his daughter's. The next day not only
the strangers but the girl and all her things had vanished, and in
her room instead were found two images of the Dioscuri and some
silphium on a table (cf. Plut. *non posse suaviter vivi* 22. 1103a).

This is one story about Phormio. But there is another, from
Theopompus, which explains his inclusion with Aristeas and the
rest in the Clementine passage ('Suidas', *s. Φορμίων*):

He was a Crotoniate,[31] and was wounded at the battle of the Sagra.
As the wound proved difficult to heal, he received an oracular bidding
to go to Sparta; there the first person to invite him to dinner would
cure him. On his arrival at Sparta he had just dismounted from his
chariot, when a young man extended such an invitation. After dinner
his host asked him the reason for his journey, and, when he heard about
the oracle, took some scrapings from his spear (ἀποξύσας τοῦ δόρατος)
and placed them on the wound. After Phormio left, he was about to
ascend his chariot, as he thought, when he found himself grasping the
handle of his own front door back in Croton. On another occasion he
was celebrating the *Theoxenia*, when the Dioscuri [who were presumably his guests at the sacral entertainment] invited him to go to Cyrene
to meet Battus; and he stood up holding a stalk of silphium (καὶ
ἀνέστη τε ἔχων σιλφίου καυλόν).

Here, not only does Phormio undergo a miraculous transportation in the body from Sparta to Croton, but there is in the last
sentence an obscurely worded reference to a transportation in
the spirit, a soul-journey. He is invited to meet King Battus of
Cyrene because he is another seer (he is presumably the Battus
who is said by Clement, immediately before the passage under
discussion [T. 21], to have compiled a treatise known as the
Mantic Art of the Argonautic diviner Mopsus. The original Battus
who founded Cyrene introduced the rites of the Dioscuri there
(schol. *ad* Pind. *Pyth.* v. 10)). Silphium was the principal export of
Cyrene (cf. Plaut. *Rud.* 629 ff.; Hdt. iv. 169; connected with
Battus, Ar. *Pl.* 925); when Phormio got up out of his trance
(ἀνέστη) he was holding a stalk of it, proof that he had not merely
been dreaming. The story can be nicely paralleled from Jacobus

de Voragine: a lady who was devoted to the Virgin was unable owing to the absence of her chaplain to hear mass on the festival of the Purification. She entered her chapel and fell into a trance before the altar, wherein she found herself in a magnificent church ('subito in excessum mentis facta videbatur sibi se in quadam ecclesia pulcherrima et speciosa collocatam esse'), and seemed to hear mass celebrated by Christ Himself in the presence of the Virgin. At the end she refused to surrender to an acolyte the candle she had been given; there was a somewhat unseemly struggle, the candle broke in two, and she came to herself in her own chapel holding half of it ('ad hanc igitur vehementem fractionem illa subito ad se rediit, et se iuxta altare ubi se posuerat inveniens cereum fractum in manu sua repperit' (*Legenda Aurea* 37 —*de Purificatione B.V.M.*)).[32]

There can be little doubt that the first Phormio story, given by Pausanias, is more primitive in form than the second, given by Theopompus. It embodies a theme common in folk-lore, in which a god in human guise visits some mortal and makes a request which is refused; the mortal is punished for his refusal. Here, the images and the silphium are the signatures, as it were, of the Dioscuri, left to inform Phormio who his guests really were. In the second story elements of the first are taken and adapted to an entirely new setting. The bodily transportation of Phormio's daughter becomes a bodily transportation of Phormio himself (like the bodily transportation of Aristeas from the fuller's shop, of Empedocles in the περὶ τῆς ἄπνου, and of Cleomedes from the chest in Astypalaea); Phormio's unwitting entertainment of the Dioscuri becomes a deliberate entertainment at the *Theoxenia*; Cyrene, the provenance of the Dioscuri in the first story, becomes the goal of a trance journey in the second, because at Cyrene dwells the seer Battus; the silphium, evidence of the guests' identity in the first story, becomes in the second evidence that Phormio's soul has actually made the journey.

This is complicated enough to suggest that the second story is a *literary* adaptation of the first; which is confirmed by the fact that the author has complicated it still further by introducing elements of extraneous legends. The oracular instruction about who should be Phormio's healer and the method by which the cure was effected are a variation on the story, treated by Sophocles and Euripides, of Telephus, whose wound, inflicted by Achilles, festered incurably till he was told by Apollo that the dealer of the wound would heal it; as happened when Achilles was persuaded to scrape some rust from his spear on to it (ἀποξύ- σαντος τῆς μελίας τὸν ἰόν: Apollod. *Epit.* iii 17–20, with Frazer's note). Clearly, then, the young man in Sparta who invites Phormio to dinner is the warrior who wounded him in the battle of the Sagra, and as clearly he is one of the Dioscuri, who helped the Locrians to victory over the Crotoniates at the Sagra by fighting at their side, according to Trogus (Justin xx. 3)—a romantic elaboration of what may quite well have been an historical fact: that Sparta, on being asked for help against Croton by the Locrians, said she would send them the Dioscuri, who then travelled back with the Locrian ambassadors symbolically (cere- monial couches were prepared for them on the ship: Diod. Sic. viii. 32). There is yet another variant of the Telephus theme con- nected with the battle of the Sagra, to be found in Pausanias (iii. 19. 11 ff.) and Conon (fr. 1. 18 = Phot. *Bibl.* 133b): a Crotoniate called Leonymus or Autoleon was wounded in the chest or thigh by Ajax, who was fighting for the Locrians. As the wound would not heal he consulted Delphi, and was sent to Leuke Nesos, a sort of Island of the Blest in the Euxine, where he was cured by the ghost of Ajax, met other heroes, and was given a message for Stesichorus by Helen. This looks to me like another literary invention, related to the second Phormio story indeed, but as cousin rather than as progenitor.

The personages in the Clementine passage are now seen to have much in common. Abaris, Aristeas, Epimenides, Zoroaster, Em- pedocles, and Empedotimus were all associated with Pythagoras (and it will not escape attention that Phormio too lived in Croton, where Pythagoras himself taught for twenty years); Pythagoras, Empedocles, Epimenides, also possibly Aristeas and Zoroaster, were reincarnated; Pythagoras, Abaris, Aristeas, Epimenides, Zoroaster, and Phormio all had trance experiences, 'journeys in the soul', while Empedotimus had a revelation of a similar nature 'in the body', and Empedocles experimented with the cataleptic trance and may have obtained such revelations from his subject at second hand; finally, Pythagoras, Empedocles, Zoroaster, Abaris, and Empedotimus are known to have featured in dialogues by Heraclides Ponticus, and Empedotimus is an invention of Heraclides. Most of the tales about these people we have seen to be current by the end of the fourth century B.C., some could not have been earlier than that century, and indeed the whole theme of knowledge 'gained in the soul' while the body is left as if dead appears to be derived in the first place from the Platonic myth of Er. All these similarities are best explained as the work of one adapter or editor living in the fourth century, and the weight of evidence points to Heraclides as the man.

If this argumentation is correct, the stories I have been discussing, and especially the two versions of the Phormio story, provide us with a good sample of the way Heraclides went to work, more extensive than, though not dissimilar from, the samples of his treatment of Abaris and his arrow or the Gallic capture of Rome. He would take some strange tale and use elements therefrom to construct an even stranger, shaping it to conform to a pattern of association with Pythagoras, reincarnation, trance journeyings of the soul, divination and supernaturally acquired knowledge, intercourse with the gods, who 'have a concern for human affairs' (fr. 75 W.); the bizarre is enhanced by the introduction of magi, Sibyls (cf. frr. 130, 131 W., and note 25), Hyperboreans, outer continents, and so on; and other tales and earlier literature are laid under contribution. An example of this is his treatment of Empedocles in the περὶ τῆς ἄπνου [153 f.] : much of it can be seen to be developed from things in Empedocles' own writings—his friend Pausanias with whom he discourses is the addressee of the περὶ φύσεως (fr. 1); the cataleptic woman herself may have been suggested by the promise that Empedocles makes to Pausanias, that after studying his teachings he will be able to bring the dead back to life (fr. 111. 9); the translation of Empedocles to heaven is based on what he himself says about the ultimate lot of the good man (fr. 146); while the translation and its circumstances, the heavenly light and the great voice[33] summoning

Empedocles, are surely borrowed from Sophocles' account of the supernatural summons and disappearance of the hero Oedipus at Colonus (*O.C.* 1621–65), and from Euripides (*Bacch.* 1078):

ἐκ δ' αἰθέρος φωνή τις, ὡς μὲν εἰκάσαι
Διόνυσος, ἀνεβόασεν· ὦ νεανίδες,
ἄγω τὸν ὑμᾶς κἀμὲ τἀμά τ' ὄργια
γέλων τιθέμενον· ἀλλὰ τιμωρεῖσθέ νιν.
καὶ ταῦθ' ἅμ' ἠγόρευε καὶ πρὸς οὐρανὸν
καὶ γαῖαν ἐστήριξε φῶς σεμνοῦ πυρός.

And there came a voice from heaven—Dionysus, at a guess—crying: 'Maenads, I have brought you the man who mocked you and me and our rites: now punish him.' And with these words a pillar of divine fire was set between earth and sky.

It must have been just such a command to punish impiety that the mysterious voice gave from the bronze laurel in the market-place at Metapontum when the girl Pharsalia came wearing the golden wreath stolen from Delphi by Philomelus [123]; and the fate that befell her at the hands of the maddened seers was exactly that of Pentheus at the hands of the maddened Bacchae. This tale must have been invented between 356 B.C., when Philo-melus rifled the Delphic treasures (cf. Diod. Sic. xvi 30), and Theopompus, who is our earliest authority for it. It would then fit Heraclides chronologically, and it shows several Heraclidean idiosyncrasies: Aristeas and the Hyperboreans, the seers, the divine intervention and the threatening voice, the distorted bor-rowing from Hdt. iv. 15—Herodotus' 'statue dedicated to Aristeas and surrounded by laurels' has become a bronze laurel; and Aristeas did *not* say in the Herodotean account that he had come from the Hyperboreans. We even have the account, quite pos-sibly historical, of which it could be a typically Heraclidean elaboration. This we owe to Plutarch, who says that the golden wreath was a dedication of the Cnidians (not the Lampsacenes), and that a mob of young men, excited with cupidity for the pre-cious object, tore Pharsalia to pieces in their struggles for it near the temple of Apollo in Metapontum (*Pyth. orac.* 8). The more fanciful version handed down by Theopompus could well have appeared in Heraclides' book περὶ εὐσεβείας, from which is preserved an example of divine vengeance wreaked upon the sacrilegious (fr. 46 W.).

Another personage relevant to an investigation of the Aristeas saga appeared in the work of Heraclides. This was Aristaeus, the son of Apollo and Cyrene. Cicero says: 'We have it that the Ceans are wont to observe carefully the rising of Sirius, and to deduce therefrom the healthfulness of the ensuing season, as Heraclides Ponticus writes. For if the star presents a dim and misty appearance the atmosphere must be dense and torpid, so that its effluence (*adspiratio*) will be oppressive and unhealthy; but if it shines brightly it is a sign that the atmosphere is rarefied and clean, and so salubrious' (*Div.* i. 130 = fr. 141 W.). In chapter 9. 2 of the excerpts *de rebus publicis*, ascribed by the codices to a Heraclides,[34] is the following fragment (the chapter is about Ceos): 'They say that Aristaeus learnt the care of flocks and herds from the Nymphs, and beekeeping from the Brisae; when plants and animals were dying, by reason of the etesian winds blowing [πνεῖν AB, δείπειν (*supra scripto* πνεῖν) C, λείπειν *Schneidewin*]. . . .'[35] This provides a link between the Ciceronian passage and a scholium on Apollonius Rhodius (ii. 498):

When the Dog Star was oppressing the Cyclades with its heat and for long causing drought and embarrassment, the Ceans as the result of an oracle summoned Aristaeus the son of Apollo and Cyrene from Phthia. He, accompanied by some Arcadians, came to Ceos and founded the temple of Zeus Ikmaios, in order to cause rain; and he appeased the Dog Star. And he ordered the Ceans to observe the rising of the Dog Star each year under arms and to sacrifice to it. It was as a result of this that the etesian winds blow, and cool the earth in the summer heat [cf. Call. *Aet.*, fr. 75. 32–37]. So Greece was freed from the drought.

(Apollonius himself says much the same in ii. 516–27: the oracle mentioned by the scholiast was given by Apollo, though the poet does not say that it was the Ceans specifically who summoned Aristaeus; the latter left Phthia at the bidding of Apollo and settled in Ceos—he too, then, had received an oracle (519).)

This account of Aristaeus can be expanded yet further from Diodorus (iv. 82):

They say that Aristaeus, after the death of Actaeon, visited his father's oracle, where Apollo foretold to him his migration to Ceos and the honours he would receive from the Ceans. He went to the island, and as Greece was suffering from a plague [λοιμοῦ: Apollonius (ii. 519) says they summoned Aristaeus λοιμοῦ ἀλεξητῆρα] he sacrificed on behalf of all the Greeks.[36] As this took place at the rising of Sirius, when the etesian winds happened to be blowing, the plague ended . . . [here ensues what appears to be an aside by Diodorus]. They say that Aristaeus left offspring in Ceos and returned to Libya to his mother, then sailed for Sardinia, which island, captivated by its beauty, he reduced from wilderness to cultivation. There he begot two children, Charmus and Polycarpus. Afterwards he visited other islands and spent some time in Sicily, where he was inspired by the fruitfulness of the island to give the natives the benefit of his own discoveries [the arts of beekeeping, &c.]. For this reason they say that Aristaeus receives divine honours from the Sicilians above all others, especially from those who harvest the olive. Finally they tell how he went to Dionysus[37] in Thrace, was initiated into his mysteries, and passing his time with the god learnt much of utility from him. After dwelling some time in the neighbourhood of Mount Haemus he disappeared (ἄφαντον γενέσθαι), and has earned worship not only there among the barbarians but also in Greece.[38]

This I suspect to be all Heraclidean: the association with, and instruction by, divine beings (cf. Zoroaster [159], Epimenides [156], and Phormio's friendship with the Dioscuri [162]); the consultation of the oracle (Heraclides was fond of oracles, cf. frr. 46b, 50, 65, 130, 136, 138 W.); the ambivalent attitude to the miraculous, which is sometimes accepted, sometimes explained away (the prayer to avert the drought or plague was successful because it coincided with the blowing of the etesian winds; this looks as if it were a scientific explanation of a tradition in which the winds blew as a result of Aristaeus' supplications. Compare the method of prognostication from the look of the Dog Star in Cicero, the varied theories of Empedocles' end, the scientific explanation of catalepsy and of Epimenides' ability to do without food).

The several references here to the conferment of divine honours on Aristaeus as a teacher of men are also remarkable, and recall what we have heard of Pythagoras, Empedocles, Hermotimus, and Aristeas himself. In fact, there are two further points of contact with traditions about Aristeas: the mysterious final disappearance of Aristaeus, and the special reverence in which he was held by the Sicilians. There is good evidence for this last in Cicero (*Verr.* II. iv. 128), and it accounts for the curious story that the Proconnesian was worshipped by the Sicilians [129 f.]. This is not, I think, a *confusion* of Aristeas with Aristaeus, so much as deliberate adaptation or contamination of two different traditions in the manner of Heraclides: on the foundation that the Sicilians give heroic honours to Aristaeus because he helped farmers has been erected the fiction that they give heroic honours to Aristeas the Proconnesian because he helped philosophers—or more properly, perhaps, a philosopher, Pythagoras, to whom Aristeas imparted, or with whom he discussed, divine knowledge gained 'in the soul'.[39] (Though we know of 'Pythagoreanism' in Sicily—at Acragas—as early as the first quarter of the fifth century B.C., there is no evidence that the Master himself was ever there: but the scene of Pythagoras' discussion with Abaris in the περὶ δικαιο-σύνης of Heraclides was the court of Phalaris, tyrant of Acragas.)

It is by a similar postulate that I would account for the appearance of 'Aristeas of Metapontum' in the catalogue of early Pythagoreans [142]. It was in Heraclides' manner to use the same characters in different works: Pythagoras featured not only in the proem to the περὶ τῆς ἄπνου but also in the *Zoroaster*, the περὶ δικαιοσύνης, and with Empedotimus; Abaris, in the περὶ δικαιο-σύνης, and he must at least have been mentioned in the περὶ τῶν εἰς Ἄβαριν ἀναφερομένων, as was Aristeas not only in one of the works on oracles but very possibly also in the περὶ τῆς ἄπνου; his name occurred too in yet another book, which we have not before considered—probably *On the Date of Homer and Hesiod*.

The Christian Father, Tatian, is concerned to show [T. 27] that Moses was 'not only older than Homer, but older than all the writers that were before Homer: older than Linus, Philammon, Thamyris, Amphion, Musaeus, Orpheus, Demodocus, Phemius, the Sibyl, Epimenides of Crete, he who went to Sparta, Aristaeus of Proconnesus, who wrote the *Arimaspea*, Asbolus the Centaur, Isatis, Drymon, Euclus the Cyprian, Horus the Samian, and

Pronapides the Athenian'.[40] The Heraclidean provenance of this list is immediately indicated by the characterization of Epimenides: it was that earlier incarnation of Epimenides [161], for the contemporary of Pythagoras was certainly not older than Homer. And this indication is reinforced by the fact that Heraclides elsewhere spoke of the Sibyl (as older than Orpheus—fr. 130 W.), and of Linus, Philammon, Thamyris, Amphion, Demodocus, and Phemius as early musicians, to whom he actually assigns not only historicity but works (fr. 157 W.): to Philammon a 'Birth of Leto and of Artemis and Apollo',[41] to Thamyris a 'Titanomachia', to Demodocus a 'Sack of Troy' and 'Marriage of Aphrodite and Hephaestus' (obviously suggested by *Od.* viii. 492 ff. and 266 ff.), to Phemius a 'Homecoming of Agamemnon's Army' (from *Od.* i. 326 f.).[42] Heraclides may have dated Aristeas early because of the chronology of Herodotus (iv. 15), or because he thought that the one-eyed Arimaspi were the model for Homer's Cyclopes, which seems to have been the reason why someone made Aristeas a teacher of Homer [T. 7; 26].[43]

But if Aristeas wrote the *Arimaspea* before Homer's time he could not have conversed in the flesh with Pythagoras, who for Heraclides, as we have seen, was a contemporary of Phalaris. He must, then, have done so either in a later incarnation, or in the spirit, as a ghostly manifestation. I believe that it was the latter, an elaboration by Heraclides of the Herodotean tale of the appearance of Aristeas' ghost in Italy centuries after his disappearance; that not only did Heraclides speak of appearances of Aristeas in Sicily but also in Metapontum (as in Herodotus; hence Aristeas is called a Metapontine in Iamblichus' list); that he claimed to have come from Apollo's country, the land of the Hyperboreans (in Herodotus he said that he was the companion of Apollo, and he had told of the Hyperboreans in his poem); that he imparted to Pythagoras knowledge of things terrestrial and celestial which he had gained when his soul was freed from its body [121 f.]; and that the Metapontines set up a bronze laurel in commemoration of this visitation [123] (in Herodotus it had been a statue of Aristeas surrounded by real laurels). My argument is spun from such slender threads that it is unwarrantedly audacious to conjecture in which dialogue this interview may have occurred; nevertheless, it would suit quite well one of the works *On the Soul*, in which we know Heraclides was at pains to prove the actual existence of the Hyperboreans (fr. 102 W.).

I would venture farther and put it that we possess a fragment of this discourse of Aristeas. There is in 'Suidas' this curious entry (*s.* Ἄβαρις) : 'The Avars were utterly wiped out by the Bulgars. These Avars drove out the Sabinores, having themselves been compelled to emigrate by tribes inhabiting the shores of the Ocean but driven out of their country by a fog bred of the Ocean overflowing and by the appearance of a multitude of griffins, about which there was a saying [oracle?] that they would not stop until they had devoured the entire human race. Under pressure from these terrors they assaulted their neighbours, who, proving weaker than the invaders, had to emigrate' (ὅτι τοὺς Ἀβάρις οἱ Βούλγαροι κατὰκράτος ἄρδην ἠφάνισαν. ὅτι οἱ Ἀβάρις οὗτοι ἐξήλασαν Σαβίνωρας, μετανάσται γενόμενοι ὑπὸ ἐθνῶν οἰκούντων μὲν τὴν παρωκεανῖτιν ἀκτήν, τὴν δὲ χώραν ἀπολιπόντων διὰ τὸ ἐξ ἀναχύσεως τοῦ Ὠκεανοῦ ὁμιχλῶδες γινόμενον, καὶ γρυπῶν δὲ πλῆθος ἀναφανέν· ὅπερ ἦν λόγος [*leg.* λόγιον?] μὴ πρότερον παύσασθαι πρὶν ἢ βορὰν ποιῆσαι τὸ τῶν ἀνθρώπων γένος. διὸ δὴ ὑπὸ τῶνδε ἐλαυνόμενοι τῶν δεινῶν τοῖς πλησιοχώροις ἐνέβαλλον· καὶ τῶν ἐπιόντων δυνατωτέρων ὄντων οἱ τὴν ἔφοδον ὑφιστάμενοι μετανίσταντο). This is clearly a weird distortion of Herodotus' summary of the account given in the *Arimaspea* about the migratory pressures of the central Asiatic peoples ([T. 1]: αἰεὶ τοῖσι πλησιοχώροισι ἐπιτίθεσθαι—cf. τοῖς πλησιοχώροις in 'Suidas'). There it was not 'the inhabitants of the shores of the Ocean' (i.e. the Hyperboreans, 'whose country extended to the sea') who began the movement as here, but the inland Arimaspi; there the griffins were not a mob that suddenly appeared and threatened the destruction of mankind but the permanent guardians of the gold of those parts. The fog and the inroads of the Ocean (ἀνάχυσις τοῦ Ὠκεανοῦ) are an importation (Heraclides knew about the Atlantic tides: fr. 117 W.) ; it is noteworthy that one of the things that the soul of Aristeas saw in its flight between heaven and earth in the account of Maximus was 'inroads of the sea' (ἀναχύσεις θαλάττης [122]).[44]

This seems, then, to be from Aristeas, but it is not the Aristeas of the *Arimaspea*. I think that we have here another Heraclidean adaptation: he has worked up hints given by the author of the *Arimaspea* as reported in Herodotus' summary, and put them into the mouth of Aristeas in his own work. But why should this fantasy come to be mixed in with the history of the Avars in 'Suidas'' article? Because the Avars have the same name as Abaris the Hyperborean, and Heraclides' Aristeas was giving the reason why Abaris was coming to Greece: for help against a scourge that was already causing his countrymen to move, and threatened to be universal ('they say that on the occasion of a world-wide plague Greeks and barbarians consulted Apollo, who bade the Athenians pray on behalf of all [cf. 168, and note 36]. Many peoples sent ambassadors to them, among whom came Abaris from the Hyperboreans', Harpocr. *s.* Ἄβαρις). A memory of this, I suggest, has caused the muddle in 'Suidas' (the relevant passage is not in Priscus (Müller, *F.H.G.* iv. 104 f.)).

It is, then, in the Aristeas of Heraclides that we should see the origin of Aristeas the Pythagorean, the seer, traveller 'in the soul', and religious teacher, now well fitted to have a *Theogony* ascribed to him [31 f.]; it is the source of that dichotomy in the tradition about the limit of Aristeas' travels [133 f.], and accounts for the date given by 'Suidas' for Aristeas, the fiftieth Olympiad [126]: that is, in the time of Phalaris (who was 'tyrant of the whole of Sicily in the fifty-second Olympiad', according to 'Suidas', *s.* Φάλαρις), with whom, according to Heraclides, Pythagoras was contemporaneous [169].

What manner of man was the author of these curiosities? Heraclides was born in Heraclea Pontica some time between 388 and 373. From there he moved to Athens, in 364 or earlier, and joined the Academy (Voss 8 ff.). Voss disbelieves Diogenes' statement (v. 86) that Heraclides also heard the Pythagoreans, but on insufficient grounds; there is no impossibility in it, for a younger contemporary, Aristoxenus, was a pupil of Xenophilus, one of the 'last of the Pythagoreans', at Athens. In 338 Heraclides was nearly elected to the headship of the Academy in succession to Speusippus; after this narrow defeat he returned to Heraclea, where he was still alive about 315 (Voss 18 f.). There is a tradition that made him a Peripatetic also, and Sotion said that he was a disciple of Aristotle, but this can hardly mean that he was a member of the Lyceum (Voss 13 f.). He must indeed have known Aristotle well when they were both pupils of Plato (there was little difference in their ages), but I think that his characterization as a Peripatetic is based on no more than the wide extent of his interests, in the way of that school.

He was said to be very fat, gentle, and dignified in appearance; and Diogenes has a queer tale to tell about his end (v. 91). Heraclea was suffering from a famine, and the people consulted Delphi for a remedy. Heraclides bribed the envoys to produce a forged oracle, to the effect that the city must crown him with a gold crown and give him heroic honours after his death; but as he was being crowned in the theatre he was seized with a fit. The author of this story was the liar Hermippus, to whom perhaps should also be ascribed what looks like a sequel (preserved through Demetrius Magnes and Hippobotus: D.L. v. 90; cf. H.P., fr. 17 W.): when on the point of death, Heraclides ordered a confidant to substitute a snake for his corpse upon the bier, whose appearance would lead the onlookers to suppose that the dead man had become a hero (cf. Cumont 394); but the fraud was discovered. Here it looks as if Heraclides' own propensities—his interest in oracles, the punishment for impiety, the conferment of divine honours upon men, even his suggestion of deception in the attainment of the latter (cf. Empedocles)— have been turned against him: the fiction has been built up out of hints gleaned from his own work, even as he himself had built up such fictions out of hints gleaned from the work of others.

Even the forged oracle in this tale may be an extension of the reputation which Heraclides had for the perpetration of literary forgeries. For not only did he invent works which he ascribed to fictitious personages [170], but he forged 'plays of Thespis' [20], and at least two oracles which he quotes are highly suspect.[45] We have already seen reason to believe that the fragments of the *Arimaspea*, if not genuine, are fourth-century forgeries [20]: in Heraclides we may have their author.

It is clear that any evidence about anything that can be traced to the authority of Heraclides must be treated with the greatest reserve. It is also clear that it cannot be peremptorily dismissed as sheer invention, for the elements out of which he moulded his fancies were often provided by earlier literature or tradition. The difficulty is to distinguish these elements from the peculiar twist that he has given them. We are not, for instance, entitled to conclude that Aristeas had no connexion with Pythagoras before Heraclides; indeed, there is reason to suppose the contrary.

A reader of Herodotus' story about the appearance of Aristeas' ghost at Metapontum must wonder about both the message the apparition gave and the choice of messenger. Why did he say that Apollo visited the Metapontines alone of the Italiotes, and why should it be Aristeas who was selected to announce this, an antique poet from an island on the other side of the Greek world, having no connexion with Metapontum? It is a type of story to appeal to the Pythagorean mind[46]—the still-living soul of Aristeas reincarnated in the raven and accompanying Apollo, the favourite god of Pythagoreanism.[47] It will not be forgotten that Pythagoras ended his days at Metapontum, after he had left Croton; and at the latter place he had been dubbed, according to Aristotle (*ap.* Ael. *V.H.* ii. 26), 'the Hyperborean Apollo'. Why *Hyperborean*? We may have here an important clue: for the Hyperboreans, the special people of Apollo, figured in the *Arimaspea*. What is more, they were the prototypes of an important side of the Pythagorean way of life, for Hellanicus, in a fragment which has signs of deriving from Aristeas' poem, said that they 'practised righteousness by abstaining from meat and living on fruit' [71 f.]. It is, then, possible that the answer to all these questions is this: that Pythagoras, who particularly reverenced Apollo, the god of music, was also specially interested in the *Arimaspea*, whose author had clearly been a favourite of the same god, having been possessed by him. In the poem it was stated that a feature of the righteousness of the Hyperboreans was their vegetarianism; it would follow that vegetarianism must particularly commend itself to their god, and so Pythagoras adopted it.[48] From his support of his tenet by appeal to this authority, and from his demeanour as of one more than human (cf. Aristotle *ap.* Iambl. *V.P.* 31), he came to be called by the Crotoniates 'the Hyperborean Apollo'—whether seriously or in jest does not matter: it was taken seriously by his disciples. After the move to Metapontum from Croton it occurred to them to try to win countenance for their sect by introducing the idea there that their leader was the embodiment of Apollo, who thus favoured the Metapontines alone with his presence. The introduction was engineered by means of a 'supernatural revelation'; and what better instrument could be chosen to make such a revelation than that poet who had been beloved by both Apollo and Pythagoras, who had himself sung of the Hyperboreans, Aristeas of Proconnesus?[49]

VIII

CONCLUSION

In the survey of possible debtors to the *Arimaspea* I said that primary clues would be provided by what Herodotus tells us of the poem's contents: mention in other authors of one or more of the Issedonians, Arimaspi, griffins, and possibly Hyperboreans, would make a significant context. In this way, by interlocking one with another, a number of passages were brought under review. Moreover, besides establishing an upper terminus for the poem (the Cimmerian invasion of Asia Minor), the résumé of Herodotus also revealed an important fact about the poet: his veracity. He gave an historically true account of the westerly pressure of the peoples of the steppe, and his one-eyed men and gold-guarding monsters were actual creatures of central Asiatic folk-lore. Claims, then, for borrowings from the *Arimaspea* should fulfil two requirements to be acceptable: their matter should be in, or at least near, a significant context in the sense outlined above, and should reflect historical truth about, or the actual folk-lore of, the Eurasian and central Asiatic regions. It remains to summarize the results of these tests.

The Rhipaean mountains. Damastes repeats Aristeas' order of peoples from the Scyths to the outer sea, omitting the griffins. Between the Arimaspi and the Hyperboreans he places the Rhipaean mountains, always snow-bound, from which Boreas begins his course. They were incredibly high, according to Aristotle. Pliny puts this range near the Arimaspi, in the region called 'Featherful' (*Pterophoros*) from the perpetual snows; the North Wind has his origin from a cave there which bears his name. According to the pseudo-Plutarch the so-called Cave of Boreas was by the river Tanais. Caves of the Winds appear in the folk-lore of northern Asia, and there was a famous one near the Dzungarian Gate.

There are indications that this range was not originally called

'Rhipaean' but 'Caucasus'. The pseudo-Plutarch says that the Caucasus was at first called 'the Lair of Boreas'; Aeschylus, in a significant context, puts his—immensely high—Caucasus in the place normally assigned to the Rhipaeans; later geographers sometimes identified the Rhipaeans with the Caucasus, or held that the former were a continuation of the latter; the source of the Tanais was located in both.

The Region of Feathers. This, associated by Pliny with the Rhipaean mountains and Arimaspi, was reported by the Scyths and their neighbours (Issedonians?) as hindering sight and progress, according to Herodotus. As it is also put by an early Chinese source in central or northern Asia it must have been a piece of local folk-lore. The fact that it was impossible to see there may underlie descriptions of the Rhipaeans as murky or benighted (e.g. Sophocles, Pliny), and account for the strange mis-statement of Hippocrates, that Scythia is perpetually fog-bound (in a passage where he speaks of the Rhipaeans in language like that of Damastes).

The Arimaspi. They are said by Herodotus to steal gold from the griffins. For Aeschylus they are one-eyed horsemen living by an auriferous river; Dionysius also places them by a river, in company with the griffins. In art the opponents of the griffins are sometimes depicted as horsemen. Robbers who seize their loot and flee on horseback occur in old central Asiatic story, and the Arimaspi might have been some of the first Mongols to learn to ride. Gold is found in plenty in some parts of central Asia—even in rivers, though Aeschylus' Pluton *might* only 'flow with gold' because it was used for washing the ore.

The griffins. Pausanias actually says that the *Arimaspea* described them as a mixture of lion and eagle. As such they were a Mediterranean conceit, though the old Chinese tell of a 'winged tiger' in the neighbourhood of the one-eyed Kuei. Central Asiatic tales ascribed to monstrous ants the role of Aristeas' griffins; they apparently extruded the gold as they made their holes, as the griffins are said to do by Pliny (Dionysius says they dug it up).

Gorgons and Graeae. Aeschylus, in a significant context, locates them strangely, apparently in the north-east of the world (Pindar puts the Gorgons near the Hyperboreans) : they live in darkness, and the Graeae are 'swan-shaped'. Central Asiatic lore knows of fierce and ugly 'swan-maidens', who live in Stygian darkness and can fly.

Amazons. In the same context, Aeschylus places Amazons oddly, by the Sea of Azov. Amazons sometimes replace male warriors in artistic grypomachies. Actual sociological features of aboriginal tribes could explain their location in Scythia.

Cannibals figure in significant contexts in Pliny and others and are mentioned among Scythian peoples by Herodotus. The one-eyed men themselves are said to be cannibals in a Ukrainian tale about the Tatars.

The Issedonians. These were not on the north-easterly trade-route, and Aristeas is the only Greek we know who claimed to have reached them. It may be assumed therefore that Herodotus' account of their customs comes from the *Arimaspea.* This account need not have been an invention; in fact it is very unlikely to have been, for, strange as Issedonian manners would have appeared to a Greek, they all have historical parallels. Herodotus' statement that they 'faced' the Massagetae may not be from the poem (there is no reason to suppose that his other statement, that they were to the east of the Argippaei, was), though his poetic language here may point to it. According to Zenothemis (supported perhaps by a muddled remark of Aelian), they lived by a river. Alcman spoke of the Issedonians (as well as the Rhipaeans, dark and forested); he, therefore, together with the Kelermes grypomachy, gives us a lower terminus for the *Arimaspea.*

One of the doublet stories which Herodotus tells about the Scythian prince Colaxais and his two brothers may come from the *Arimaspea,* as Alcman also seems to have known the name (*Colaxes?*). (It may be remarked that this type of folk-tale, of the successful youngest brother and his two unsuccessful elder brothers, though common among some other peoples was foreign to ancient Greece.)

I would claim the *Phasis-Tanais* and the *vegetarianism* of the Hyperboreans for the *Arimaspea* on other grounds: the former because Aeschylus so identified them in the *Prometheus* trilogy, which seems to have contained so much from this early poem (and such an identification could only have been made very early); the latter, by linking a fragment of Hellanicus with the use made of Aristeas by the first Pythagoreans. There may be more matter from the *Arimaspea* lurking in other passages I have discussed in the course of this book; but if so, I do not see how it can be isolated.

I end with an hypothesis which embodies my main conclusions and, I think, 'saves the phenomena' economically. I beg the reader to forgive the categorical tone of this, which is not intended to reflect the certainty of revelation.

Aristeas the son of Caystrobius flourished in Proconnesus in the third quarter of the seventh century before Christ. He was devoted to Apollo, with a fervour more commonly felt by the initiates of Dionysus for their god. At this time the Greeks were reconnoitring the west and north coasts of the Black Sea, 'beyond' the north wind Boreas, whose home was popularly thought to be in Thrace. It must have seemed that they were penetrating the regions of the blessed Hyperboreans, the favourites of Apollo, and when news of such an expedition from Cyzicus reached Proconnesus Aristeas felt impelled to join it in order to find the country of his god. This urge was so compulsive that it took the form of a psychosomatic disturbance which to his fellow citizens seemed to be a death and resurrection, and to Aristeas himself to constitute actual possession by Apollo.

Aristeas' goal proved to be more distant than he had expected. The home of Boreas was not in Thrace after all; but, undaunted, Aristeas landed, perhaps in the neighbourhood of the Sea of Azov, and headed inland, determined to find it. But now he had no bearings, and no way of identifying Boreas save by its force and bitterness; so the course of his slow progress came to be directed into the teeth of the east rather than of the north wind. This reorientation would have been aided by the fact that the Scythian tribes, on whose hospitality he must have depended, were themselves still strung out over the Eurasian steppe in the act of migration, and would naturally pass him back along the way they themselves had come. As he went, he seemed to recognize features of legend that he had heard at home—the

Phasis of Argonautic story in the Tanais, Amazons in the masculine ladies of the Sauromatae. His Scythian hosts also told him of
the patriarch from whom they were descended.

At last, in the region of the head waters of the Ishim, he passed
from the Scythians to another people, the Issedonians. Among
them he sojourned for some time, and from them he learned news
of what he sought. They told him that beyond them were lofty
storm-wrapt mountains—the western outliers of the central
Asiatic highlands—which they called by a name Aristeas interpreted as 'Caucasus', whence a furious wind issued from a cavern.
This cavern he took to be the source of the 'blasts of Boreas',
beyond which the Hyperboreans must live their idyllic life; and
when his informants also told him of the settled civilization of
the cereal-eating Chinese, whose territory extended from beyond
the mountains down to the sea, he thought they were speaking of
these very Hyperboreans.

Almost within sight of success, however, he heard also of
dangers and terrors ahead. The Issedonians said that they had
been pushed away from the mountains by the Arimaspi, whom
they described as horsemen having only one eye. These people
now dwelt about an auriferous river, and purloined the gold of
those parts from the guardianship of swift and fierce monsters.
Whether the name 'griffin' given to these was Issedonian or
not, their shape was Greek, conferred upon them by Aristeas
himself from his memory of half-leonine, half-aquiline monsters
he had seen depicted by artists at home. Similarly also, when he
was told of other monsters living in the region of darkness,
hideous and murderous 'swan-maidens' who could doff their
feathers and become hags, Aristeas identified them with the
Gorgons and Graeae of Greek legend. The list of horrors was
capped with tales of cannibals (though these may have been
Scythian rather than Issedonian lore) and a land where ever-
falling feathers hampered sight and progress. Aristeas decided
to turn back.

Of the Issedonians themselves he noted that they were a
nomadic (or semi-nomadic) people, whose women did a man's
job, and who venerated their fathers to the extent of eating them

when dead and preserving their skulls, encased in gold, as cult objects. He may have added that their (southern) neighbours were the Massagetae.

On his return to Proconnesus more than six years after he had set out, Aristeas related his experiences in a hexameter poem, which Greeks later called the *Arimaspea*. In this he faithfully distinguished his own first-hand witness from hearsay, and also reported accurately the westerly drive of the peoples of the Eurasian steppe which had already caused the Cimmerian invasion of Asia Minor.[1] After this he disappeared a second time from Proconnesus, perhaps on another expedition to the land of the Hyperboreans, from which there was to be no homecoming; it is pleasing to fancy that this time his persistence was rewarded, and that he ended his days in China!

The poem quickly contributed to literature, art, and geography. Through it Scythia became known as the home of griffins, and Greek artists used them, and their rivalry with the savage Arimaspi, as a decorative motif for wares destined for the Scythian market; whence native Scythian artists then borrowed the griffin. Aristeas' identification of the Argonautic Phasis with the Tanais did not hold for long, but explorers who knew the *Arimaspea* and were looking for the lofty range of Caucasus in that area thought they had found it in the high mountains bordering the eastern shores of the Euxine, which as a result were to bear the name thereafter.

A Hesiodic poet portrayed the griffin, after the *Arimaspea*; and from it Alcman learned of the gloomy, wooded mountain of the storm-wind, of the Issedonians, and of the Scythian Colaxes. The Scythian Amazons reappear in Pindar, Aeschylus, and Euripides, and a later Greek attempt to account for their presence there is preserved by Herodotus. It is these Amazons who sometimes replace male warriors in the grypomachies of vase-painters. Aristeas' unorthodox location of the Gorgons in the neighbourhood of the Hyperboreans is repeated by Pindar and Aeschylus. His Caucasus, home of Boreas, which was not heard of again by the Greeks until the time of Alexander, suffered a dichotomy at the hands of Ionian geographers, on the one hand being mistaken for the range which still bears its name, and on the other being slewed round to the proper position of Boreas, the cardinal north, to form a non-existent 'Rhipaean' range spanning northern Europe and Asia from west to east. The effect of this can still be seen in Aeschylus' curious position for his Caucasus, in the pseudo-Plutarch's statement that the Caucasus was once called 'the Lair of Boreas', and in ancient theories that the Rhipaeans were a spur of the Caucasus.

If 'Longinus' has preserved for us a genuine fragment of the *Arimaspea*, Aristeas also told of a sort of mermen leading a miserable existence in the waves of the sea; but the authenticity of this as of the other professed quotations from the poem is still debatable. The work was yet current in the fifth century B.C., but may soon have disappeared: it does not seem to have been known to the Alexandrian librarians, and Latin authorities, though they know of Aristeas, do not name his poem or even give any hint that he composed a *poem* at all. We need not suppose that anyone ever produced another, spurious, *Arimaspea* in its entirety: the fragments we possess may be no more than faked 'quotations' from it in a prose work—perhaps by Heraclides Ponticus in the fourth century B.C., who practised literary forgery and was interested in Aristeas, Hyperboreans, and the bizarre.

Even so, at least those fragments preserved by Tzetzes may embody matter derived from the genuine *Arimaspea* through the mediation of Ionian geographers; and it is probably thanks to such intermediaries that Hellenistic and Roman writers occasionally reproduce matter from the authentic *Arimaspea* that is not in Herodotus' summary.

The poem was known to another devotee of Apollo, Pythagoras of Samos. From it he learned that Apollo's righteous Hyperboreans were vegetarians, and so adopted as a religious tenet a practice so acceptable to his god, and earned himself the nickname of 'the Hyperborean Apollo'. After his enforced move from Croton to Metapontum, his followers, to win esteem for their master's teachings in the new place, put about the story of a divine revelation that the Metapontines had been especially favoured by a visitation of the god, and chose as the vehicle for this revelation the ghost of Aristeas, Apollo's possessed and Pythagoras' own authority for one of his most striking injunctions.

This early connexion of Pythagoras with Aristeas was exploited further in the fourth-century Academy, by Heraclides Ponticus, who moulded a number of earlier misty 'mystery-men' to a set pattern of friendship with Pythagoras, wonder-working, reincarnation, divination, and trance. In the trance state, when their bodies lay as if dead while their souls wandered forth, these people gained preternatural knowledge not only of far parts of the earth but of divine truths. The inspiration for this idea of Heraclides came from his master Plato, but its particular application to Aristeas was no doubt suggested to him by Herodotus' story of Aristeas' apparent death, resurrection, and subsequent ghostly reappearance far from Proconnesus.

It was under the influence of the popular Heraclides that for later generations Aristeas became a 'theologian', and the extraordinary journey he had actually made in the body became a mythical journey that he made in the spirit; and his association, whether as ghost or reincarnation, with Pythagoras in the same author's imagination caused his date to be given in the sixth century B.C. The reputation of the old wizard of Proconnesus lingered on in nearby Byzantium until the fourteenth century; it may still linger somewhere today, connected as ever with strange things, for the ship which in 1938 fished up a living coelacanth, as it were from the Mesozoic era, was called *Aristea*.

NOTES (pp. 1–14)

CHAPTER I

1. The translations of Herodotus in this book are based on that by Rawlinson (Everyman ed.).

2. Stephanus Byzantius, s. Ἰσσηδόνες, who may owe this information to the work of Alexander Polyhistor (first century B.C.) περὶ τῶν παρ' Ἀλκμᾶνι τοπικῶς εἰρημένων (or ἱστορημένων)—cf. s. Ἀράξαι, Ἀσσός.

3. If the form used by Alcman were really Ἀσεδόνες or Ἀσσεδόνες (vid. Meineke's app. crit. to Stephanus), or Ἐσσεδόνες (Schneidewin, Coniectanea Critica 28), this theory could hardly be maintained. But it may in fact have been Ἀσσηδόνες (Lobel in The Bodleian Quarterly Record iv (1923), 48: Pap. Ox. 1611 appears to give Ἀσσηδών as an alternative form of Ἰσσηδών, cf. Herodian, περὶ μονήρους λέξεως α' 9₁₇). It may be just worth noting that the places apropos of which Stephanus mentioned the work of Alexander named in note 2 both begin with A, and the other strange places which Stephanus says occurred in Alcman also begin with A—Ἀννίχωρον and Ἄρυββα. There are few other references to Alcman in Stephanus; perhaps for some reason he knew only that part of Alexander's book that dealt with names beginning with A. The Romans spell this people with an initial E (Val. Fl. vi. 750 perhaps excepted), the second syllable being long in the poets.

4. I am not completely convinced that ἡμῖν in Od. i. 10 (τῶν ἁμόθεν γε, θεά, θύγατερ Διός, εἰπὲ καὶ ἡμῖν) is not the equivalent of μοι in l. 1. The καί in l. 10 might be taken (i) with τῶν (= the companions of Odysseus)— 'tell us [poet and audience] of these men too [as well as of Odysseus]': but this seems an incredible postponement; (ii) with ἡμῖν—'tell us too [as well as other poets and audiences] of these things (τῶν)': but ἁμόθεν—'taking up the tale from any point you like'—implies that there was a corpus of the adventures of Odysseus already in existence, and the poet could hardly thus assume that his audience was ignorant of them; (iii) with ἡμῖν—'tell me too [as well as other poets who have sung of Odysseus] of these things': this seems to me the most natural, but the lack of certain parallels counsel caution.

5. I wish I could be sure that these curious people were not the same as the Sciapods, who lay on the ground and shaded their bodies from the sun with their single huge feet as with a parasol (Ctesias ap. Harpocr. s. Σκιάποδες; Plin. N.H. vii. 23).

6. Il. i. 53–58, x. 465–70, xxii. 331–6; Od. i. 126–31, xix. 4–9, xxiv. 57–62; Hes. Op. 83–88, 618–23, Scut. 261–6; Call. H. iv 28–33, fr. 260. 62–67; Ap. Rhod. i. 569–74, iv. 1318–23; Simias, fr. 1. 1–6, fr. 6; Delphic oracles ap. Hdt. vi. 86 γ 2. 1–6, vii. 140. 2. 1–6.

7. Epicharmus ἐν Ἡρακλεῖ τῷ παρὰ Φόλῳ (fr. 7. 2) has the earlier sense οἴομαι δ' οὐδεὶς ἑκὼν πονηρὸς οὐδ' ἄταν ἔχων. So too Aesch., fr. 401 Sidgwick, though the fragment is suspect (the sense of l. 1, ζόης πονηρᾶς θάνατος αἱρετώτερος, may have been rather that of fr. 90, βίου πονηροῦ θάνατος

εὐκλεέστερος but glossed by ll. 2 f. to give it the meaning of, for example, Eur. *Hec.* 377 f.). The meaning of 'grievous' assigned to the word at Ar. *Pl.* 352 (τουτὶ πονηρὸν φαίνεται τὸ φορτίον) ill suits the context, which requires something like 'here's a load of mischief', 'a bad lot' (cf. Eur. *I.T.* 1306).

8. As it happens, we are able to witness the digestive process applied to the very fragment of the *Catalogus* under consideration, in the account of the ἐπιπώλησις of the herds of Augeas in the Ἡρακλῆς λεοντοφόνος ([Theocr.] xxv. 85 ff.). Here we meet ἀπειρεσίων in l. 100, πολύρρηνες in l. 117, ἀφνειὸν μήλοις in l. 119, and εἰλιπόδεσσιν in l. 131.

9. It is odd that nearby are two words recurring in fr. 4—ἀνθρώπων and ἀφνειότατος (*Il.* xx. 217; 220). Does this mean that frr. 3 and 4 were in fact closely conjoined? Dion. P. 953 is also related to *Il.* xx. 222.

10. Hesychius has a gloss πευκαλεῖται· ξηραίνεται. ἢ ἀντὶ τοῦ ζητεῖται. Ἀριστέας. Onions (*Origins of European Thought* 31) suggests that this may be the Proconnesian or the grammarian: the fragments of the former (if they are his) do not show any propensity for rare words, and why should Hesychius quote this unmetrical form? The latter seems more likely (for him cf. Varro, *L.L.* x. 75).

11. Fränkel (320, n. 6) thinks that the repetition might be deliberate; but what the point could then be is obscure.

12. It *may* be evidence of oral composition: cf. Dodds on 'decayed' epithets, in Platnauer's *Fifty Years of Classical Scholarship* 14 f., 34. If so, it would argue for the genuineness of the fragment.

CHAPTER II

1. The authority who reports Heraclides' fraud was a contemporary, Aristoxenus, a malicious man (cf. fr. 67), who, however, may here be telling the truth [VII].

2. Galen, *in Hippocr. de nat. hom.* (xv. 109) (where we should read [ἢ] περὶ τὰς ἐπιγραφάς?). Juba II was also duped: *David. scholl. Aristot.* 28a Brandis, quoted by Mullach, *Philosophorum Graecorum Fragmenta* i. 411.

3. *Consolatio*: no. 283 N. (*fr. phil.* ix M. for fragments of the genuine work). See J. A. Farrer, *Literary Forgeries* 5 ff. Φοινικικά: Farrer 191. If the *Culex* extant in the first century A.D. was not the poem we now possess we should have another example; but this is quite uncertain.

4. My supplementation was published by C. A. Trypanis in his Loeb edition of the fragments of Callimachus (98 f.).

5. Pfeiffer in his edition of Callimachus (on fr. 186. 12) regards it as uncertain whether Callimachus did in fact identify the two peoples. But surely *H.* iv. 291 ff. proves it: there either the 'daughters of Boreas' must be Arimaspian, or the Arimaspi must stand for the Hyperboreans. The former would be hard to maintain in the face of the names and parentage of the girls (cf. Hdt. iv. 35 (Opis); [Plato], *Axiochus* 371a (Opis and Hecaerge); Serv. auct. *ad Aen.* xi. 532; Hec. Abd. *ap.* Diod. Sic. ii. 47. 7 (descendants of Boreas held hereditary sway over the Hyperboreans)).

6. *Not* stated by the scholiast on Ar. *Pax* 1270, as Schmid–Stählin assert (i. 205).

7. Meuli (156 f.) thinks more highly of the value of this tradition: for him it is evidence that the Arimaspi are one-eyed infernal beings of Altaic-Turkic and Mongol myth, beings, like the Hyperboreans, not of this world: 'offenbar ist es sehr gute gelehrte Überlieferung, wenn Antimachos, Kallimachos und andere die Arimaspen den Hyperboreern gleichsetzen, und für die endgültige Deutung der Arimaspen wird man dies beachten müssen'; griffins (= dragons defending the Golden Mountain of God) and Arimaspians are genuine products of Scythian folk-lore, 'die nicht in goldsandhaltigen Wüsten oder in Gebirgen mit Goldgruben wohnen, sondern in einem mythischen Jenseits, wie die Hyperboreer; einem Jenseits, in das der Schamane zu reisen pflegte'.

That we are dealing here with traces of genuine 'Scythian' folk-lore I have no doubt; but I doubt very much if the Hyperborean–Arimaspian tradition goes any way to proving the supernatural status of the Arimaspi in that folk-lore. The important point for my present purpose is that this tradition does *not* derive from (the 'shamanizing'!) Aristeas (who plants his Arimaspi very firmly on this earth, calling them ἄνθρωποι (fr. 4. 1; ἄνδρες in fr. 1), who press upon their neighbours the Issedonians).

8. It has been suggested that *de subl.* 10. 5 f. is from Posidonius' σύγκρισις Ὁμήρου καὶ Ἀράτου (Schmid–Stählin ii. 477, n. 4). If so, and if 10. 4 (which is closely connected with 10. 5—cf. ὁ μὲν γὰρ . . . ποιήσας . . . ὁ δὲ Ὅμηρος) is carried with it, it merely takes our problem one stage farther back.

9. Abominable Snowmen? In Pliny's time Imaus ('Snowy', cf. *N.H.* vi. 64: this is correct) was the name given to the easternmost portion of the Himalayas (cf. Strab. 519). Everest expeditions of recent years have heard and told of the swiftness of the Snowman, and the reversal of his feet (he has thus acquired a common characteristic of supernatural beings in the East)! These *silvestres homines* are the ἄγριοι ἄνθρωποι of Megasthenes *ap.* Strab. 711.

10. Cf. Hdt. iv. 64 f.; Anon. Vat. 49.

11. Cf. Antonius Diogenes (508 = Phot. *Bibl.* 109b).

12. Anon. Vat. 50.

13. A similar story in Fife not so long ago (*County Folklore* vii. 11)!

14. On the strength of this chapter of Gellius a predilection for the marvellous has been ascribed to the Magnesian Hegesias (e.g. in Schmid–Stählin ii. 207; Smith, *Dictionary of Greek and Roman Biography* ii. 368). It may be so, but I see that an Agesias of Megara is quoted by the Vatican paradoxographer (1). Is this really our man?

15. Cf. Sen. *Ep.* 90. 16.

16. It could underlie the whole of the second chapter of *N.H.* vii, in spite of the references therein to Cicero and Varro (13; 18; cf. 19): Isigonus used Varro (Schmid–Stählin ii. 420).

17. Eudocia (or whoever the author of the *Violarium* was) may have been led to alter καὶ καταλογάδην Θεογονίαν εἰς ἔπη ᾳ to καὶ Θεογονίαν πάνυ καλῶς through puzzlement at the conjunction of καταλογάδην, 'in prose', with ἔπη, a word usually used of hexameter lines (for its use of prose lines see Crönert 127).

18. I agree with Jacoby (i. 519): 'daß Dionys noch eine prosaschrift des

Aristeas besaß, ist nicht zu entnehmen.' It is not clear from Clement's
Μελησαγόρου γὰρ ἔκλεψεν. ... ὁ Προκοννήσιος Βίων, ὃς καὶ τὰ Κάδμου
τοῦ παλαιοῦ μετέγραψεν κεφαλαιούμενος (Strom. vi. 26. 8) whether the
abridgement of Cadmus by Bion was a frank summary or an intended
forgery. In the context it looks as if some dishonesty is imputed to Bion; if
so, it need only mean that Dionysius here is giving one example from each
of his two categories—writings by Cadmus have survived but are of doubtful authenticity, those of Aristeas have perished.

19. Nissen (299) thinks that Gell. ix. 4 is evidence that there were yet
other books of marvels besides the *Arimaspea* passing under the name of
Aristeas; but the only evidence that Aristeas may have been the author of
anything other than the *Arimaspea* and the (improbable) *Theogony* is the
dubious T. 28 (and what the 'spurious poems' of Peisander there mentioned may have been about we have no idea).

20. The list does not profess to be exhaustive.

CHAPTER III

1. The only exceptions are fr. 3 of Aristeas himself and a line of Zenothemis which may well be based on something in the *Arimaspea* [68]. Mela
(ii. 9; 13) compounds Hdt. iv. 26 and 65.

2. L. & S.[8] are surely wrong in preferring ῥιπαί here, and interpreting
'[the quarter of] the night storms'. See Jebb's note.

3. Cf. Plin. *N.H.* iv. 89; Ant. Diog. (510 = Phot. *Bibl.* 110b–11a). Both
contain errors which should not be imputed to the scientists, represented by,
for example, Cleomedes i. 7; Geminus, *El. astr.* 6 (Geminus here gives the
explanation of *Od.* x. 82–86 by Crates of Mallus: Homer places his Laestry-
gonians near the Arctic circle where ἡ δύσις παράκειται τῇ ἀνατολῇ. That
Homer shows here some inkling ('folk-memory'?) of conditions in the far
north has been accepted by some modern scholars (Minns 436 f.); but
difficulties remain, and it may be that Laestrygonia is a purely imaginary
country enjoying a perpetual twilight).

4. The possibility can almost be discounted that Alcman's fragment refers
to some mountain in Arcadia, near the Rhipe of *Il.* ii. 606. This place was
unknown to the ancient commentators (Strab. 388; Paus. viii. 25. 12; cf.
Page 122). The scholiast on *O.C.* 1248, who quotes the lines of Alcman
and presumably knew their context, does not take them so, though he
must be mistaken in placing the mountain in the far west (a deduction
from ἐννύχιαι).

5. Either both poles or the north must be meant. The ancient notion that
the north pole was higher than the south is well known; but it would not be
natural for a Roman to confine to the south pole a description applying
equally well to either. *Ima* here has the sense of *extrema*: cf. Varr. Atac., fr.
14. 1 f. 'at quinque aetheriis zonis accingitur orbis, ac vastant imas hiemes
mediamque calores'; and Lucan's own use of *infima* at viii. 464. *Iacet*, while
playing upon *ima*, has a metaphorical sense, 'lies torpid and useless'. I say
this because modern scholars have tended to follow Burmann in understanding this passage to refer to the south pole.

6. Not all scholars are agreed on this. Some hold that Anaximenes conceived of the whole plane of the earth's surface as sloping from N. to S. This can only be reconciled with Anaximenes' other theory, that the earth floats on air like a lid (Diels–Kranz i. 94. 24 ἐπιπωματίζειν), if he thought of the earth as a cross-section of a cylinder with the upper surface bevelled. Such an interpretation is obligatory if Anaximenes really held that the motion of the heavenly bodies is lateral in one plane, like that of a millstone, &c. (ibid. i. 92. 16 ff.; 93. 20 f.). But the analogies may be a misunderstanding by later doxographers; for the visible paths of the heavenly bodies appear to be far from lateral, except to dwellers in very high latitudes. I agree with Kiessling that for Anaximenes the heavenly bodies describe their orbits in two planes—in a more vertical one above the horizon and in a lateral one below, or more properly along, it. According to Kiessling the sun is masked at night by the high outer rim of the earth's disk, though he allows that Anaximenes may have reinforced his argument by calling in the aid of the Rhipaean mountains. Though agreeing with much of Kiessling's impressive exposition, I think that he, in common with the supporters of the 'sloping earth' interpretation, credits Anaximenes with more sophistication than he merits. See Zeller–Mondolfo, *La Filosofia dei Greci* I. ii. 219 f.; *P.–W.* iA. 848–50. The (or some) Epicureans appear to have suggested obscuration of the sun by a northern mountain range as the (or more probably, after their manner, one possible) explanation of night; Anaximenes need have been no subtler (Avien. *Or. Mar.* 644–73; the sense seems clear in spite of an unfortunate lacuna in the text. The passage is discussed by Kiessling, *P.–W.* iA. 852 ff. Kiessling (ibid. 850 ff.) would also ascribe a similar view to Heraclitus (fr. 120)—unconvincingly, I think).

7. τὰ δὲ κατύπερθε πρὸς βορέην ἄνεμον τῶν ὑπεροίκων τῆς χώρης. How and Wells seem to me to be wrong in treating ὑπεροίκων as possessive—'lands that lie above to the north, of those who dwell in the upper parts of the country'. I take the ὑπέροικοι to be the same as the περίοικοι of c. 31.

8. ὑπὸ πτερῶν κεχυμένων. The verb combines the ideas of both *falling* and *heaping up*.

9. This was suggested by A. A. Blakeway (C. M. Bowra, *Greek Lyric Poetry* 66).

Aristeas' form of the name might have been Κόλαξος (Hec. Mil. said there was a branch of the Colchians called Κοραξοί—Steph. Byz. *s.v.*), but perhaps Κολάξης is more likely: a Scythian prince Colaxes appears in Valerius Flaccus (vi. 48 ff.), descended from an ἔχιδνα μιξοπάρθενος like Scythes, who corresponds to Colaxais in the Greek version of the Scythians' descent given by Herodotus (iv. 8–10). Either Κόλαξος or Κολάξας could give Alcman's Κολαξαῖος (Schwyzer, *Griechische Grammatik* i. 467).

10. The phrase recurs, in a different sense, in Eur. (*Phoen.* 1058).

11. Cf. Wilamowitz, *Aischylos-Interpretationen* 156 f. (I take it that Wilamowitz means we must not imagine Aeschylus 'reaching for' his *Arimaspea* (or any other authority) when he decided to write of 'Scythian' geography, rather than as Meuli (154, n. 2): 'bei Aisch. Prom. 803 ff. ist nach Wilamowitz . . . nicht Aristeas als Quelle anzunehmen'.)

12. πρῶτος is surely a mistake in the papyrus for πρῶτον—'H. says that Saneunus was the first to discover', rather than 'H. was the first to say'. It looks like an extract from one of those lists of discoverers or inventors popular from Heraclides Ponticus on. Scythians as inventors of bronze: see Jacoby's note on this fragment of Hellanicus. Jacoby says that 'Scythian iron' is not unusual, though he refers only to Sept. 817 (= 818 Murray). His qualms because Herodotus (i. 215) says there was no iron in the country of the Massagetae seem unnecessary: it was true, but Scythia was far away.

13. I follow Bothe here in printing with a capital: cf. the other named rivers Pluton (806), Aethiops (809), Nile (812). And οὐ ψευδώνυμον loses all point if we are not told what the name is to which it refers (cf. 85). This punning figure was liked by the Greeks (cf. Arist. Rhet. ii. 23); ὑβριστήν would turn it into a riddle! So the scholiast took it, and provided an answer: τὸν Ἀράξην, παρὰ τὸ ἀράσσειν καὶ ἠχεῖν τὰ κύματα αὐτοῦ (cf. Strab. 531; Steph. Byz. s. Ἀράξης). That he was guessing is indicated by his prefixing the article; but if he really read Ἀράξην it would be interesting (the Araxes flows into the Tanais and rises in Parnassus (i.e. Paropamisus = Indian Caucasus), according to Aristotle, Meteor. i. 13).

14. The epithet εὐίππους has a Scythian or northerly connotation: cf. the Ὑπερβόρεοι εὐίπποι of the Catalogus [23 f.] (Hyperboreans are equated with Scythians by the sixth-century Ionian Ananius (fr. 4. 3)).

15. νοητέον δὲ νῦν, φασί, Καύκασον τμῆμά τι τοῦ προειρημένου Ταύρου βορειότατον, περὶ τὴν Κρονίαν ἀνῆκον θάλασσαν, οὗ μέρη καὶ τὰ πρὸ τούτων γραφέντα Ῥιπαῖα ὄρη. It is not clear whether οὗ refers to Καύκασον or Ταύρου: the latter seems indicated by καί (the Rhipaeans as well as the Caucasus are a far-northern spur of the Taurus—hence also τμῆμά τι). Yet cf. schol. ad Dion. P. 666: τὸν Καύκασον περὶ τὴν Κρονίαν θάλασσαν ὑποτίθεται, καὶ μέρη αὐτοῦ τὰ Ῥιπαῖα βούλεται εἶναι, καὶ τὸν Καύκασον τμῆμα εἶναι τοῦ Ταύρου (= Eustathius?); Mela i. 109; Pliny, N.H. vi. 15 (the Rhipaeans are an extension of the Caucasus).

16. In the codices of Dion. Hal. (Ant. Rom. i. 61. 1) Atlas is said to have been an Arcadian king who dwelt περὶ τὸ λεγόμενον Καυκάσιον ὄρος. Is this something more than a mere misreading (of Καυκώνιον? so C. Jacoby), and should it be connected in some way with the 'Hyperborean Atlas' (Apollod. ii. 5. 11)?

17. For example, Ἀβασίας Freshfield (supposed to mean 'land of the Abasci', a Scythian tribe north of Colchis (Arrian, Periplus Ponti 11): but the name Ἀβασία is not vouched for, and the Abasci appear to be late); Χαλυβίας Schütz (not vouched for, and paleographically unlikely); Ἀρίας Heimsöth (unmetrical?). W. Ridgeway's justification of Ἀραβίας from Xen. Cyrop. vii. 4 and 5; viii. 6; and Plaut. Trin. 933 ff. (Transactions of the Cambridge Philological Society ii (1881-2), 179 f.) does not convince me: it is not surprising that Xenophon knew of the small district called Arabia on the border of Commagene (it is presumably the Arabia of Pliny, N.H. v. 85 f.; vi. 129), but it would be surprising if Aeschylus had known of it; and I find it hard to treat the Plautine passage as a serious piece of geography (yet Professor Lloyd-Jones has pointed out to me that the Medicean

scholiast's metrical comment on *P.V.* 436 (πῶς τὴν Ἀραβίαν Καυκάσῳ συνῴκισεν;) may come from Comedy, which would make the reading of our text, if not authentic, at least very early). I note a river Arabis near Colchis ('Scylax', *Periplus* 83)!

18. Burges himself appears to have favoured this view (see Paley on *P.V.* 421). Avars are supported by D. W. Freshfield in *The Academy*, 15 (Jan.–June, 1879), 566 (contradicted by A. R. Fairfield, ibid. 16, 33; further correspondence between the protagonists, ibid. 68, 105).

19. The modern Don enters the sea through a multiplicity of channels in a rapidly growing delta (Minns 21): in classical times it was δίστομος (Anon. *Periplus Ponti Euxini* 49 = 'Scymnus' 871 ff.; Pliny, *N.H.* vi. 19. According to Strabo (493) these mouths were sixty stades apart; seven, according to Artemidorus (*ap.* schol. *ad* Dion. P. 14)—presumably ζ' in error for ξ'). Anyway, the arm of the sea, some forty miles long and fifteen broad, through which the Don is approached, would condition explorers' minds to the idea that they were entering a strait.

20. See Jacoby on Hec., fr. 18.

21. A quite different history for the intercontinental boundary is suggested by Jacoby (on Hec., fr. 195): (i) it is the Colchian Phasis of the Argonautic legend (the Phasis-Rion), leading to the Ocean; (ii) later it is moved north to the Hypanis-Kuban and the Cimmerian Bosporus (the latter is also called Tanais by some authorities); (iii) finally it is moved yet farther north to the Don, which is then called Tanais. Whereas Hecataeus meant (i) in his *Histories* he meant (ii) in his geographical work. This theory solves some anomalies in Hecataeus—it explains why certain tribes near the Caucasus are said to be, some in Asia, some in Europe; and why Phanagoria and environs are in Asia but the Dandarii, just to the north, in Europe. Yet there are still difficulties. The only ancient author to call the (or a!) Hypanis the boundary between Europe and Asia is Cornelius Gallus (*ap.* Vib. Seq. 11); Jacoby says this is 'aus gelehrter hellenistischer quelle' (this is the only certain remnant of Gallus we have!)—it is more likely to be a mere slip. And though Hecataeus put the Dandarii in Europe he put a tribe to the north of these, and to the south-east of the Tanais mouth, in Asia (cf. Jacoby on fr. 216)! The whole question is complicated by the fact that our sources for Hecataeus' views are sometimes palpably inaccurate in referring a place to Europe or Asia (cf. Jacoby on fr. 193). But it is clear that for Hecataeus the Phasis-Rion was not the intercontinental boundary; for myself, I am inclined to think the Phasis-Tanais was, as for Aeschylus.

(This is not a fragment of Hecataeus of Miletus but of Hecataeus of Abdera, if Röper's (most attractive) emendation of ὡς Ἑκάταιος †εφοτιεις† to εἴφ' ὁ Τήιος is accepted (cf. Diels–Kranz ii. 240. It was accepted later by Jacoby himself: 264 F 13). I do not understand Jacoby's argumentation when he says on the authorship that 'die ableitung des Tanais aus dem Araxes kann nur ein sehr alter autor gegeben haben'. This may (or may not) be true of the original author of the idea, but it in no way helps towards choosing between the earlier and the later Hecataeus here. Why should this author be any older than Aristotle, who says exactly the same?)

22. Antonius Diogenes also appears to have taken his heroes through

the Tanais into the northern ocean: διὰ τοῦ Πόντου καὶ ἀπὸ τῆς κατὰ Κασπίαν καὶ Ὑρκανίαν θαλάσσης πρὸς τὰ Ῥιπαῖα καλούμενα ὄρη καὶ τοῦ Τανάιδος ποταμοῦ τὰς ἐκβολὰς ἀφιγμένοι, εἶτα διὰ τὸ πολὺ τοῦ ψύχους ἐπὶ τὸν Σκυθικὸν ἐπιστραφέντες ὠκεανόν (507 = Phot. Bibl. 109a).

23. A general contraction, or underestimation, of distances may explain the curious error in 725 f., where Salmydessus is spoken of as near Themiscyra (about five hundred miles away!). Aeschylus' mistake is anyway less gross than Lucan's at viii. 540 ('vada testantur iunctas Aegyptia Syrtes').

24. If the position of the Phasis suggested above is right, the Arimaspi would not be far from it. There is a tradition that they helped the storm-bound Argonauts (Steph. Byz. s. Εὐεργέται). (The Ariaspi got the name Εὐεργέται from confusion with Arimaspi— or vice versa (cf. Q. Curt. vii. 3. 1)? See Tomaschek in P.–W. ii. 826 f.)

25. Jacoby (i. 353) states unequivocally that the name Hybristes conceals the Tanais. This would fit the ancient reputation, and the ancient etymology, of Tanais (cf. Mela i. 115; Tanais διὰ τὸ τεταμένως ῥεῖν, Eustathius et schol. ad Dion. P. 14; cf. [Plut.], fluv. 14), but not the account of Aeschylus, whose Hybristes must empty, not into the Palus Maeotis, but into the Euxine to the west of it. This is one requirement which any identification of the Hybristes must fulfil; another is, that it should have the Maeotian-Amazons on its eastern bank. If the Maeotians/Sauromatae did in pre-classical times in fact dwell to the west of the Tanais, as may be indicated in Herodotus' story of the Amazons being washed ashore on the west side of the Palus Maeotis, we could perhaps identify the Hybristes with the Borysthenes (or the Hypanis-Bug) without more ado; yet perhaps it is a mistake to try to identify it with any one river: a *conflation* of the Tanais with the Borysthenes or the Hypanis would be preferable, as it would enable us to account for Aeschylus' self-contradiction in putting the Scythians on the western shore of the Palus Maeotis in 417 ff., when in 709 ff. they are away to the west of the Hybristes. There is no need to suppose that the process of conflation (if such there was) was conscious: it may have been inadvertent, and aided by the fact that Aeschylus' authority gave no names to the rivers he described.

26. For dating the Pontic colonies I follow R. M. Cook. Archaeological discoveries (at present to seek) may, of course, necessitate the abandonment of this position.

Rhys Carpenter (59) thinks that there was nothing to take the Greeks into the Black Sea before the Cimmerian invasion of Asia Minor, and therefore that the localization of the Argonautic legend could not have been much earlier than mid-seventh century. Indeed, in an article entitled 'The Greek Penetration of the Black Sea' (*A.J.A.* lii (1948), 1 ff.) he argues that it would have been impossible for ships to enter the Euxine against the current of the Thracian Bosporus before the invention of the penteconter (which he suggests took place c. 700): 'The years just before or just after 680 B.C. [Carpenter's approximate foundation-date for Chalcedon] must be our choice for the sensational event which was to become so mighty in legend—the first passing of a Greek ship into the Black Sea' (9).

27. Megasthenes' ants inhabit a mountain plateau in Dardistan. The

Indians distract the insects with lumps of meat, and apparently use yokes of horses, not camels, in their forays (Müller compares Dio Chrys. 35. 24. Is his reading of ἱπποζυγίοις an emendation?). Herodotean reminiscence: the ants are as big as or bigger than foxes; perhaps the meat-bait was suggested by Hdt. iii. 111. 3. Pliny's account of the ants (*N.H.* xi. 111) is mainly a blend of Megasthenes and Herodotus.

28. Jacobs's insertion of οἱ before τὸν χρυσὸν φυλάττοντες I think obscures the sense: οὐκ ἂν διέλθοιεν requires a protasis. I have not followed Hercher in showing a lacuna before καλοῦνται, but have supplied οἱ before τούτοις, considering this to be but a specimen of Aelian's fatuous style (cf. ix. 36 ὄρνιθες ὅσοι θαλάττης ἔντροφοι καί εἰσι καὶ νομίζονται).

29. Griffins in India, ants in Ethiopia: Philostr. *vit. Ap.* vi. 1; cf. iii. 48.

30. ἐλαίαισι [ἐλάαισι Brunck] περιχλωρῆσιν ἐρυμνάς Tz.

31. The reeds are first heard of from Herodotus, the *Indian* Dog-men from Ctesias (Dog-men in Libya already in Hdt. iv. 191; where Hesiod and Aeschylus (Strab. 299) put them is not certain): see references by Mayhoff on Pliny, *N.H.* vii. 21 and 23, to which add (on the reeds) Strab. 710-11; Varr. Atac., fr. 20 Baehrens; Marcianus, *Periplus maris exteri* i. 44 (*G.G.M.* i. 537). On Dog-men see also Yule ii. 311; 228.

32. τὸν Fränkel: τοῦ cod. For Apollo's temple among the Hyperboreans cf. Her. Pont., fr. 51 W.; Paus. x. 5. 9 (cf. Arist., fr. 3; Strab. 421; Philostr. *vit. Ap.* vi. 10 f.; Plut. *Pyth. orac.* 17); Hec. Abd. *ap.* Diod. Sic. ii. 47. 2; Iambl. *V.P.* 91.

33. Cf. Alcaeus' *Hymn to Apollo* (fr. 307). Because I think the narrator was air-borne I have not followed Wilamowitz in emending l. 5 περί (= 'in the neighbourhood of '; cf. περί ... νήσους in 7 f.) to παρά. Apollo carried off Cyrene thus (Pind. *Pyth.* ix. 5 ff.), and also perhaps Stratonice, a daughter of Porthaon, according to a new fragment of the *Catalogus* to be published by Lobel.

34. It *could* be Cleinis' soul in ecstasy, but there is no hint of this in Antoninus.

35. For example, v. 584 *Choaspes*; 596 *Iaxartes*; vi. 193 *Strymon*; 201 *Tyres*; 220 *Rhyndacus*; 618 *Hebrus*.

36. If correct, this would rule out the identification of the Campasus with the Cambyses, which flowed into the river Cyrus or the Caspian.

37. I am inclined to date the beginning of *Il.* xiii to about the middle of the seventh century—the time of the earliest probings of Greek exploration to the west and north-west of the Euxine: the Scythians' dietary habits are known, but not the name 'Scythian'. It may be conjectured that the author of these lines (as of *Il.* ix. 5) lived on the Asiatic coast of the Propontis—the natural base for such exploration (this is confirmed by his apparent knowledge that the highest point of Samothrace is visible from the Troad (Carpenter 36)). But there seems to me no reason to assume indebtedness to the *Arimaspea* here.

38. From Clem. Alex. His subsequent words, τοὺς ἑξακονταετεῖς οὗτοι ἔξω πυλῶν ἄγοντες ἀφανίζουσιν, may not be from Hellanicus: note the reversion to direct speech. They are perhaps a muddle in Clement's own mind of the Hyperboreans' suicide before reaching senility (Pliny, *N.H.* iv.

89; Mela iii. 37), of stories of the Massagetae who kill off their old folk (Hdt. i. 216. 2), and of something like Mimnermus' αἲ γὰρ ἄτερ νούσων τε καὶ ἀργαλέων μελιδωνέων ἑξηκονταέτη μοῖρα κίχοι θανάτου (fr. 6).

39. Schmid–Stählin ii. 678; but cf. *P.–W.* v. 925.

40. So Lindsay: *an divitiis pici?* (*pici divitiis Non*. But both the Plautine codices and Nonius have the same word order.) '*Picos veteres esse voluerunt, quos Graeci grypes appellant*' Nonius 152; but see J. O. Thomson in *C.R.* 70 (1956), 3.

41. The Loeb editors of Ennius and Varro have been unnecessarily perverse about this fragment: Warmington (*Remains of Old Latin* i. 392) thinks *decem* qualifies the unnamed antecedent of *quas*; though Varro, who presumably knew what it was, clearly did not. The reference is presumably to nuggets not only of rare quality but of exceptional size. Kent, in his edition of Varro's *L.L.* (i. 328), takes *fodere* to mean *infodere*, so giving the verb an unusual sense and the Arimaspians an unusual role.

42. iii (comm.), 53: 'man tut H. schwerlich unrecht, wenn man ihn unmittelbar hinter Aristeas stellt, der φοιβόλαμπτος γενόμενος von den Skythen zu den apollinischen Hyperboreern gelangt [not so!] . . . es ist ein unterschied mehr der zeit als des literarischen γένος, wenn er seinen reiseweg — die zwischenhaltung eines "landsmannes" als vermittler seiner kenntnisse (Rohde Rom.[2] 238 [? 228]) ist nach den parallelen unwahrscheinlich — genau beschreibt' [how is it known that Aristeas did not describe his journey in detail?]. Hecataeus, then, visited the Hyperboreans in person; and Jacoby ingeniously reconstructs his route: from Teos by Phanagoria and the Tanais to the Caspian [not necessary], thence to the north-eastern ocean and along its coast.

CHAPTER IV

1. I am not sure how much weight should be given to this testimony. Huc, who was in Lhasa 1845/6, says that the bodies of the dead were cut up and fed to the dogs, in the 'most complimentary' form of burial (ii. 251 f.).

2. Landor (i. 55) remarks on the general superiority of Tibetan women to the men, and says that 'the ladies of the Forbidden Land seem to have it all their own way'. Huc notices the free and active life led by the women of Tibet (ii. 176).

3. This observation of Marco has also been noticed by How and Wells (on Hdt. iii. 105).

4. All that I have to say about these Chinese sources (including the translations) I owe to the kindness of Professor D. Hawkes.

5. *Chao Hun. Ch'u Tz'ŭ*, 9/4b in the *SSŭ Pu Ts'ung K'an* edition (Hawkes 104).

6. Both the Dog Jung and the Kuei were real people against whom the Chinese made war.

7. *Shan Hai Ching*, *S.P.T.K.* ed. B/55a–56a. Is the 'winged tiger' that neighbours the ants significant for the griffin story?

8. 'Sea' in these contexts appears to connote something like the Greek Oceanus.

9. In the context it appears that this is an error for 'north-west to north-east'.

10. *Shan Hai Ching*, B/43a–43b.

11. *Huai Nan Tzu, S.P.T.K.* ed. 4/7b.

12. A one-eyed giant features in a thirteenth/fourteenth-century Mongolian story like that of Odysseus and Polyphemus. But variants of this tale are so widespread that it has little evidential value for my purpose. See Frazer's Loeb ed. of Apollodorus, ii. 404 ff. (452 ff. for the Mongolian legend).

13. I am indebted to Mr. L. D. Reynolds for the translation of this passage.

14. An account of an illustrated Chinese 'Book of Monsters' is given by de Mely in *Revue archéologique* iii (1897), 367 ff. It notices one-eyed men; dog-headed men, the males of whom barked only and could not understand speech, though the females could speak and understood Chinese; pygmies, who are attacked by cranes; men with horses' legs; wild men with hairy bodies and pendulous breasts (Abominable Snowmen?); long-lived men; and men with fishes' bodies (these can be traced back to the fourth century B.C.: one of the 'Heavenly Questions' (T'ien Wen) is 'where does the man-fish live?'—immediately after a reference to long-lived men (Hawkes 49).

The pygmies and cranes are strange. They are put in India by Megasthenes (Strab. 711). They appear of course in *Il.* iii. 3 ff. (For geranomachies in Greek art of the seventh century B.C. see Dunbabin 79; 87.)

15. *Gnomon* 9 (1933), 567 f.; Meuli 156 f. [185 f.]; Phillips 174. It appears to be accepted also by Dodds (141) and Bowra (1). Furtwängler's view is rather different: the griffins are treasure-guarding dragons, their Arimaspian enemies are goblins (Roscher i. 1768).

16. Cf. Yule 311 f.; 228 (on Dog-heads).

17. This survey is based on the admirable disquisitions of Prinz and Ziegler (art. 'Gryps' in *P.–W.* vii), where references to illustrated examples will be found. See also Furtwängler in Roscher (*Gryps*: illustrated); Leibovitch in *Bulletin de l'Institut d'Égypte* xxv (1942/3), 183 ff. (illustrated); Phillips 172.

18. That lions were known in neolithic times as far north as lat. 46 is proved by a clay model of one that was unearthed at Schipenitz (ref. in note 19).

19. There is no room in this scheme for the 'griffin' which was discovered on a late neolithic site (perhaps *c.* 2400–1700 B.C.) at Schipenitz (Bukowina) (Gordon Childe in *Journal of the Royal Anthropological Institute* liii (1923), 281; 283). The finds here included some painted pottery with animal figures. Most of these, though stylized, are not monstrous; but one, a silhouette in profile of a couchant four-legged creature with animal's muzzle, prick-ears, tail curved over body, and sharp claws on the hind feet, has also a distinct forward-tilted hump rising from the shoulders, which might be meant for wings. Childe calls this a griffin; and, while not ruling out the possibility that the wing-like projection may be due to accident or to a later stain, is himself convinced by close examination that it was part of the original figure.

20. Is it because the one-eyed Arimaspians were shaggy all over that

later poets and artists so represented the one-eyed Cyclopes (e.g. Theocr. xi. 50; Ov. *Met.* xiii. 846 f.; Philostr. *Imag.* ii. 18. 3: ὄρειός τε καὶ δεινὸς γέγραπται χαίτην μὲν ἀνασείων ὀρθὴν καὶ ἀμφιλαφῆ πίτυος δίκην, καρχάρους δὲ ὑποφαίνων ὀδόντας ἐκ βορού τοῦ γενείου στέρνον τε καὶ γαστέρα καὶ τὸ εἰς ὄνυχα ἧκον λάσιος πάντα; cf. Call. *H.* iii. 76)?

21. Dr. Paul Jacobsthal expressed the opinion to me, in 1953, that the artist was an Ionian living in a Greek colony in south Russia; he dated the mirror to *c.* 575 B.C. Otherwise, he said, he agreed in the main with Payne (*Necrocorinthia* 231).

22. But ἐπίγρυπος in Hdt. ii. 76.

23. Thus attaching ὀρθόποδος ὑπὲρ πάγου to the verb τράφη, with the other adverbial phrases, rather than to ἄμιππος, whatever that means (perhaps 'stabled with the horses' of the wind-god? The passage is discussed by Lloyd-Jones in *C.Q.* li (1957), 24 ff., who does not, however, consider this possibility. If this phrase *is* to go with ἄμιππος then no particular πάγος need be meant, as far as I can see). Πάγος means 'a precipitous excrescence' ('hill' is insufficiently precise); sometimes the 'precipice' itself (Hes. *Scut.* 439), and this might be its sense here, the cave being then imagined as situated in a mountain side above a precipice.

24. The Cave of Boreas appears again in Callimachus (*H.* iv. 62 ff., where note the odd epithet in l. 65, ἑπτάμυχον βορέαο παρὰ σπέος), who located it not in the Rhipaean mountains but in the Haemus range. So too Apollonius Rhodius (i. 211 ff.) puts Boreas' home in north Thrace, near the 'Sarpedonian rock'—also known to Sophocles (fr. 637: ἡμεῖς δ' [Cleopatra speaking?] ἐν ἄντροις [Bergk: ἄστροις] ἔνθα Σαρπηδὼν πέτρα) and Simonides (schol. *ad* Ap. Rhod. i. 212). It could be that Boreas' cave was first located in Haemus and then moved to the Rhipaeans; but this would make the belief Greek, and if so why do the other Greek winds not live in caves? I think that the cave was brought to Haemus from the Rhipaeans, under the influence of Homer's '*Thracian* Boreas'.

25. The same story was told in Britain, of a mighty wind issuing from the Peak Cavern in Derbyshire (Gervase of Tilbury, *Otia Imperialia* 24; 117 Liebrecht; cf. Camden's *Britannia* 495 (trans. Gibson; London, 1695)).

26. Rubruck only in fact—if even he? Cf. Humboldt ii. 501 f.

27. But see Atkinson 472.

28. The Spirit of Chung Mountain, who blows hard and soft to cause winter and summer [82] *may* help to take the tradition back to the third century B.C. (or earlier); and a Chinese poem of about that date mentions a 'Cave of the Winds' (location not stated) (Hawkes 79).

29. *E.R.E.* ii. 689 ff.; Rohde [ii] 233 f.

30. Himself a 'blameless' Hyperborean? The name is clearly a pseudonym.

31. Apparently first suggested by Gladisch (in Roscher i. 2829), and followed by Tomaschek (764 ff.), Minns (113 f.), Casson (*C.R.* xxxiv (1920), 3), G. F. Hudson (*Europe and China* 27 ff.), and Sykes (*Quest for Cathay* 19 f.).

32. I do not see why Farnell ([i] iv. 100) calls it a 'foolish etymology' (Dodds (162) thinks it is probably the right one after all). References to discussions of the problem will be found in Guthrie (78 f.) and D. L. Page, *Sappho and Alcaeus* 251. The modern etymologies are two: (1) Ὑπερβόρεοι is

a vulgar corruption of ὑπέρβοροι which may have been a north Greek form
of ὑπέρφοροι, which is supposed to mean 'carriers over' and to be connected
with περφερέες, the name by which Herodotus says the escort was called
which accompanied the annual gifts sent by the Hyperboreans to Delos *via*
the Adriatic, Dodona, Euboea, and Tenos (Pausanias much later gives a
different route, through Sinope). This would make the legend of the Hyperboreans Delian, for no such gifts were sent to Delphi. But (*a*) there appears
to have been a Delphic version of the Hyperborean legend as early as *c*.
600 B.C. (our evidence for this—Alcaeus—is much earlier than for the Delian);
this has to be dismissed as 'rivalry with Delos'; (*b*) why should gifts sent
from the north of Greece to Delos follow such a roundabout route? (2) The
root of the word is a pre-Greek word for 'mountain' (the Slavonic *gora*
is adduced, though its relevance to seventh-century Greece is obscure); and
Bora was the name of a mountain in Macedonia, according to Livy. This
would make the legend of the Hyperboreans Delphic (they dwelt 'beyond
the mountain' from Delphi). Then what about the Hyperborean offerings
to Delos? Where did they come from, and why were none sent to
Delphi?

Yet these offerings seem to have been historical. C. T. Seltman ingeniously
suggests (in *C.Q.* xxii (1928), 155 ff.) that they really emanated from a
Graeco-Getic [?] offshoot of the Milesian colony of Istrus (founded 656 B.C.),
descendants of settlers who had moved well inland up the Danube valley.
The route by which the offerings were sent according to Herodotus (iv. 33)
may have been cut in the fourth century B.C. by Celtic eastward migration,
and so diverted to that given by Pausanias (i. 31. 2, where Arimaspians and
Issedonians are inserted to push the Hyperboreans farther away). Connexion
of the Delphic Apollo with the Hyperboreans was due to deliberate Delphian
invention, to rival Delos.

The theory is an attractive one, so long as it is understood to apply only
to the source of the 'Hyperborean' offerings, and not to account for the
origin of the Hyperboreans themselves. If it is right, the offerings could not
have started before the second half of the seventh century; more probably
later, as the foundation-date for Istrus which Seltman accepts may well be
too early, and the archaeological evidence he mentions from the Danube
valley is not earlier than the sixth century. This would make his account
of the beginning of the Delphic–Hyperborean connexion hard to maintain.
(This Delphic connexion seems to me to indicate that the Hyperboreans
existed in the Greek imagination before their offerings.)

Our earliest mention of the Hyperboreans (apart from Aristeas) is
probably in a fragment of the Hesiodic *Catalogus* (before 600 B.C.? cf.
Schmid–Stählin I. i. 269). There they are called εὔιπποι, and so are clearly
merged with the northern nomads [189]. There is no certainty about even
the approximate date of the Homeric Hymn to Dionysus (vii), which Guthrie
(*O.C.D. s.* 'Hyperboreans') says contains the first mention of them (28 f.).
I would note that here they appear to be located *overseas*, though this could
not be pressed; they are at least 'at the back of beyond'.

I am disposed to incline to the view that Page says the evidence favours:
that in origin the Hyperboreans are not a real people but a folk-memory

—'the earlier settlement of an Apollo who spread with his worshippers southward over the Greek mainland'.

33. J. Legge, *The Chinese Classics* III. i. 151. Some of this work, but not all, belongs to the sixth century A.D.; but Mr. Geoffrey Bownas tells me that this particular note is probably to be dated to the end of the fourth century B.C. Cf. Hennig 23 ff.; Alföldi, *Gnomon* ix (1933), 566.

34. Dodds 162. Baring-Gould is reminded by these swan-maidens of the Phorcides of the *P.V.* (*Curious Myths of the Middle Ages* 568).

CHAPTER V

1. Hecataeus may have been following Aristeas here; but it should be noted that he called the Issedonians 'Scythians' also (fr. 193), which Aristeas did not.

2. φθειροτραγέουσι. To save the reputation of the Budini How and Wells wish to render this 'eat fir-cones'.

3. These are a puzzle. Elks and reindeer have been proposed, but neither of these is aquatic. Rawlinson's seals are surely impossible? Minns (105) on second thoughts would see otters in the θηρία τετραγωνοπρόσωπα, and take ἐνύδριες as water-snakes; I suppose people who ate lice might also hunt water-snakes! How and Wells suggest that the square-faced animals were mink.

4. Representative of the principal schools of thought. There seems no point in trying to be exhaustive here. References to the ideas of other authorities will be found in the works summarized.

5. Erman 211 on the Bashkirs and the bird-cherry; 297 on *aschy*: 'the Bashkirs denominate every acid, especially the sour juices which they mix with their milk, by a word which is written *atchui* in Russian, and they call the cherries themselves *tchia*, a word formed, probably, from the same root'; 'the word for sour, among the Tatars of Kasan, is *atchi*. The Sclavonian is quite different.' The word in fact is Turkish (*áći* or *akśi*: Minns 109).

6. [42], and Kiessling in *P.–W.* iA 846 ff. But there is no reason to suppose that this notion was as early as Aristeas.

7. This would not mean that the whole area was inhabited by Issedonians but that it was the region over which the horde moved its flocks for pasture.

8. A seventh-century Greek in a strange land could not have known his bearing in relation to his home at all accurately, and must have found it exceedingly difficult to maintain a course in one direction consistently over a long period. Though sailors already knew how to get a rough bearing from Ursa Major (*Od.* v. 277), the science of navigation by the stars was rudimentary. This may have been the chief reason why the early Greek mariners tended to coast and avoid the open sea if possible (that they had no fear of the open sea if they were sure of making a correct landfall is indicated by the fact that the regular trade-route to India lay across the Indian Ocean, once the regularity of the monsoons had been discovered (Plin. *N.H.* vi. 100 ff.)). The stars would be even less use to an explorer travelling in the daytime over featureless plains.

(The other constellations mentioned in *Od.* v. 271 ff., Boötes and the Pleiads, would not help Odysseus much in finding his way, though they might tell him the time (the Pleiads were of more importance to farmers). It is surprising how unobservant the Greeks were for long about the heavens, until they learned more from the peoples of the Middle East in the fourth century B.C. It does not appear that they realized the superiority of the Little over the Great Bear for orientation until then (or even then: cf. Arat. *Phaen.* 36–44). Before then too the only constellations our authors name are the Great Bear, Boötes, Orion, the Pleiads, and the Hyades (the mention of Aquila at *Rhesus* 530 rather points to a post-Euripidean date for the play). There is no *first-hand* evidence that they had any knowledge of the planets either until the end of the fifth century, in Xenophon (*Mem.* iv. 7. 5), apart from the obvious Venus. The *names* of the planets are even later: Plat. *Tim.* 38 d; *Epin.* 986 e ff.; Seneca (*N.Q.* vii. 3. 2) says 'Eudoxus primus ab Aegypto hos motus [*sc.* of the planets] in Graeciam transtulit'.)

9. Cf. the brief Peripatetic treatise, *Ventorum situs et cognomina.*

10. As also at *Od.* xiv. 403 f., if 'the Syrian island' is Syros and 'Ortygia' Delos (east of Syros). But this is uncertain (cf. Kirk and Raven, *The Presocratic Philosophers* 52 ff.).

11. ὑπὲρ Κρήτης at *Od.* xiv. 300 may mean 'to the south of Crete' ('above Crete' from the point of view of the Ionian poet).

12. The 'tilted disk' theory is ascribed to Anaxagoras, Leucippus, and Democritus in the fifth century (Diels–Kranz ii. 5. 34; 22. 11; 71. 17; 78. 12; 107. 4; cf. Hdt. i. 142. 2); it may have been held by Anaximenes in the sixth [188]. It persisted even after the discovery of the sphericity of the earth. Cf. the Pythagorean view quoted by Aristotle, *cael.* ii. 285b; Virg. *G.* i. 240 f.; Macrob. *S.S.* ii. 5. 22.

13. A beginning is being made with ἀπηλιώτης, an Eastern Ionic word; the consummation of the process is to be seen in Arist. *Meteor.* ii. 6.

14. Though not exactly: the name given to the true north wind was more often Aparctias (Arist. *Meteor.* ii. 6; [Arist.], *de mundo* 394b29—βορέαι is also a generic name for winds ἀπὸ ἄρκτου, 394b20; Pliny, *N.H.* ii. 119; Favorinus *ap.* Aul. Gell. ii. 22; Vegetius iv. 38; Lydus, *mens.* iv. 76).

15. The name 'Arimaspian' *may* be Mongol (äräm däk means 'one-eyed' among the Mongols, according to Laufer 452). The etymology is uncertain; if known, it need only tell us what language the *Issedonians* spoke, of course. We hear of a king of the Iazyges called Βανάδασπος (Dio Cass. lxxi. 16), and an Iberian Ἀμάζασπος (*I.G.* xiv. 1374). These are late (second century A.D.), but if anything weigh against a Mongolian origin for Ἀριμασπός.

If the Arimaspi were Mongols, they must have been among the first of their race to learn to ride the horse (cf. C. W. Bishop in *Antiquity* xiv (1940), 314; Phillips 173, and further in *Artibus Asiae* xx (1957), 160 f.). Mongols are not hairy, but the Arimaspi might have got their reputation for hairiness from their garments: '[the Tatars'] shoubes or gownes are hayrie on the outside, and open behinde, with tailes hanging downe to their hammes' (Carpini (Beazley 109)).

16. The modern name, Hindu Kush, was used *c.* 1332 by Ibn Batuta, who explains it as (Persian) 'Hindu killer' (*E.B.* xiii 514b). *Kush* might be related in some way to *Caucasus* (cf. Thomson 126), but even so whether as progenitor or descendant cannot be told.

CHAPTER VI

1. c. 1 quotes Theopompus by name; c. 5 has two stories about Pherecydes which are branded as falsifications of Theopompus' making by Porphyry (*ap.* Euseb. *P.E.* x. 3. 6 ff.).

2. Cf. Plut. *gen. Socr.* 23. 592c–d (where he is called Hermodorus, a psychological mistake of Plutarch, presumably, caused by the fact that 'Hermodorus'' soul remembered its experiences in and out of its various bodies by the gift of Hermes (D.L. viii. 4 f.), rather than a copyist's error as Rohde thought ([i] 331, n. 112)).

3. Was Hermotimus originally a local hero-prophet (cf. Amphiaraus and Orpheus), and were his enemies, the Cantharidae, the clan of a rival prophet (cf. the Cragalidae and Delphi, Parke i. 342 f.)?

4. i. 519. I do not understand his remark 'die schriften der wundermänner Abaris und Aristeas sind wahrscheinlich nur erfindung Lobons'.

5. See Rohde's art. '*Γέγονε* in den Biographica des Suidas' (*Kleine Schriften* i. 114 ff. = *R.M.* xxxiii (1878), 161 ff.). Rohde thinks that the coupling of Cyrus with Croesus must indicate the capture of Sardis by the former, and that the variants in the date of the Olympiad are to be explained by the postulate that one tradition has preserved the first figure of *νη'*, the other the second (*Kl. Schr.* i. 136). This is plausible, but a less likely corruption than the one I suggest.

'Suidas' normally uses *γέγονε* in the sense of *ἤκμαζε*, much more rarely in the sense of *ἐγεννήθη* (ibid. 177).

6. [i] 329. The earliest date for the Metapontine appearance Rohde makes to be 434, but I would not allow some of his premisses—for example, he postulates the Cimmerian invasion as a *terminus post quem* (thus assuming the identity of Aristeas with the author of the *Arimaspea* that Herodotus knew). In [ii] 186, n. 1, on the other hand, Rohde moves the date of the Metapontine appearance back some sixteen years, to *c.* 450, and appears to feel no qualms about this; but here he takes no account of the Cimmerian invasion (though the poem still features in his train of reasoning), and anyway makes the foundation-date of Proconnesus too early.

7. One naturally takes this to mean 'in *many* places', though I suppose strictly it need mean only 'more than one' (cf. Eur. *Hel.* 587 f.). Even so, the testimony would be non-Herodotean.

8. Cf. Nilsson [i] 104. In the case of the honours paid by the Abderites to Timesius (Hdt. i. 168) it is not clear whether his grave was there or not (*ἐξελασθείς* could mean that his followers were driven out, but he himself was killed).

9. Cf. Boyancé 234. Boyancé thinks it was probably heroization, and in Pythagoras' case widespread in Magna Graecia, not confined to the place where he ended his days.

10. Has the tradition passed through the hands of some joker like Hermippus (cf. his account of the death of Pythagoras (D.L. viii. 40), and of the works of Zoroaster (Pliny, *N.H.* xxx. 4))? Hermippus may have been guying Heraclides Ponticus in particular (cf. Lévy [i] 39 ff.).

11. Meuli (154, n. 2) also rejects Schwyzer's emendation, but for a bad

reason: 'die . . . Worte ὡς ἐγὼ συμβαλλόμενος ἐν Προκοννήσῳ τε καὶ Μεταποντίῳ εὕρισκον verbieten wohl diese Änderung; mit (τὰ) ἐν Μεταποντίῳ kann doch H. nicht seinen eigenen Aufenthalt, sondern nur die ἐπιδημία des Aristeas gemeint haben.' συμβαλλόμενος does not here mean 'comparing' but 'calculating'; not τὰ ἐν Μεταποντίῳ but τὰ ἔτεα is to be understood as its object (cf. ii. 31). The emendation was published in *Philologische Wochenschrift* (1922), 528.

12. Proconnesus may not have been founded from Miletus direct, but from one of the Milesian colonies on the east coast of the Propontis, perhaps through fear of the oncoming Cimmerians (e.g. from Cyzicus, itself founded *c.* 675?—cf. *J.H.S.* lv. 146). But this is sheer speculation. For the little that is known of the history of Proconnesus see F. W. Hasluck in *J.H.S.* xxix (1909), 6 ff.

13. 157 f. Herodotus was only too pleased to have everything as rational as possible, 'selbst . . . wenn . . . die wunderbare Schnelligkeit der Reise von Prokonnesos nach Artake nicht wegzubringen war . . . An Stelle dieser ursprünglicheren Sagen haben die Griechen von Prokonnesos und Kyzikos eine Erzählung gesetzt, die den Wundermann seine Reise ganz leibhaftig, unter möglichster Ausschaltung alles Übernatürlichen, ausführen liess'. But it is not so much the speed of Aristeas' journey from Proconnesus to the mainland as the speed of the Cyzicene's in the reverse direction which is really anomalous.

14. The story from Heraclides Ponticus (*ap.* D.L. viii. 5) about Hermotimus identifying Euphorbus' shield in the temple of Apollo at Branchidae, and himself being a previous incarnation of Pythagoras, is insufficient to establish that Hermotimus had any strong or traditional connexion with Apollo (though there was a temple of Apollo in the Clazomenian territory—Strab. 645). Hermotimus is not numbered among Pythagoras' incarnations in the lists of Dicaearchus and Clearchus (Aul. Gell. iv. 11. 14); that of Hermippus is probably derived from Heraclides (cf. Lévy [i] 40; so also Tert. *anim.* 28; Porph. *V.P.* 45).

15. Cf. xxxi. 10: Δημήτριος ὁ Φαληρεὺς . . . καθάπερ χρησμῳδῶν . . . εὐστόχως τούτους τοὺς λόγους ἀποπεφοίβακεν. It should be said that in neither of these passages can we be sure how far the words are those of Diodorus or of his excerptor; not that it matters a great deal as we have the use of φοιβάζειν by Lycophron.

16. Pausanias does not call these men φοιβόληπτοι, but the fact that they were ἱεροὶ τῷ θεῷ suggests it. If so, Apollo's possession of his devotees (Frazer's suggestion that they may have been scapegoats seems to me unhappy) at Hylae and his possession of Aristeas have features akin to Dionysiac frenzy: superhuman physical feats (cf. Eur. *Bacch.* 755–8) and compulsive wandering.

Plutarch (*E ap. Delph.* 20) preserves a tantalizing bit of information: certain Thessalian priests on days of ill-omen withdrew into the solitudes and were said to be 'ruled by Apollo' (φοιβονομεῖσθαι). Plutarch guesses that this means they kept themselves pure; but it is an odd word, and one would like to know more.

17. Carpenter (161) discounts theories that Aristeas was an epileptic.

CHAPTER VII

1. Theano, the wife of Pythagoras, was probably an invention of the fourth century B.C. Our earliest authority for her is Hermesianax (fr. 7. 85 f. Powell (*Collectanea Alexandrina* 100)), who flourished in the early third; the line ascribed to Empedocles by Hippobotus *ap.* D.L. viii. 43 is probably spurious (cf. fr. 155). The name may have been suggested by that of the wife of the mythical king Metapontus (Theano perhaps as early as Euripides: Hyg. *Fab.* 186); or by the Thracian Theano of *Il.* xi. 224 *al.* (a number of the names of 'early Pythagoreans' in Iamblichus' catalogue are taken from Homer).

2. There are other mathematical works ascribed to an Aristaeus, who may have been a real person. His *Solid Loci* was used by Euclid (Heath, *Greek Mathematics* i. 438); and if he is the same Aristaeus who wrote a *Comparison of the Five Figures* he would probably have flourished in the fourth century B.C. (after Theaetetus; cf. ibid. i. 162).

3. Hippasus is listed as a Sybarite, whereas he is a Metapontine or a Crotoniate elsewhere (D.L. viii. 84; Iambl. *V.P.* 81); Timaeus, elsewhere a Locrian (e.g. Plat. *Tim.* 20; [Arist.] *mir. ausc.* 178), is here a Crotoniate or a Parian. That Aristeas should be classed as a Metapontine therefore causes me no misgiving (especially as it can be explained [170]); nor that he should then become a Crotoniate, in view of the way in which Croton and Metapontum, from being both intimately connected with Pythagoras, were interchanged (cf. the confusion about Hippasus already mentioned; Diels-Kranz i. 102.16 (contrast 20 f.); Plut. *Rom.* 28 [128]).

4. Cf. Lévy [i] 37 ff. Hermippus' story was known to the schol. *ad* Soph. *El.* 62 and to Tertullian (*anim.* 28). The latter calls the οἰκίσκος in which Pythagoras lay hid by Gregory's word, *adyta*.

5. I am unable to agree with Dodds about this. Nor are the stories about Hermotimus and Abaris in point here, as far as I can see (Dodds 141).

6. In the tradition of the wandering poetic διάνοια may be the souls of the vaporous poets which Trygaeus met in the sky grubbing among the clouds for matter (Ar., *Pax* 827 ff.). This passage implies the notion of soul-journeys during life; the poets themselves were perhaps asleep! Cf. Pind., fr. 116, where Dodds (104) infers that soul-journeying is meant.

7. The idea of the pettiness of mundane affairs is already present in Plato (e.g. *Theaet.* 173e).

8. Who ἱστορίαν τινὰ τοιαύτην πρῶτος παραδέδωκεν θαυμασίαν. I suspect πρῶτος: that it cannot here have a temporal sense is shown (*a*) by the tense of the verb, (*b*) by the existence of the Platonic precedent, the myth of Er, on which indeed Proclus is here commenting!

9. It is noteworthy that Timarchus' soul escaped from his body through the sutures of his skull (τῆς κεφαλῆς ἅμα ψόφῳ προσπεσόντι πληγείσης, τὰς ῥαφὰς διαστάσας μεθιέναι τὴν ψυχήν), like that of Dr. Wiltse [139]. A similar sensation experienced at the onset of catalepsy is recorded in R. C. Johnson's *Watcher on the Hills* (51). According to the Tibetan *Book of the Dead* (ed. W. Y. Evan-Wentz (1949), 91 f.), the most desirable outlet for the

soul of the dying is through the sutures of the skull. The idea looks as if it may be connected with a belief that the soul is introduced into the embryo through the fontanelle.

10. And is nicely parodied by Lucian (*Philops.* 22 ff. Cf. Wehrli on H.P., fr. 92).

11. From which it might be inferred that for Empedotimus the circle of the Milky Way is at the same distance from the earth as the circle of the sun—it is the boundary of Pluto's realm, Hades. This would accord with a Pythagorean belief that the Milky Way marks a former orbit of the sun (Arist. *Meteor.* 1. 8. 345ª14). For Cicero (*rep.* vi. 16) the Galaxy is, and for Manilius (i. 758 ff.) it may be, the seat of the souls of the blessed; for Statius (*Silv.* i. 2. 51 ff.), the seat of the gods themselves. I do not know whether there is any significance in the fact that the Milky Way intersects the Zodiac in the sign of Scorpio (Man. i. 690), where was the way by which Hercules went to the gods [151].

12. Cf. Arist. *de anima* i. 3. 10, ὁ Τίμαιος φυσιολογεῖ τὴν ψυχὴν κινεῖν τὸ σῶμα κτλ., where he means ὁ Πλάτων ἐν Τιμαίῳ (36e). Cf. Ammonius, *de interpr.* 133, 16 Busse (= Diels–Kranz i. 223. 12).

13. It became an eschatological commonplace, apparently: Porph. *ap.* Stob. i. 447. 5, ἡ λεγομένη καὶ νομιζομένη τῶν ἐν Ἅιδου τρίοδος.

14. And Clearchus, fr. 10 may be a parody of Heraclides (D.L. viii. 4 f.).

15. This, in conjunction with *in remp.* ii. 119 [151], disproves Lévy's interpretation of Varro's *mortalem aspectum detersus* (ⁱⁱ 155, n. 2). Cf. Wehrli's note on H.P., fr. 91.

16. A belief ascribed to Pythagoras himself by Diodorus (xviii. 1. 1), which need mean no more than that it was held by Pythagoreans. It was accepted by Aristotle (*ap.* Sext. Emp. πρὸς φυσικούς i. 20 f. = Ross, *Works of Aristotle Translated* xii. 84: cf. Jaeger, *Aristotle* 161 f.). It was a piece of popular lore (cf. *Il.* xvi. 843 ff.; Plat. *Apol.* 39c; Harland and Wilkinson, *Lancashire Folk-lore* 104), taken up by savants looking for proof of the soul's divinity.

17. Cf. Arist. *Eud.*, fr. 1 (*Aristotle Translated* xii. 16). Is the flood that which overwhelmed Helice and Bura (Heraclides Pont., fr. 46 W.)?

18. Though the fact that the *Theages* is quoted might have some significance. Heraclides has been suggested as the author of this dialogue (A. E. Taylor, *Plato*⁵ 534). Even the reference to Execestus could be from Heraclides. He and Aristotle were exact contemporaries, and must have known each other well in the Academy. This makes it impossible to pronounce on their literary relationship.

19. Once Gauls have become Hyperboreans it is a short and logical step to see the Rhipaean mountains in the Alps: Steph. Byz. *s.* Ὑπερβόρεοι (Protarchus); Posidonius *ap.* schol. *ad* Ap. Rhod. ii. 675 (this scholiast also tells us that Hec. Abd. said that the Hyperboreans existed in his time).

20. This seems to have been a separate work from the περὶ δικαιοσύνης (or ὁ πρὸς Ἄβαριν λόγος Procl. *in Tim.* 141d = fr. 36 Voss), of which *Abaris* may have been an alternative title (perhaps fr. 73 W. should rather be assigned to the περὶ δικαιοσύνης; but cf. fr. 75 W. with Iambl. *V.P.* 218).

περὶ τῶν πρὸς Ἄβαριν ἀναφερομένων naturally means 'concerning the sayings [or writings] ascribed to Abaris', (not 'remarks addressed to A.', which Voss (57) thinks possible): it may have been about his χρησμοί (Ap. mir. 4 (Theopompus); schol. ad Ar. Eq. 729; Lycurgus, fr. 85; Suid. s. Ἄβαρις).

21. Accepting the convincing thesis of Boyancé (Revue des Études anciennes xxxvi. 321 ff.) that Iambl. V.P. 215–21 is a summary of the περὶ δικαιοσύνης; I am sure that it is a summary of some Heraclidean dialogue, but not so sure which one.

22. Cf. Dodds 161, n. 33; Meuli 160.

23. The function of the arrow in Aristotle's account (Iambl. V.P. 140–3, if it is from Aristotle; Ross accepts it, Aristotle Translated 135) seems to have been that of a guide: whether Abaris rode on it is not clear. Anyway, see note 18 above.

24. Of the nicknames given to the 'pupils of Pythagoras' Abaris, Epimenides, and Empedocles [143], the last, in the form κωλυσανέμας, was known to Timaeus (D.L. viii. 60), a younger contemporary and (hostile) user of Heraclides (the most improbable tradition that Empedocles was a pupil of Pythagoras also comes from Tim. (D.L. viii. 54), perhaps from the same source as κωλυσανέμας). If this trio of nicknames were really coeval, as is suggested by their conjunction in the later authorities, Heraclides must almost certainly have been their inventor.

25. See Bidez–Cumont i. 80–84; ii. 63–66. Aristoxenus (fr. 13) was using Heraclides. Lydus (mens. iv. 42) provides the link whereby we can draw on Antonius Diogenes (507 ff. = Phot. Bibl. 109 ff.) to extend our knowledge of Heraclides' Zoroaster: what Dercyllis is said in Photius' epitome to have heard from Astraeus about Pythagoras and Mnesarchus is given at greater length by Porphyry (V.P. 10–14). Antonius claimed to have authority for his fantasies in ancient writers; unfortunately Photius does not preserve their names, but Heraclides was clearly one. Noteworthy also is the location of the Sibyl in the moon in Antonius, with which should be compared a passage in Plutarch, very Heraclidean in its interest in oracles and its proposal of a 'scientific' explanation of them (Pyth. orac. 9. 39c–d; cf. ser. num. vind. 22. 566d; and, for the proximity of the moon to the island of the Hyperboreans, Hec. Abd. ap. Diod. Sic. ii. 47).

Wehrli's assignation of frr. 69 and 70 to the Zoroaster cannot be supported: the original of the magus who claimed at the court of Gelo to have circumnavigated Africa was surely Sataspes (Hdt. iv. 62), not Zoroaster—even though the historical Sataspes was unsuccessful.

26. ο[ἱ μὲν οὐ] τὸν Ἡρά φασιν εἶναι τὸν πατέρα τοῦ μύθου τοῦδε παντός, ἀλλὰ Ζωροάστρην, καὶ ὡς τοῦδε τοῦ ὀνόματος ἐγκειμένου τὴν γραφὴν ἐκδεδώκασιν, ὥσπερ καὶ ὁ Ἐπικούρειος Κολώτης. I take it that Proclus means that some texts of the Platonic myth had actually been edited with the name of Zoroaster substituted for that of Er, and is not referring to the apocryphal work of Zoroaster quoted by Clement (Strom. v. 103), as Bidez–Cumont think (ii. 160).

27. The real Zoroaster could never have made such a claim himself: metempsychosis was not a tenet of true Mazdaism (Bidez–Cumont i. 28). If Aristeas was anywhere said to have had a number of incarnations,

Democharis [25] might have been the father of one of them; but 'Suidas' [Hesychius'] doubt about his subject's paternity may be ascribable to simple confusion with some other Aristeas.

28. It must surely have been this antique Zoroaster who was descended from 'one of the invaders from the continent beyond the Great Sea'. This continent was originally a passing fancy of Plato (*Tim.* 24a), later taken up and developed by someone on lines suggested by the accounts of the inhabitants of Atlantis in the *Timaeus* and the *Critias*, and blended with the myth of the discourse of Silenus to Midas mentioned by Aristotle in the *Eudemus* (Ross, *Aristotle Translated* xii. 18 f.) (cf. Xen. *Anab.* i. 2. 13). The author of this development may have been Theopompus (*ap.* Ael. *V.H.* iii. 18 = Jacoby ii B. 551 f.), but it has the look to me of a Heraclidean fable. This continent was 'beyond the Great Sea' (schol. *ad Alcib.*—cf. H.P., fr. 102 W.[157]), ἔξω τούτου τοῦ κόσμου, inhabited by a sort of super-Hyperboreans (Theopompus).

I see that Bidez–Cumont (i. 14) suggest Heraclides as possibly the author of the tradition that made Zoroaster the descendant of one of the immigrants from this outer continent. The tradition would perhaps be at least as early as Hermippus if I am right in emending Arnobius, *adv. nat.* i. 52 (Bidez–Cumont ii. 15) 'age veniat, quaeso, per igneam zonam Magus inferiore [interiore *cod.*] ab orbe Zoroastres, Hermippo ut assentiamur auctori'. I find Bidez–Cumont's explanation of this passage, after Kroll, quite unconvincing: the *ignea zona* is naturally the διακεκαυμένη, and Zoroaster (or his progenitor) may have come from a part of the great continent in the southern hemisphere (often thought of as lower than the northern [117]). Arnobius would be sneering at an impossible story: no one could travel through the uninhabitable torrid zone!

29. λέγεται δὲ ὡς καὶ πρῶτος αὐτὸν Αἰακὸν λέγοι, καὶ Λακεδαιμονίοις προείποι τὴν ὑπ' Ἀρκάδων ἅλωσιν προσποιηθῆναί τε πολλάκις ἀναβεβιωκέναι. The last word could merely refer to 'returning to life' after catalepsy (cf. ἀναβιούς of Er in *rep.* x. 614b), but the ref. to Aeacus can only be understood as meaning a previous incarnation. The text appears to be corrupt; perhaps we should read πρῶτον [so Casaubon] αὐτὸν Αἰακὸν λέγοι ⟨γεγονέναι⟩ (for the Greek cf. i. 25, αὐτὸς δέ φησιν . . . μονήρη αὐτὸν γεγονέναι). Cf. Dodds 143.

30. Diogenes (i. 115) says it was at Orchomenus that they were taken; either this is an event otherwise unknown, or it is a slip, perhaps of Theopompus, who knew of the prophecy. Κρησί here also seems to be a mistake (for Λακεδαιμονίοις: see note 29 above).

31. He is called a Crotoniate also by Cratinus in his *Trophonius* (Meineke, *F.C.G* .ii. 143; I agree with Meineke that there can be no doubt that he is the same as the Phormio called ὁ Λάκων by Pausanias and Clement: see his useful discussion, ibid. 1227 ff.). Kock and Meineke assign this play to the elder Cratinus, rather than to the younger (fourth century). Such slight evidence as there is seems to me to suggest the latter: fr. 1 M. (221 K.), about abstention from the τρίγλη, τρυγών, and μελάνουρος, looks like a dig at one form of Pythagoreanism, for which these creatures were tabu (D.L. viii. 33; cf. the Hippocratic treatise περὶ ἱερῆς νούσου 2; Arist. *ap.* D.L. viii. 19); and

Pythagoreans were a favourite butt of the Middle Comedy (cf. Diels–Kranz i. 479 f.).

32. For a curious account of a modern 'journey in the soul' confirmed by an *apport* see Nandor Fodor, *On the Trail of the Poltergeist* 91 ff.

33. A mysterious voice from heaven addresses Epimenides in D.L. i. 115 (from Theopompus). Cf. Cleonymus and Thespesius [148 f.]. (But Bidez thinks Heraclides did *not* invent the Empedoclean translation: *Vie d'Empédocle* 35 ff.)

34. Müller (*F.H.G.* ii. 197 ff.) discusses various theories about its authorship. He is inclined to accept much of it (including this chapter) as ultimately Heraclidean.

35. Cf. Empedocles—D.L. viii. 60: also derived from Heraclides?

36. So the pious Aeacus (a previous incarnation of Epimenides, it will be remembered) prayed on behalf of all the Greeks for delivery from a drought (Isocr. *Euag.* 14 f.; Clem *Strom.* vi (= Euseb. *P.E.* x. 2. 8); Diod. Sic. iv. 61. 2). So too the Athenians pray on behalf of all the world for delivery from a universal plague (Harpocr. *s. Ἄβαρις*; cf. schol. *ad* Ar. *Eq.* 729).

37. Dionysus Brisaeus? Cf. Macrob. *Sat.* i. 18. 9; *Et. magn. s. Βρισαῖος*. The *Brisae* taught Aristaeus beekeeping [167]. (On the name *Brisae* see D. Detschew, *Die thrakischen Sprachreste* 89 f.)

38. Cf. also a fragment of Sallust (*ap.* Serv. *ad Geor.* i. 14); Nigidius Figulus *ap.* schol. *in* Germ. *Arat.* 287; Paus. x. 17. 3 f.

39. Such a blending of the two personages might help to explain the fact that later authorities sometimes call Aristeas *Aristaeus* (Pausanias actually uses both forms [T. 4; 6]).

40. Asbolus the Centaur (surely a figure to appeal to Heraclides!) is the Ἄσβολος οἰωνιστής of the Hesiodic *Shield* (185); Euclus the Cyprian was said to have prophesied that Homer would be born in Cyprus, and forecast the Persian war (Paus. x. 24. 3; 14. 6); Pronapides was supposed to have been a goodly poet and teacher of Homer (Diod. Sic. iii. 67. 5).

41. Λητοῦς τε καὶ Ἀρτέμιδος καὶ Ἀπόλλωνος γένεσιν δηλῶσαι ἐν μέλεσι. Leg. Λητοῦς τόκον [Ἀρτέμιδος καὶ Ἀπόλλωνος γένεσιν]?

42. In the assignation of works to such characters as these we can see the beginning of the process carried farther by Lobon and others later [25].

43. Euphorion made Homer a contemporary of Gyges (Clem. *Strom.* i. 21 = Jacoby ii. 579): because of a supposed connexion with Aristeas?

44. But Maximus uses the phrase elsewhere (xxvi. 1a: ἀναχύσεις θαλάττης ποταμῶν ἐκβολάς, ἀέρων μεταβολάς).

45. (1) The elegiac couplet with the pentameter first about the lovers Chariton and Melanippus who conspired against Phalaris (fr. 65 W. Cf. Ael. *V.H.* ii. 4; Suid. *s. Φάλαρις*; Oenomaus *ap.* Euseb. *P.E.* v. 35. 3). It seems to be based on the fourth-century Pythagorean tale about Phinteas and Damon and the tyrant Dionysius (Iambl. *V.P.* 233 ff., from Aristoxenus). Phalaris' unwonted leniency to his would-be assassins earned him from Apollo a postponement of his fate for two years—an idea suggested by Hdt. i. 91. (2) fr. 138 W.: apparently an order to Xerxes to abstain from sacrilege, which is a conflation of Hes. *Op.* 27, Empedocles, fr. 141, and

perhaps an oracle given to Jason of Pherae in 370 B.C. (cf. Parke in *A.J.P.* lxi (1940), 78 f. Parke thinks that the Heraclidean oracle is genuine).

46. Cf. Tournier 45; Meuli 159.

47. Cf. Empedocles, frr. 134; 140. Apollo is frequently associated with Pythagoras in later tradition.

48. It would be safer to say 'was confirmed in his adoption of it'; but, whatever psychological causes we may believe to underlie the practice of religious vegetarianism (Dodds 154; 175), the fact that there is no first-hand evidence for this practice in Greece before Pythagoras—quite the reverse—indicates that he introduced it, and prompts the question, Why?

49. My theory would imply that the authorship of Aristeas was evident from the poem itself. This is not in the least improbable: he may have been addressed in the vocative by other personages in it.

CHAPTER VIII

1. Though the Cimmerians of the *Odyssey* (xi. 13 ff.) have moved from the world of fact to that of fancy, and are not, I think, to be located anywhere on this earth, the poet had heard from somewhere that the real Cimmerians had dwelt in a 'region of darkness'—the north [40]. I believe that it was Aristeas who first told the Greeks whence their Cimmerian invaders had come (having himself been told by the Scyths): criticizing the theory that the Cimmerian raids in Asia Minor gave an impulse to Greek colonization in the Black Sea, Cook (79) says 'it would be remarkable if at that critical time the Ionians had tried to plant colonies in the hornets' nest'; indeed it would—if they knew where the nest was! But how could they know?

TEXTS AND FRAGMENTS

1. HERODOTUS iv. 13

   [*Arimaspeorum* fr. 1] ἔφη δὲ Ἀριστέης ὁ Καϋστροβίου ἀνὴρ Προκοννήσιος, ποιέων ἔπεα, ἀπικέσθαι ἐς Ἰσσηδόνας φοιβόλαμπτος
   γενόμενος, Ἰσσηδόνων δὲ ὑπεροικέειν Ἀριμασποὺς ἄνδρας μουνοφθάλμους, ὑπὲρ δὲ τούτων τοὺς χρυσοφύλακας γρῦπας, τούτων δὲ
   τοὺς Ὑπερβορέους κατήκοντας ἐπὶ θάλασσαν. τούτους ὦν πάντας
   πλὴν Ὑπερβορέων ἀρξάντων Ἀριμασπῶν αἰεὶ τοῖσι πλησιοχώροισι
   ἐπιτίθεσθαι, καὶ ὑπὸ μὲν Ἀριμασπῶν ἐξωθέεσθαι ἐκ τῆς χώρης
   Ἰσσηδόνας, ὑπὸ δὲ Ἰσσηδόνων Σκύθας, Κιμμερίους δὲ οἰκέοντας ἐπὶ
   τῇ νοτίῃ θαλάσσῃ ὑπὸ Σκυθέων πιεζομένους ἐκλιπεῖν τὴν χώρην.

2. HERODOTUS iv. 16

   [fr. 2] οὐδὲ γὰρ οὐδὲ Ἀριστέης, τοῦ περ ὀλίγῳ πρότερον τούτων
   μνήμην ἐποιεύμην, οὐδὲ οὗτος προσωτέρω Ἰσσηδόνων αὐτὸς ἐν
   τοῖσι ἔπεσι ποιέων ἔφησε ἀπικέσθαι, ἀλλὰ τὰ κατύπερθε ἔλεγε
   ἀκοῇ, φὰς Ἰσσηδόνας εἶναι τοὺς ταῦτα λέγοντας.

3. TZETZES, *Chiliades* vii. 676–9; 686–92

   καὶ ὁ Φερένικός φησι περὶ Ὑπερβορέων,
   ὥσπερ καὶ ὁ Ζηνόθεμις, ὁμοῦ καὶ Ἀριστέας,
   ὁ Ἀριστέας ὁ σοφός, ὁ τοῦ Καϋστροβίου,
   οὗπερ αὐτὸς μὲν ἔπεσιν ἐνέτυχον ὀλίγοις

   . . . .

   καὶ Ἀριστέας δέ φησιν ἐν τοῖς Ἀριμασπείοις·
   [fr. 3] Ἰσσηδοὶ χαίτῃσιν ἀγαλλόμενοι ταναῇσι·
   [fr. 4] καὶ †σφᾶς† ἀνθρώπους εἶναι καθύπερθεν ὁμούρους
   πρὸς βορέω, πολλούς τε καὶ ἐσθλοὺς κάρτα μαχητάς,
   ἀφνειοὺς ἵπποισι, πολύρρηνας πολυβούτας.
   [fr. 5] ὀφθαλμὸν δ᾽ ἔν᾽ ἕκαστος ἔχει χαρίεντι μετώπῳ,
   χαίτῃσι⟨ν⟩ λάσιοι, πάντων στιβαρώτατοι ἀνδρῶν.

4. PAUSANIAS i. 24. 6

   [fr. 6] τούτους τοὺς γρῦπας ἐν τοῖς ἔπεσιν Ἀριστέας ὁ Προκοννήσιος μάχεσθαι περὶ τοῦ χρυσοῦ φησιν Ἀριμασποῖς τοῖς ὑπὲρ

Ἰσσηδόνων· τὸν δὲ χρυσόν, ὃν φυλάσσουσιν οἱ γρῦπες, ἀνιέναι τὴν
γῆν· εἶναι δὲ Ἀριμασποὺς μὲν ἄνδρας μονοφθάλμους πάντας ἐκ
γενετῆς, γρῦπας δὲ θηρία λέουσι εἰκασμένα, πτερὰ δὲ ἔχειν καὶ
στόμα ἀετοῦ. καὶ γρυπῶν μὲν πέρι τοσαῦτα εἰρήσθω.

5. 'LONGINUS', de sublimitate 10. 4

ὁ μὲν γὰρ τὰ Ἀριμάσπεια ποιήσας ἐκεῖνα οἴεται δεινά·
[fr. 7] θαῦμ' ἡμῖν καὶ τοῦτο μέγα φρεσὶν ἡμετέρῃσιν.
ἄνδρες ὕδωρ ναίουσιν ἀπὸ χθονὸς ἐν πελάγεσσι·
δύστηνοί τινές εἰσιν, ἔχουσι γὰρ ἔργα πονηρά,
ὄμματ' ἐν ἄστροισι, ψυχὴν δ' ἐνὶ πόντῳ ἔχουσιν.
ἦ που πολλὰ θεοῖσι φίλας ἀνὰ χεῖρας ἔχοντες
εὔχονται σπλάγχνοισι κακῶς ἀναβαλλομένοισι.

6. PAUSANIAS v. 7. 9

Ἀρισταῖος δὲ ὁ Προκοννήσιος, μνήμην γὰρ ἐποιήσατο Ὑπερβορέων καὶ οὗτος, τάχα ἄν τι καὶ πλέον περὶ αὐτῶν πεπυσμένος εἴη
παρὰ Ἰσσηδόνων, ἐς οὓς ἀφικέσθαι φησὶν ἐν τοῖς ἔπεσιν.

7. STRABO 21

τάχα δὲ καὶ τοὺς μονομμάτους Κύκλωπας ἐκ τῆς Σκυθικῆς
ἱστορίας μετενήνοχε· τοιούτους γάρ τινας τοὺς Ἀριμασποὺς φασιν,
οὓς ἐν τοῖς Ἀριμασπείοις ἔπεσιν ἐνδέδωκεν Ἀριστέας ὁ Προκοννήσιος.

8. PLINY, Naturalis Historia vii. 10

sed iuxta eos, qui sunt ad septentrionem versi, haut procul
ab ipso aquilonis exortu specuque eius dicto, quem locum Ges
clithron appellant, produntur Arimaspi, quos diximus, uno
oculo in fronte media insignes. quibus adsidue bellum esse
circa metalla cum grypis, ferarum volucri genere, quale vulgo
traditur, eruente ex cuniculis aurum, mira cupiditate et feris
custodientibus et Arimaspis rapientibus, multi, sed maxime
inlustres Herodotus et Aristeas Proconnesius scribunt.

9. AULUS GELLIUS ix. 4. 1–4

cum e Graecia in Italiam rediremus et Brundisium iremus
egressique e navi in terram in portu illo inclito spatiaremur...
fasces librorum venalium expositos vidimus. atque ego avide

statim pergo ad libros. erant autem isti omnes libri Graeci miraculorum fabularumque pleni, res inauditae, incredulae, scriptores veteres non parvae auctoritatis: Aristeas Proconnesius et Isigonus Nicaeensis et Ctesias et Onesicritus et Philostephanus et Hegesias; ipsa autem volumina ex diutino situ squalebant et habitu aspectuque taetro erant.

10. DIONYSIUS HALICARNASSEUS, *Thucydides* 23

οὔτε γὰρ διασώζονται τῶν πλειόνων αἱ γραφαὶ μέχρι τῶν καθ' ἡμᾶς χρόνων οὔθ' αἱ διασωζόμεναι παρὰ πᾶσιν ὡς ἐκείνων οὖσαι τῶν ἀνδρῶν πιστεύονται· ἐν αἷς εἰσιν αἵ τε Κάδμου τοῦ Μιλησίου καὶ Ἀρισταίου τοῦ Προικοννησίου καὶ τῶν παραπλησίων τούτοις.

11. 'SUIDAS'

Ἀριστέας, Δημοχάριδος ἢ Καϋστροβίου, Προικοννήσιος, ἐποποιός· τὰ Ἀριμάσπεια καλούμενα ἔπη· ἔστι δὲ ἱστορία τῶν Ὑπερβορέων Ἀριμασπῶν, βιβλία γ'. τούτου φασὶ τὴν ψυχήν, ὅταν ἐβούλετο, ἐξιέναι καὶ ἐπανιέναι πάλιν. γέγονε δὲ κατὰ Κροῖσον καὶ Κῦρον, Ὀλυμπιάδι ν'. ἔγραψε δὲ οὗτος καὶ καταλογάδην Θεογονίαν, εἰς ἔπη ͵α.

Cf. EUDOCIA, *Violarium* clvii

Ἀριστέας Δημοχάριδος ἢ Καϋστροβίου, Προκοννήσιος, ἐποποιός. συνέθηκε τὰ Ἀριμάσπεια καλούμενα ἔπη (ἔστι δὲ ἱστορία τῶν Ὑπερβορέων Ἀριμασπῶν, βιβλία τρία), ἔγραψε καὶ Θεογονίαν πάνυ καλῶς.

12. HERODOTUS iv. 14–15

καὶ ὅθεν μὲν ἦν Ἀριστέης ὁ ταῦτα ποιήσας, εἴρηκα· τὸν δὲ περὶ αὐτοῦ ἤκουον λόγον ἐν Προκοννήσῳ καὶ Κυζίκῳ, λέξω. Ἀριστέην γὰρ λέγουσι, ἐόντα τῶν ἀστῶν οὐδενὸς γένος ὑποδεέστερον, ἐσελθόντα ἐς κναφήιον ἐν Προκοννήσῳ ἀποθανεῖν, καὶ τὸν κναφέα κατακληίσαντα τὸ ἐργαστήριον οἴχεσθαι ἀγγελέοντα τοῖσι προσήκουσι τῷ νεκρῷ. ἐσκεδασμένου δὲ ἤδη τοῦ λόγου ἀνὰ τὴν πόλιν ὡς τεθνεὼς εἴη ὁ Ἀριστέης, ἐς ἀμφισβασίας τοῖσι λέγουσι ἀπικνέεσθαι ἄνδρα Κυζικηνὸν ἥκοντα ἐξ Ἀρτάκης πόλιος, φάντα συντυχεῖν τέ οἱ ἰόντι ἐπὶ Κυζίκου καὶ ἐς λόγους ἀπικέσθαι. καὶ τοῦτον μὲν ἐντεταμένως ἀμφισβατέειν, τοὺς δὲ προσήκοντας τῷ νεκρῷ ἐπὶ τὸ κναφήιον παρεῖναι ἔχοντας τὰ πρόσφορα ὡς ἀναιρησομένους. ἀνοιχθέντος δὲ τοῦ οἰκήματος οὔτε τεθνεῶτα οὔτε ζῶντα φαίνεσθαι Ἀριστέην. μετὰ δὲ ἑβδόμῳ ἔτεϊ φανέντα αὐτὸν ἐς Προκόννησον ποιῆσαι τὰ ἔπεα τὰ νῦν ὑπ' Ἑλλήνων Ἀριμάσπεα καλέεται, ποιήσαντα δὲ ἀφανισθῆναι τὸ δεύτερον. ταῦτα μὲν αἱ πόλιες αὗται λέγουσι, τάδε δὲ οἶδα Μεταποντίνοισι τοῖσι ἐν Ἰταλίῃ συγκυρήσαντα μετὰ τὴν ἀφάνισιν τὴν δευτέρην Ἀριστέω ἔτεσι τεσσεράκοντα καὶ διηκοσίοισι, ὡς ἐγὼ συμβαλλόμενος ἐν Προκοννήσῳ τε καὶ Μεταποντίῳ εὕρισκον. Μεταποντῖνοί φασι αὐτὸν Ἀριστέην φανέντα σφι ἐς τὴν χώρην κελεῦσαι βωμὸν Ἀπόλλωνος ἱδρύσασθαι καὶ Ἀριστέω τοῦ Προκοννησίου ἐπωνυμίην ἔχοντα ἀνδριάντα παρ' αὐτὸν στῆσαι· φάναι γάρ σφι τὸν Ἀπόλλωνα Ἰταλιωτέων μούνοισι δὴ ἀπικέσθαι ἐς τὴν χώρην, καὶ αὐτός οἱ ἔπεσθαι ὁ νῦν ἐὼν Ἀριστέης· τότε δέ, ὅτε εἵπετο τῷ θεῷ, εἶναι κόραξ. καὶ τὸν μὲν εἰπόντα ταῦτα ἀφανισθῆναι, σφέας δὲ Μεταποντῖνοι λέγουσι ἐς Δελφοὺς πέμψαντας τὸν θεὸν ἐπειρωτᾶν ὅ τι τὸ φάσμα τοῦ ἀνθρώπου εἴη. τὴν δὲ Πυθίην σφέας κελεύειν πείθεσθαι τῷ φάσματι, πειθομένοισι δὲ ἄμεινον συνοίσεσθαι. καὶ σφέας δεξαμένους ταῦτα ποιῆσαι ἐπιτελέα. καὶ νῦν ἕστηκε ἀνδριὰς ἐπωνυμίην ἔχων Ἀριστέω παρ' αὐτῷ τῷ ἀγάλματι τοῦ Ἀπόλλωνος, πέριξ δὲ αὐτὸν δάφναι ἑστᾶσι· τὸ δὲ ἄγαλμα ἐν τῇ ἀγορῇ ἵδρυται.

13. TZETZES, *Chiliades* ii. 723–35

> ὁ Ἀριστέας μὲν υἱὸς ἦν τοῦ Καϋστροβίου,
> τῷ γένει Προικονύήσιος τῶν εὐγενῶν καὶ πρώτων.
> οὗτος χαλκείῳ παρεισδὺς θνήσκει καὶ πίπτει νέκυς.
> κλείσας δ' εὐθέως ὁ χαλκεὺς ἐκεῖνο τὸ χαλκεῖον
> τοῖς συγγενέσι τὸ δεινὸν λέγει τοῦ Ἀριστέα.
> οἱ δὲ δραμόντες ὀδυρμοῖς πάντες πρὸς τὸ χαλκεῖον,
> ἀνοίξαντες οὐδὲν εὗρον, οὐ νέκυν οὐδὲ ζῶντα.
> μετὰ δ' ἑπτὰ χρόνους φανεὶς πάλιν ὁ Ἀριστέας,
> ἔπη τὰ Ἀριμάσπεια λεγόμενα συγγράφει.
> καὶ πάλιν ἀφανίζεται τὸ δεύτερον καὶ θνήσκει.
> καὶ μετὰ διακόσια δὶς εἴκοσι τὰ ἔτη
> ἐφ' Ἡροδότου γέγονε, καὶ πάλιν ἀνεφάνη,
> ὥσπερ φησὶν Ἡρόδοτος· εἰ δ' ἀληθὲς οὐκ οἶδα.

Cf. *Chiliades* iv. 521 f.

καὶ Ἀριστέας ἅμα,
ὁ Ἀριστέας ὁ σοφὸς ὁ τοῦ Καϋστροβίου,
⟨sc. τῷ ἀποθνήσκειν τε καὶ ζῆν ἐφρόνει μέγα⟩.

14. APOLLONIUS, *Mirabilia* 2

Ἀριστέαν δὲ ἱστορεῖται τὸν Προκοννήσιον ἔν τινι γναφείῳ τῆς Προκοννήσου τελευτήσαντα ἐν τῇ αὐτῇ ἡμέρᾳ καὶ ὥρᾳ ἐν Σικελίᾳ ὑπὸ πολλῶν θεωρηθῆναι γράμματα διδάσκοντα. ὅθεν πολλάκις αὐτῷ τοῦ τοιούτου συμβαίνοντος καὶ περιφανοῦς γιγνομένου διὰ πολλῶν ἐτῶν καὶ πυκνότερον ἐν τῇ Σικελίᾳ φανταζομένου οἱ Σικελοὶ ἱερόν τε καθιδρύσαντο αὐτῷ καὶ ἔθυσαν ὡς ἥρωι.

15. PLINY, *Naturalis Historia* vii. 174

reperimus inter exempla ⟨*sc.* uti de homine ne morti quidem debeat credi⟩ ... Aristeae etiam ⟨*sc.* animam⟩ visam evolantem ex ore in Proconneso corvi effigie, magna quae sequitur hanc fabulositate.

16. PLUTARCH, *Romulus* 28

ἔοικε μὲν οὖν ταῦτα [the mysterious disappearance of Romulus, his subsequent reappearance and deification] τοῖς ὑφ᾽ Ἑλλήνων περί τε Ἀριστέου τοῦ Προκοννησίου καὶ Κλεομήδους τοῦ Ἀστυπαλαιέως μυθολογουμένοις. Ἀριστέαν μὲν γὰρ ἔν τινι κναφείῳ τελευτῆσαί φασι καὶ τὸ σῶμα μετιόντων αὐτοῦ τῶν φίλων ἀφανὲς οἴχεσθαι· λέγειν δέ τινας εὐθὺς ἐξ ἀποδημίας ἥκοντας ἐντυχεῖν Ἀριστέᾳ τὴν ἐπὶ Κρότωνος πορευομένῳ.

17. ORIGEN, *contra Celsum* iii. 26

ἴδωμεν δὲ καὶ ἃ μετὰ ταῦτα λέγει ὁ Κέλσος, παρατιθέμενος ἀπὸ ἱστοριῶν παράδοξα καὶ καθ᾽ αὐτὰ μὲν ἀπίστοις ἐοικότα ὑπ᾽ αὐτοῦ δὲ οὐκ ἀπιστούμενα ὅσον γε ἐπὶ τῇ λέξει αὐτοῦ. καὶ πρῶτόν γε τὰ περὶ τὸν Προκοννήσιον Ἀριστέαν, περὶ οὗ ταῦτά φησιν· "εἶτ᾽ Ἀριστέαν μὲν τὸν Προκοννήσιον ἀφανισθέντα τε οὕτως δαιμονίως ἐξ ἀνθρώπων καὶ αὖθις ἐναργῶς φανέντα καὶ πολλοῖς ὕστερον χρόνοις πολλαχοῦ τῆς οἰκουμένης ἐπιδημήσαντα καὶ θαυμαστὰ ἀγγείλαντα, καὶ τοῦ Ἀπόλλωνος ἐπισκήψαντος τοῖς Μεταποντίνοις ἐν θεῶν μοίρᾳ νέμειν τὸν Ἀριστέαν, τοῦτον οὐδεὶς ἔτι νομίζει θεόν." ἔοικε δὲ εἰληφέναι τὴν ἱστορίαν ἀπὸ Πινδάρου καὶ Ἡροδότου [cf. 27 ἢ Ἡρόδοτος μὲν καὶ Πίνδαρος ἀψευδεῖν παρὰ σοὶ νομίζονται . . . ;] [Origen then repeats T. 12 *verbatim*].

Cf. AENEAS GAZAEUS, *Theophrastus* lxxxv. 993 Migne [a careless compilation from Origen, it would appear]

Πίνδαρος δὲ ὁ Θηβαῖος καὶ Ἡρόδοτος Ἀλικαρνασσεὺς Ἀριστέα φασὶ τὸν Προκοννήσιον εἰσελθόντα παρὰ τὸν κναφέα ἐν Προκοννήσῳ, ἐκεῖ καὶ τεθνάναι· καὶ ἀφανισθέντα Κυζικηνοῖς φανερῶς διαλέγεσθαι· καὶ διακοσίοις ὕστερον ἔτεσι καὶ τεσσαράκοντα ἐν Ἰταλίᾳ Μεταποντίνοις ὀφθῆναι, καὶ κελεύειν ἑαυτὸν θυσίαις τιμᾶν, καὶ τὸν Ἀπόλλωνα· συνείπετο γάρ, ἔφη, τῷ Ἀπόλλωνι τότε κόραξ, ὑπάρχων ὁ νῦν Ἀριστεύς· καὶ τοὺς Μεταποντίνους πέμψαντας εἰς Δελφοὺς ἐρωτᾶν τὸν Ἀπόλλωνα εἰ χρὴ τῷ Ἀριστεῖ πείθεσθαι· καὶ τὴν Πυθίαν χρῆσαι ὡς πειθομένοις ἄμεινον ἔσται. καὶ νῦν ἀνδριὰς ἕστηκεν ἐπωνυμίᾳ Ἀριστεύς, παρ' αὐτῷ τῷ ἀγάλματι τοῦ Ἀπόλλωνος. καὶ ὡς θεοῖς ἀμφοτέροις ἡ θυσία κοινὴ νομίζεται.

18. ATHENAEUS xiii. 605c–d

Φαρσαλίᾳ τῇ Θεσσαλίδι ὀρχηστρίδι δάφνης στέφανον χρυσοῦν Φιλόμηλος ἔδωκε, Λαμψακηνῶν ἀνάθημα. αὕτη ἡ Φαρσαλία ἐν Μεταποντίῳ ὑπὸ τῶν ἐν τῇ ἀγορᾷ μάντεων, γενομένης φωνῆς ἐκ τῆς δάφνης τῆς χαλκῆς, ἣν ἔστησαν Μεταποντῖνοι κατὰ τὴν Ἀριστέα τοῦ Προκοννησίου ἐπιδημίαν, ὅτ' ἔφησεν ἐξ Ὑπερβορέων παραγεγονέναι, ὡς τάχιστα ὤφθη εἰς τὴν ἀγορὰν ἐμβαλοῦσα, ἐμμανῶν γενομένων τῶν μάντεων διεσπάσθη ὑπ' αὐτῶν. καὶ τῶν ἀνθρώπων ὕστερον ἀναζητούντων τὴν αἰτίαν εὑρέθη διὰ τὸν τοῦ θεοῦ στέφανον ἀνῃρημένη.

19. MAXIMUS TYRIUS x. 2 f.

Προκονησίῳ ἀνδρὶ τὸ μὲν σῶμα ἔκειτο ἔμπνουν μέν, ἀλλ' ἀμυδρῶς καὶ ἐγγύτατα θανάτου· ἡ δὲ ψυχὴ ἐκδῦσα τοῦ σώματος, ἐπλανᾶτο ἐν τῷ αἰθέρι, ὄρνιθος δίκην, πάντα ὕποπτα θεωμένη, γῆν, καὶ θάλατταν, καὶ ποταμούς, καὶ πόλεις, καὶ ἔθνη ἀνδρῶν, καὶ παθήματα, καὶ φύσεις παντοίας· καὶ αὖθις εἰσδυομένη τὸ σῶμα καὶ ἀναστήσασα, ὥσπερ ὀργάνῳ χρωμένη, διηγεῖτο ἅττα εἶδέν τε καὶ ἤκουσεν, παρ' ἄλλοις ἄλλα.

20. MAXIMUS TYRIUS xxxviii. 3c–f

ἐγένετο καὶ ἐν Προκοννήσῳ ἀνὴρ φιλόσοφος, ὄνομα Ἀριστέας·
ἠπιστεῖτο δὲ αὐτῷ οὐχὶ σοφία τὰ πρῶτα, διότι μηδένα αὐτῆς
διδάσκαλον προΰφερεν. πρὸς οὖν δὴ τὴν τῶν ἀνθρώπων ἀπιστίαν
ἐξεῦρεν λόγον· ἔφασκεν τὴν ψυχὴν αὐτῷ καταλιποῦσαν τὸ σῶμα,
ἀναπτᾶσαν εὐθὺ τοῦ αἰθέρος, περιπολῆσαι τὴν γῆν τὴν Ἑλλάδα καὶ
τὴν βάρβαρον, καὶ νήσους πάσας, καὶ ποταμούς, καὶ ὄρη· γενέσθαι
δὲ τῆς περιπολήσεως αὐτῇ τέρμα τὴν Ὑπερβορέων γῆν· ἐποπτεῦσαι
δὲ πάντα ἐξῆς νόμαια καὶ ἤθη πολιτικά, καὶ φύσεις χωρίων, καὶ
ἀέρων μεταβολάς, καὶ ἀναχύσεις θαλάττης, καὶ ποταμῶν ἐκβολάς·
γενέσθαι δὲ αὐτῇ καὶ τὴν τοῦ οὐρανοῦ θέαν πολὺ τῆς νέρθεν σαφεστέραν.

21. CLEMENS ALEXANDRINUS, Stromata i. 21

προγνώσει δὲ καὶ Πυθαγόρας ὁ μέγας προσανεῖχεν αἰεὶ Ἄβαρίς
τε ὁ Ὑπερβόρειος καὶ Ἀριστέας ὁ Προκοννήσιος Ἐπιμενίδης τε ὁ
Κρής, ὅστις εἰς Σπάρτην ἀφίκετο, καὶ Ζωροάστρης ὁ Μῆδος Ἐμπε-
δοκλῆς τε ὁ Ἀκραγαντῖνος καὶ Φορμίων ὁ Λάκων, ναὶ μὴν Πολυ-
άρατος ὁ Θάσιος Ἐμπεδότιμός τε ὁ Συρακούσιος ἐπί τε τούτοις
Σωκράτης ὁ Ἀθηναῖος μάλιστα.

22. IAMBLICHUS, Vita Pythagorica 138

καὶ τοῦτό γε πάντες οἱ Πυθαγόρειοι ὁμῶς ἔχουσι πιστευτικῶς,
οἷον περὶ Ἀρισταίου τοῦ Προκονησίου καὶ Ἀβάριδος τοῦ Ὑπερ-
βορέου τὰ μυθολογούμενα, καὶ ὅσα ἄλλα τοιαῦτα λέγεται. πᾶσι γὰρ
πιστεύουσι τοῖς τοιούτοις, πολλὰ δὲ καὶ αὐτοὶ πειρῶνται.

23. GREGORIUS NAZIANZENUS, Oratio iv (adversus Iulianum i) 59

ταῦτα μὲν παιζέτωσαν παρ᾽ ἐκείνοις Ἐμπεδοκλεῖς καὶ Ἀρισταῖοι
καὶ Ἐμπεδότιμοί τινες καὶ Τροφώνιοι καὶ τοιούτων δυστυχῶν
ἀριθμός· ὧν ὁ μὲν τοῖς Σικελικοῖς κρατῆρσιν ἑαυτὸν θεώσας, ὡς
ᾤετο . . . τῷ φιλτάτῳ σανδάλῳ κατεμηνύθη παρὰ τοῦ πυρὸς
ἐκβρασθέντι . . . οἱ δὲ ἀδύτοις τισὶν ἑαυτοὺς ἐγκρύψαντες ὑπὸ
τῆς αὐτῆς νόσου καὶ φιλαυτίας, εἶτ᾽ ἐλεγχθέντες, οὐ μᾶλλον ἐκ τῆς
κλοπῆς ἐτιμήθησαν ἢ ἐκ τοῦ μὴ λαθεῖν καθυβρίσθησαν.

24. PROCLUS, in Platonis rem publicam ii. 113

καὶ γὰρ ἐφ᾽ ἡμῶν τινες ἤδη καὶ ἀποθανεῖν ἔδοξαν καὶ μνήμασιν

ἐνετέθησαν καὶ ἀνεβίωσαν καὶ ὤφθησαν οἱ μὲν ἐγκαθήμενοι τοῖς
μνήμασιν, οἱ δὲ καὶ ⟨ἐφ⟩εστῶτες· καθάπερ δὴ καὶ ἐπὶ τῶν πάλαι
γεγονότων ἱστοροῦνται καὶ Ἀριστέας ὁ Προκοννήσιος καὶ Ἑρμότιμος
ὁ Κλαζομένιος καὶ Ἐπιμενίδης ὁ Κρὴς μετὰ θάνατον ἐν τοῖς ζῶσιν
γενόμενοι.

25. STRABO 589

ἐντεῦθέν [Proconnesus] ἐστιν Ἀριστέας ὁ ποιητὴς τῶν Ἀριμασπείων καλουμένων ἐπῶν, ἀνὴρ γόης εἴ τις ἄλλος.

26. STRABO 639

τινὲς δὲ διδάσκαλον Ὁμήρου τοῦτόν [Creophylus] φασιν, οἱ δ᾽
οὐ τοῦτον ἀλλ᾽ Ἀριστέαν τὸν Προκοννήσιον.

Cf. EUSTATHIUS, ad Il. ii. 730

τινὲς δὲ καὶ διδάσκαλον Ὁμήρου τὸν Κρεώφυλον εἶπον· ἕτεροι δὲ
Ἀρισταῖον τὸν Προκοννήσιον, ὡς καὶ ταῦτα ὁ γεωγράφος [Strabo]
ἱστορεῖ.

27. EUSEBIUS, *Praeparatio Evangelica* x. 11. 27 (= TATIANUS, *ad
Graecos* 41)

τὸ δὲ νῦν ἔχον, σπευστέον μετὰ πάσης ἀκριβείας σαφηνίζειν ὡς
οὐχ Ὁμήρου μόνον πρεσβύτερός ἐστιν ὁ Μωσῆς, ἔτι δὲ καὶ τῶν πρὸ
αὐτοῦ συγγραφέων, Λίνου, Φιλάμμονος, Θαμύριδος, Ἀμφίονος,
Ὀρφέως, Μουσαίου, Δημοδόκου, Φημίου, Σιβύλλης, Ἐπιμενίδου
τοῦ Κρητός, ὅστις εἰς τὴν Σπάρτην ἀφίκετο, Ἀρισταίου τοῦ
Προκοννησίου, καὶ τοῦ τὰ Ἀριμάσπια συγγράψαντος, Ἀσβόλου τε
τοῦ Κενταύρου, καὶ Ἰσάτιδος, Δρύμωνός τε καὶ Εὔκλου τοῦ Κυπρίου,
καὶ Ὥρου τοῦ Σαμίου, καὶ Προναπίδου τοῦ Ἀθηναίου.

?28. 'SUIDAS', s. Πείσανδρος Πείσωνος

ποιήματα δὲ αὐτοῦ Ἡράκλεια, ἐν βιβλίοις β'. ἔστι δὲ τὰ Ἡρα-
κλέους ἔργα· ἔνθα πρῶτος Ἡρακλεῖ ῥόπαλον περιτέθεικε. τὰ δὲ
ἄλλα τῶν ποιημάτων νόθα αὐτοῦ δοξάζεται, γενόμενα ὑπό τε ἄλλων
καὶ Ἀριστέως τοῦ ποιητοῦ. [This form of the name is used by
Aeneas of Gaza, T. 17. The 'Pythagorean Aristeus' of Clau-
dianus Mamertus (*Stat. An.* ii. 7) may be Aristaeus rather than
Aristeas.]

BIBLIOGRAPHY

A.J.A.: *American Journal of Archaeology* (Norwood, Mass., 1897–).
A.J.P.: *American Journal of Philology* (Baltimore, 1880–).
C.A.F.: *Comicorum Atticorum Fragmenta* (ed. Kock; Leipzig, 1880–8).
C.Q.: *Classical Quarterly* (London, 1907–).
C.R.: *Classical Review* (London, 1887–).
E.B.: *Encyclopaedia Britannica* (11th ed.; Cambridge, 1910).
E.R.E.: *Encyclopaedia of Religion and Ethics* (Edinburgh, 1908–26).
F.C.G.: *Fragmenta Comicorum Graecorum* (ed. Meineke; Berlin, 1839–41).
F.H.G.: *Fragmenta Historicorum Graecorum* (ed. Müller; Paris, 1841–70).
G.G.M.: *Geographi Graeci Minores* (ed. Müller; Paris, 1855–61).
I.G.: *Inscriptiones Graecae* (Berlin, 1873–).
J.H.S.: *Journal of Hellenic Studies* (London, 1880–).
O.C.D.: *Oxford Classical Dictionary* (Oxford, 1949).
P.–W.: *Paulys Real-Encyclopädie der classischen Altertumswissenschaft* (2nd ed.; Stuttgart, 1894–).
R.M.: *Rheinisches Museum für Philologie* (Frankfurt a. M., 1842–).

ATHANASIEV, A. N.: *Russian Folk Tales* viii (Moscow, 1863).
ATKINSON, T. W.: *Oriental and Western Siberia* (New York, 1865).
BEAZLEY, C. R.: *The Texts and Versions of John de Plano Carpini and William de Rubruquis* (ed. for the Hakluyt Society; London, 1903).
BETHE, E.: 'Aristeas' (in *P.–W.* ii).
BIDEZ, J.: *Eos* (Brussels, 1945).
—— and CUMONT, F.: *Mages hellénisés* (Paris, 1938).
BOWRA, C. M.: 'A Fragment of the *Arimaspea*' (in *C.Q.* xlix (1956)).
BOYANCÉ, P.: *Le Culte des muses chez les philosophes grecs* (Paris, 1937).
BURN, A. R.: 'Dates in Early Greek History' (in *J.H.S.* lv (1935)).
CARPENTER, RHYS: *Folk Tale, Fiction and Saga in the Homeric Epics* (Berkeley, Cal., 1956).
CARRUTHERS, D.: *Unknown Mongolia* (London, 1913).
CHILDE, V. G.: *The Dawn of European Civilization* (London, 1927).
CLEMEN, C.: *Religionsgeschichtliche Erklärung des Neuen Testaments* (Giessen, 1909).
COOK, R. M.: 'Ionia and Greece, 800–600 B.C.' (in *J.H.S.* lxvi (1946)).
CORNFORD, F. M.: *Principium Sapientiae* (Cambridge, 1952).
CRÖNERT, W.: 'De Lobone Argivo' (in *Χάριτες F. Leo dargebracht*; Berlin, 1911).
CUMONT, F.: *Recherches sur le symbolisme funéraire des Romains* (Paris, 1942).
DIELS, H.: *Parmenides* (Berlin, 1897).
—— and KRANZ, W.: *Die Fragmente der Vorsokratiker* (Berlin, 1951).
DODDS, E. R.: *The Greeks and the Irrational* (Berkeley, Cal., 1951).
DUNBABIN, T. J.: *The Greeks and their Eastern Neighbours* (London, 1957).

EBERT, M.: *Südrussland im Altertum* (Bonn, 1921).

ERMAN, A.: *Travels in Siberia* (trans. Cooley; London, 1848).

FARNELL, L. R.: i *Cults of the Greek City States* (Oxford, 1896–1909).

—— ii *Greek Hero Cults and Ideas of Immortality* (Oxford, 1921).

FESTUGIÈRE, A.-J.: *La Révélation d'Hermès Trismégiste* (Paris, 1944–54).

FRÄNKEL, H.: *Dichtung und Philosophie des frühen Griechentums* (New York, 1951).

GUTHRIE, W. K. C.: *The Greeks and their Gods* (London, 1950).

HAKLUYT, R.: *Voyages* (Everyman ed.; London, 1907).

HARLAN, J.: *Central Asia* (ed. F. E. Ross; London, 1939).

HAWKES, D.: *Ch'u Tz'ŭ* (Oxford, 1959).

HENNIG, R.: *Terrae Incognitae* (Leiden, 1944).

HENNING, W. B.: *Zoroaster: Politician or Witch-Doctor?* (Oxford, 1951).

HERMANN, A.: 'Issedoi' (in *P.–W.* ix).

HOLMBERG, U.: *Finno-Ugric and Siberian Mythology* (vol. iv in *The Mythology of All Races*, ed. MacCulloch; Boston, 1927).

HOW, W. W., and WELLS, J.: *A Commentary on Herodotus* (Oxford, 1912).

HUC and GABET: *Travels in Tartary, Thibet and China* (trans. Hazlitt, ed. Pelliot; London, 1929).

HUMBOLDT, A. VON: *Asie centrale* (Paris, 1843).

JACOBY, F.: *Die Fragmente der griechischen Historiker* (Berlin, 1923–).

KIESSLING, M.: 'Hypanis' (in *P.–W.* ix).

LANDOR, A. H. S.: *In the Forbidden Land* (London, 1898).

LAUFER, B.: 'Die Sage von den goldgrabenden Ameisen' (in *T'oung Pao* ix (1908)).

LAWSON, J. C.: *Modern Greek Folklore and Ancient Greek Religion* (Cambridge, 1910).

LÉVY, I.: i *Recherches sur les sources de la légende de Pythagore* (Paris, 1926).

——ii *La Légende de Pythagore de Grèce en Palestin* (Paris, 1927).

LORIMER, H. L.: *Homer and the Monuments* (London, 1950).

MEULI, K.: 'Scythica' (in *Hermes* lxx (1935)).

MINNS, E. H.: *Scythians and Greeks* (Cambridge, 1913).

MORRISON, J. H.: 'Pythagoras of Samos' (in *C.Q.* xlix (1956)).

NILSSON, M. P.: i *A History of Greek Religion* (Oxford, 1956).

——ii *Greek Popular Religion* (New York, 1940).

NISSEN, T.: 'Die Aristeas-Legende im Idyll des Planudes' (in *Byzantinische Zeitschrift* xxxvi (1936)).

PAGE, D. L.: *History and the Homeric Iliad* (Berkeley, Cal., 1959).

PARKE, H. W., and WORMELL, D. E. W.: *The Delphic Oracle* (Oxford, 1956).

PEARSON, L.: *Ionian Historians* (Oxford, 1939).

PERROT, G., and CHIPIEZ, C.: *Histoire de l'art dans l'antiquité* (Paris, 1882–1914).

PHILLIPS, E. D.: 'The Legend of Aristeas' (in *Artibus Asiae* xviii (1955)).

REINACH, S.: *Répertoire des vases peints grecs et étrusques* (Paris, 1899 1900).

RICE, T. T.: *The Scythians* (London, 1957).

ROEBUCK, C.: *Ionian Trade and Colonization* (New York, 1959).

ROHDE, E.: i *Psyche* (trans. Hillis; London, 1925).

—— ii *Der griechische Roman* (Leipzig, 1900).

ROSCHER, W. H.: *Lexikon der griechischen und römischen Mythologie* (Leipzig, 1884–1937).

ROSTOVTZEFF, M.: i *Iranians and Greeks in South Russia* (Oxford, 1922).

—— ii *Skythien und der Bosporus* (Berlin, 1931).

SCHMID, W., and STÄHLIN, O.: *Geschichte der griechischen Literatur* (Munich, 1920).

TARN, W. W.: *The Greeks in Bactria and India* (Cambridge, 1951).

THOMPSON, M. S.: 'The Asiatic or Winged Artemis' (in *J.H.S.* xxix (1909)).

THOMSON, J. O.: *History of Ancient Geography* (Cambridge, 1948).

TISCHBEIN, J. H. W.: *Collection of Engravings from Ancient Vases* (Naples, 1791–5).

TOMASCHEK, W.: 'Kritik der ältesten Nachrichten über den skythischen Norden' (in *Sitzungsberichte der Wiener Akademien der Wissenschaften* cxvi and cxvii (1888–9)).

TOURNIER, E.: *De Aristea Proconnesio et Arimaspeo Poemate* (Paris, 1863).

TYRRELL, G. N. M.: *Apparitions* (London, 1953).

VERNADSKY, G.: *Ancient Russia* (New Haven, Conn., 1943).

VOSS, O.: *De Heraclidis Pontici Vita et Scriptis* (Rostock, 1896).

WESTBERG, F.: 'Zur Topographie des Herodot' (in *Klio* (1904)).

WINTER, F.: 'Vase aus Mylasa' (in *Mitteilungen des kaiserlich deutschen archäologischen Instituts (athenische Abteilung)*, 1887).

YULE, H., and CORDIER, H.: *The Book of ser Marco Polo* (London, 1929).

INDEX LOCORUM

GALEN   Kühn
opera
  viii. 414   155
  xv. 109   185

GALLUS   Baehrens
fragmentum p. 336   190   (*F. poet. Rom.*)

GEMINUS   Manitius
Elementa Astronomiae
  6   187

GREGORIUS NAZIANZENUS   Paris ed., 1840
Orationes
  iv (*adv. Iulianum* i) 59   T. 23; 123, 144

HARPOCRATION   Bekker
Lexicon
  Ἄβαρις   172, 205
  Κισθήνη   62
  Σκιάποδες   184

HECATAEUS ABDERITES   Jacoby
fragmenta   (*F. gr. Hist.*)
  7   185, 192, 203
  8   24
  11   24
  12   42
  13   59, 190
  14   24

HECATAEUS MILESIUS   Jacoby
fragmenta   (*F. gr. Hist.*)
  100   17
  108   17
  154   17
  163   17
  185   104
  193   197
  195   190
  203   17, 47
  204   17
  207   17
  210   188
  216   190
  284   17
  287   17
  299   17
  302   58
  323   17
  335   17

SUBJECT INDEX

Ariaspi, 191.

Aridaeus, *see* Thespesius.

Arimaspae, 72; *see also* Arimaspi.

Arimaspea, contents of, 1 ff., 4 f., 25 f., 28, 31, 32, 33, 38, 39 ff., 43 ff., 45, 60, 63, 64 f., 67 ff., 71 f., 72, 74 f., 76, 82, 92, 94, 98, 101 f., 102, 103, 110, 111, 134, 138, 171 f., 174, 176 ff., 199; date of, 3 ff., 10, 19, 40 f., 43, 110, 124 f., 132, 170, 176, 178; influence of, 7, 18, 24, 26, 31, 33, 35 f., 36 ff., 39 ff., 70 f., 73, 80, 111, 181 ff., 187, 188, 192; name, 2, 25, 32, 169, 181; nature of, 35 f., 125 f., 132 ff.; quotations from, 5, 7 ff., 20 ff., 27, 46, 63, 68, 72, 91, 110, 116, 173, 182, 185; ditto analysed, 11 ff., 185.

Arimaspi, 67, 68, 73, 107, 111, 112, 113, 116, 171, 176, 177, 191, 193, 196; in art, 6; description of, 1, 8 f., 28, 32, 39, 45, 61, 63, 64, 72, 74, 83, 170, 177, 180, 194 f.; etymology, 110, 198; Hyperborean, 22 ff., 25, 185, 186; Scythian, 23, 67, 70, 102; originals of, 80, 83 ff., 93, 108 f., 110, 118, 186, 194.

Arimaspus, king, 23.

Arimphaei, 71, 112; *see also* Argippaei.

Aristaeus, 35, 123 f., 124, 126, 130, 145, 167 ff.; of Proconnesus, 31, 33, 169, 205; Pythagorean, 142, 201, 214; *see also* Aristeas.

Aristea, ship, 183.

Aristeas, grammarian, 185; of Proconnesus, and *Arimaspea*, 1 ff., 9 f., 22, 25, 27 f., 31, 32, 39, 45, 64 f., 71 f., 76, 79, 80, 82, 92 f., 94, 100 f., 102, 104, 110 f., 113, 114, 116, 119, 124 f., 170, 172, 176, 178, 193, 197, 199, 206; other works of, 25, 31 f., 186 f.; date of, 3 f., 73, 110, 111, 117, 118, 126 ff., 131 ff., 169 f., 172, 179, 183; form of name, 35, 130, 205, 214; and Pythagoras, 142, 144, 164, 174 f.,

179, 183; ancient stories about, 2, 25, 32, 35 f., 69, 70 f., 73, 119 ff., 133 f., 138, 140, 143, 145, 147 f., 148, 153, 154, 156, 157, 163, 164, 166, 167, 168 f., 170, 174 f., 183, 204; modern theories about, 36, 111, 124 ff., 132 ff., 145, 146, 160, 179 ff., 200; *see also* Aristaeus; Aristeus.

Aristeus, 212, 214; *see also* Aristeas.

Aristotle, 157, 173, 190, 202.

Aristoxenus, 172, 185.

Artace, 2, 119, 133, 200.

Artemis, 69, 89; 'Winged', 6, 89.

As, 114.

Asbolus, 169, 205.

aschy, 105, 107, 109, 197.

Asia, 48, 50, 56, 75, 80, 82, 84, 93, 94, 96, 97 ff., 100, 101, 106, 107, 108, 109, 111, 115, 116, 118, 132 f., 150 f., 171, 176, 177, 178, 180, 181, 182, 190, 191, 192, 206.

Assyria(n), 4, 86 ff.

Astomi, 30.

Astypalaea, 129, 163.

Athena, 32.

Athens, Epimenides at, 161; Heraclides Ponticus at, 172; and worldwide plague, 205.

Atlantic Ocean, 150, 171.

Atlantis, 24, 204.

Atlas, among Hyperboreans, 189.

Attacori, 99; *see also* Uttarakuru.

Attalids, 20.

Australia, 77.

Autoleon, 164.

Avars, 54, 171 f., 190; *see also* Abaris.

Azov, Sea of, 4, 178, 179; *see also* Palus Maeotis.

Babylonia(n), 69, 86, 88, 159, 160.

Bacis, 21.

Bactria(n), 65 f., 80.

baibak, 84.

Balkhash, lake, 98.

Baltic Sea, 113.

Baltistan, 110.

I. MIRROR FROM KELERMES

II. MIRROR-HANDLE FROM ENKOMI

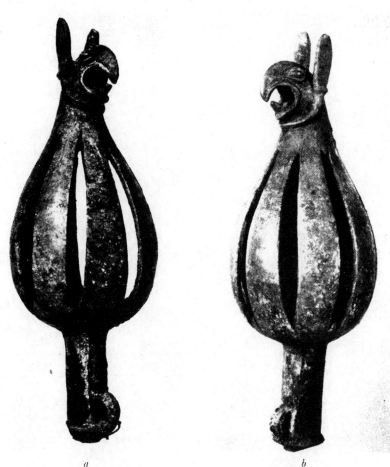

a   *b*

III. RATTLE FROM KELERMES

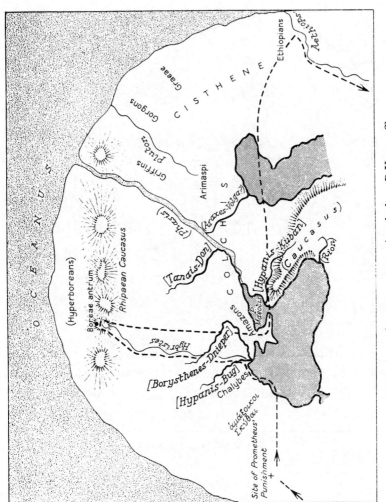

MAP I. IO'S JOURNEY. Aeschylus, *P.V.* 707 ff.

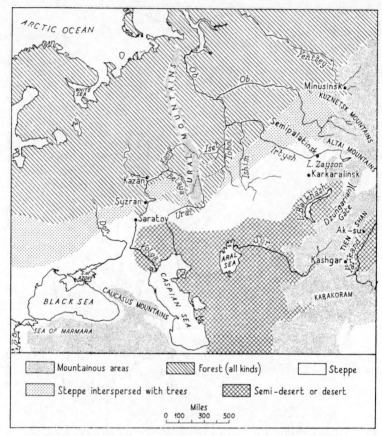

MAP II. EURASIA

OTHER TITLES IN THIS HARDBACK REPRINT PROGRAMME FROM SANDPIPER BOOKS LTD (LONDON) AND POWELLS BOOKS (CHICAGO)

ISBN 0–19–	Author	Title
8143567	ALFÖLDI A.	The Conversion of Constantine and Pagan Rome
6286409	ANDERSON George K.	The Literature of the Anglo-Saxons
8219601	ARNOLD Benjamin	German Knighthood
8228813	BARTLETT & MacKAY	Medieval Frontier Societies
8111010	BETHURUM Dorothy	Homilies of Wulfstan
8142765	BOLLING G. M.	External Evidence for Interpolation in Homer
814332X	BOLTON J.D.P.	Aristeas of Proconnesus
9240132	BOYLAN Patrick	Thoth, the Hermes of Egypt
8114222	BROOKS Kenneth R.	Andreas and the Fates of the Apostles
8203543	BULL Marcus	Knightly Piety & Lay Response to the First Crusade
8216785	BUTLER Alfred J.	Arab Conquest of Egypt
8148046	CAMERON Alan	Circus Factions
8148054	CAMERON Alan	Porphyrius the Charioteer
8148348	CAMPBELL J.B.	The Emperor and the Roman Army 31 BC to 235 AD
826643X	CHADWICK Henry	Priscillian of Avila
826447X	CHADWICK Henry	Boethius
8219393	COWDREY H.E.J.	The Age of Abbot Desiderius
8148992	DAVIES M.	Sophocles: Trachiniae
825301X	DOWNER L.	Leges Henrici Primi
814346X	DRONKE Peter	Medieval Latin and the Rise of European Love-Lyric
8142749	DUNBABIN T.J.	The Western Greeks
8154372	FAULKNER R.O.	The Ancient Egyptian Pyramid Texts
8221541	FLANAGAN Marie Therese	Irish Society, Anglo-Norman Settlers, Angevin Kingship
8143109	FRAENKEL Edward	Horace
8201540	GOLDBERG P.J.P.	Women, Work and Life Cycle in a Medieval Economy
8140215	GOTTSCHALK H.B.	Heraclides of Pontus
8266162	HANSON R.P.C.	Saint Patrick
8224354	HARRISS G.L.	King, Parliament and Public Finance in Medieval England to 1369
8581114	HEATH Sir Thomas	Aristarchus of Samos
2115480	HENRY Blanche	British Botanical and Horticultural Literature before 1800
8140444	HOLLIS A.S.	Callimachus: Hecale
8212968	HOLLISTER C. Warren	Anglo-Saxon Military Institutions
8219523	HOUSLEY Norman	The Italian Crusades
8223129	HURNARD Naomi	The King's Pardon for Homicide – before AD 1307
8140401	HUTCHINSON G.O.	Hellenistic Poetry
9240140	JOACHIM H.H.	Aristotle: On Coming-to-be and Passing-away
9240094	JONES A.H.M	Cities of the Eastern Roman Provinces
8142560	JONES A.H.M.	The Greek City
8218354	JONES Michael	Ducal Brittany 1364–1399
8271484	KNOX & PELCZYNSKI	Hegel's Political Writings
8225253	LE PATOUREL John	The Norman Empire
8212720	LENNARD Reginald	Rural England 1086–1135
8212321	LEVISON W.	England and the Continent in the 8th century
8148224	LIEBESCHUETZ J.H.W.G.	Continuity and Change in Roman Religion
8141378	LOBEL Edgar & PAGE Sir Denys	Poetarum Lesbiorum Fragmenta
9240159	LOEW E.A.	The Beneventan Script
8241445	LUKASIEWICZ, Jan	Aristotle's Syllogistic
8152442	MAAS P. & TRYPANIS C.A .	Sancti Romani Melodi Cantica
8142684	MARSDEN E.W.	Greek and Roman Artillery—Historical
8142692	MARSDEN E.W.	Greek and Roman Artillery—Technical
8148178	MATTHEWS John	Western Aristocracies and Imperial Court AD 364–425
9240205	MAVROGORDATO John	Digenes Akrites
8223447	McFARLANE K.B.	Lancastrian Kings and Lollard Knights
8226578	McFARLANE K.B.	The Nobility of Later Medieval England
9240205	MAVROGADO John	Digenes Akrites
8148100	MEIGGS Russell	Roman Ostia
8148402	MEIGGS Russell	Trees and Timber in the Ancient Mediterranean World
8142641	MILLER J. Innes	The Spice Trade of the Roman Empire
8147813	MOORHEAD John	Theoderic in Italy
8264259	MOORMAN John	A History of the Franciscan Order
9240213	MYRES J.L.	Herodotus The Father of History
8219512	OBOLENSKY Dimitri	Six Byzantine Portraits
8116020	OWEN A.L.	The Famous Druids
8131445	PALMER, L.R.	The Interpretation of Mycenaean Greek Texts
8143427	PFEIFFER R.	History of Classical Scholarship (vol 1)
8143648	PFEIFFER Rudolf	History of Classical Scholarship 1300–1850

8111649	PHEIFER J.D.	Old English Glosses in the Epinal-Erfurt Glossary
8142277	PICKARD–CAMBRIDGE A.W.	Dithyramb Tragedy and Comedy
8269765	PLATER & WHITE	Grammar of the Vulgate
8213891	PLUMMER Charles	Lives of Irish Saints (2 vols)
820695X	POWICKE Michael	Military Obligation in Medieval England
8269684	POWICKE Sir Maurice	Stephen Langton
821460X	POWICKE Sir Maurice	The Christian Life in the Middle Ages
8225369	PRAWER Joshua	Crusader Institutions
8225571	PRAWER Joshua	The History of The Jews in the Latin Kingdom of Jerusalem
8143249	RABY F.J.E.	A History of Christian Latin Poetry
8143257	RABY F.J.E.	A History of Secular Latin Poetry in the Middle Ages (2 vols)
8214316	RASHDALL & POWICKE	The Universities of Europe in the Middle Ages (3 vols)
8154488	REYMOND E.A.E & BARNS J.W.B.	Four Martyrdoms from the Pierpont Morgan Coptic Codices
8148380	RICKMAN Geoffrey	The Corn Supply of Ancient Rome
8141076	ROSS Sir David	Aristotle: Metaphysics (2 vols)
8141092	ROSS Sir David	Aristotle: Physics
8142307	ROSTOVTZEFF M.	Social and Economic History of the Hellenistic World, 3 vols.
8142315	ROSTOVTZEFF M.	Social and Economic History of the Roman Empire, 2 vols.
8264178	RUNCIMAN Sir Steven	The Eastern Schism
814833X	SALMON J.B.	Wealthy Corinth
8171587	SALZMAN L.F.	Building in England Down to 1540
8218362	SAYERS Jane E.	Papal Judges Delegate in the Province of Canterbury 1198–1254
8221657	SCHEIN Sylvia	Fideles Crucis
8148135	SHERWIN WHITE A.N.	The Roman Citizenship
9240167	SINGER Charles	Galen: On Anatomical Procedures
8113927	SISAM, Kenneth	Studies in the History of Old English Literature
8642040	SOUTER Alexander	A Glossary of Later Latin to 600 AD
8270011	SOUTER Alexander	Earliest Latin Commentaries on the Epistles of St Paul
8222254	SOUTHERN R.W.	Eadmer: Life of St. Anselm
8251408	SQUIBB G.	The High Court of Chivalry
8212011	STEVENSON & WHITELOCK	Asser's Life of King Alfred
8212011	SWEET Henry	A Second Anglo-Saxon Reader—Archaic and Dialectical
8148259	SYME Sir Ronald	History in Ovid
8143273	SYME Sir Ronald	Tacitus (2 vols)
8200951	THOMPSON Sally	Women Religious
8201745	WALKER Simon	The Lancastrian Affinity 1361–1399
8161115	WELLESZ Egon	A History of Byzantine Music and Hymnography
8140185	WEST M.L.	Greek Metre
8141696	WEST M.L.	Hesiod: Theogony
8148542	WEST M.L.	The Orphic Poems
8140053	WEST M.L.	Hesiod: Works & Days
8152663	WEST M.L.	Iambi et Elegi Graeci
9240221	WHEELWRIGHT Philip	Heraclitus
822799X	WHITBY M. & M.	The History of Theophylact Simocatta
8206186	WILLIAMSON, E.W.	Letters of Osbert of Clare
8208103	WILSON F.P.	Plague in Shakespeare's London
8114877	WOOLF Rosemary	The English Religious Lyric in the Middle Ages
8119224	WRIGHT Joseph	Grammar of the Gothic Language